Slam Dunked

*The NCAA's Shameful Reaction
to Athletic Integration
in the Deep South*

By
Ron Gomez
with Beryl Shipley

Wordclay
1663 Liberty Drive, Suite 200
Bloomington, IN 47403
www.wordclay.com

This book is a work of non-fiction. Unless otherwise noted, the author and the publisher make no explicit guarantees as to the accuracy of the information contained in this book and in some cases, names of people and places have been altered to protect their privacy.

First published by Wordclay on 4/21/2008.

ISBN: 978-1-6048-1124-7 (sc)

Printed in the United States of America.

This book is printed on acid-free paper.

Dedicated to brother Tom Shipley
a tireless seeker of truth

*Where silence would do
more harm than good,
pray for a prudent tongue
and defend yourself with the truth.*

Father Anthony Paone, S. J.
suggested by former LSU basketball
coach Dale Brown

Other books by Ron Gomez

My Name Is Ron and I'm a Recovering Legislator,
Rooftop Publishing, ISBN 978-1-60008-052-4, 2007

Neat (fiction), iUniverse, ISBN 0-595-37051-9, 2005

Pelican Games (fiction), Noble House, ISBN 1-56167766-3, 2003

Contents

Preface

For many it is hard to believe that as late as 1954, schools, universities, buses, water fountains, restroom facilities, restaurants—the whole social structure in the South—was segregated. Separate facilities of all of the above were the norm. This was perpetuated on the premise that they were "separate but equal." The famous 1954 decision by the United States Supreme Court, *Brown v. Board of Education,* changed all of that, but the transition to integration did not occur overnight. In fact, the real effects of court-mandated integration were still barely discernible in many areas of the Deep South even a decade later.

The city of Lafayette, Louisiana, located on Interstate 10 roughly between New Orleans and Houston, is the home of the University of Louisiana at Lafayette (ULL). The current population of the city and its environs is nearing two hundred thousand. Fifty years ago it was more like thirty-five thousand.

In 1954, the university was named Southwestern Louisiana Institute (SLI) and its student body numbered just more than six thousand. The name was changed in 1960 to the University of Southwestern Louisiana (USL) and again to ULL in 1999. The student population in 2007 was more than seventeen thousand.

Under the guidance of some foresighted and courageous leaders, black and white, SLI was the first all-white university in the entire South to accept undergraduate African-American students. The integration of the student body was achieved quietly and peacefully. Many have credited the relatively calm transition to the demographic makeup of the city and the area around it known as Acadiana. A large majority of the residents are of French Catholic heritage. Their ancestors were victims of British discrimination, oppression

ix

and exile in the eighteenth century, and thus the descendants were more empathetic to the black community than most.

The black population in Lafayette and Acadiana had been fairly well assimilated over the years. Partly responsible was the fact that the poor Acadians, or Cajuns, as they came to be known, mostly worked side by side with the black laborers in the agriculture-based economy of the area. There had also been considerable interracial social mixing over the years that produced many Afro-American families with French surnames and light complexions who practiced the Catholic religion.

In addition, by the mid 1950s, the oil and gas industry had attracted an influx of hard-driving, ambitious drillers and geologists who brought another distinct culture to the area. They too were openly accepted and embraced by the native population.

School integration was not totally without tension, but it was achieved without violence, without sit-ins, and without law enforcement interference.

Still, by 1965 there was not one Afro-American athlete under scholarship or participating in NCAA sports in any of the states of the Deep South. With his roots in the hills of Tennessee, Beryl Shipley, the fiery, red-haired head basketball coach of the University of Southwestern Louisiana Bulldogs changed all that. Those changes produced some of the most exciting college sports moments ever witnessed in Louisiana. They also produced great resentment and even hatred within the university and athletic community in the state, and they ultimately led to the National Collegiate Athletic Association (NCAA) eliminating the basketball program with an unprecedented suspension, or "death penalty," of two years.

Coach Shipley, aided by the research and writing skills of his older brother Tom, reveals in this book, for the first time, the questionable procedures and allegations of the NCAA. Newly discovered documents, dating back three decades, show the NCAA's actions abetting those of the racially motivated Louisiana State Board of Education and other segregationists in the '60s and early '70s who were determined to punish those responsible for integrating athletics in the state.

Beryl Shipley, a robust eighty-one-year-old at this writing, with a distinct echo of the Tennessee hills in his speech, has nurtured the burning desire through the years to have this story told as it was never told during the events that transpired.

This is that story. Admittedly there is a lingering bitterness about what the coach believes to be a miscarriage of justice. Some persons may take exception to the relating of some events in the manuscript, but it is all told based on solid research and corroborated memories.

Chapter One

"Thank God for Mickey Mouse"

By May 14, 1973, Beryl Shipley had achieved great heights of success in the basketball world. He had a nearly 70 percent winning record in his sixteen years at the University of Southwestern Louisiana in Lafayette. One of his teams had reached the final four in the NCAA College Division National Tournament in Evansville, Indiana. In their first two years in the NCAA Division I, his teams, now known as the Ragin' Cajuns, were nationally ranked in the top ten and had reached the second round of post-season tournament play. In the two years of play in the Southland Conference, USL had never lost a game. He had coached one of the most prolific scorers in college basketball, Dwight "Bo" Lamar, and had seen several of his players sign pro basketball contracts.

Beryl Shipley should have been sitting on top of his world. Instead, at 10:00 a.m. on this date, he was resigning his head coaching job. For all the satisfaction he should have had from his unprecedented tenure, the last few years were equally filled with pain, insult, and embarrassment. He had to bring his team through two years of NCAA sanctions brought about by charges stemming directly from his recruiting black players in 1966 in violation of an unwritten and unlawful but strictly enforced segregation edict placed on state university athletic teams in Louisiana.

Again in 1973, his program was under investigation by the NCAA, and it appeared his own school administration and state officials were not only abetting the inquiry but were also withholding information from him. Though there were widespread media reports of well over a hundred allegations of violations, Shipley had not seen one document. He had heard the reports. He had seen evidence of NCAA operatives on campus, but he personally had not been questioned or even advised of the charges.

The last few weeks of the basketball season had been pure hell. USL easily won the Southland Conference regular season championship for the second straight year with a perfect 12–0 record. Even though only unsupported and (then) unpublished NCAA allegations existed, because of those allegations, conference officials voted not to award the championship.

Several days later, after whipping a good Lamar University team 129–111 in Beaumont, Texas, Shipley was asked by an area sportswriter how he felt about the conference's decision. A bit sensitive from all the media speculation and sniping coming from his disgruntled and clearly envious colleagues in the conference, Shipley opined that the "Southland Conference is a Mickey Mouse league."

Mickey hadn't received such national press in decades. The story was repeated from coast to coast. Naturally the commissioner of the conference, Dick Oliver, was very unhappy. He called a meeting of all the member schools' officials, including USL Athletic Director A.G. "Whitey" Urban and the university's athletic chairman, David Fisher. It was decided (reportedly unanimously) that Shipley must properly apologize for his remarks or be banned from coaching in the conference. It is very doubtful that such an action could have been legally taken by the conference against a coach employed by a state university. Strangely the two USL officials at the meeting failed to tell Shipley of the decision, nor did the conference officially notify him until *two months later*. Even Disney's mouse would have received more courteous treatment.

In a formal letter on Southland Conference letterhead, dated May 4, 1973, Beryl received the following letter of reprimand.

> Dear Coach Shipley,
> Your criticism of the Southland Conference which appeared in print in THE PORT ARTHUR (Tex.) NEWS on Wednesday, February 7, 1973, was deplored by Faculty Athletic representatives at the annual Spring Meet in Ruston, La.
>
> Dr. David Fisher, the Southwestern Louisiana Faculty Representative, has a copy of the news column in his possession if you need it as reference material.
>
> As Commissioner of the Conference, I was instructed to privately reprimand you for your critical comment. You are herewith censured for your remarks and warned against similar statements in the future.

Further, the Faculty Representatives voted unanimously to demand an acceptable apology from you. This apology shall be in writing and directed to the President of the Conference as follows: Mr. Harold J. Smolinski, Department of Accounting, Louisiana Tech University, Tech Station, Box 5026, Ruston, Louisiana 71270.

Until the conditions of this letter are fulfilled, the Faculty Representatives have suspended you from coaching in the Southland Conference as of April 28, 1973.

Please see that this correspondence receives your immediate attention.

Sincerely,
Dick Oliver
Commissioner

It is almost beyond belief that a committee of "faculty representatives" would have the power to suspend a head coach of a major college basketball team for remarks made to a reporter. But, since the conference season had ended a couple of months earlier, and since the entire basketball season, playoffs and all, would be over before April 28, the suspension was meaningless anyway.

One week after the date of that letter, USL President Dr. Clyde Rougeau called a meeting attended by USL Vice President Ray Authement, Athletic Director A.G. "Whitey" Urban, Beryl Shipley, and the faculty chairman of athletics, Dave Fisher. It was the first time the head basketball coach had been invited for a conversation with the leadership of the university and the athletic department since rumors of an NCAA investigation had started nearly a year before.

Shipley was told he had to write the letter of apology as demanded by the conference commissioner. He was assured it was no big deal. He should just say he erred, apologize, and say he wouldn't do it again.

By this time Shipley was seething with resentment and sick of the deception being practiced and the lack of integrity exhibited by his school's administration. The camel's back was about to break. Beryl Shipley was about to decide that he no longer cared to associate or be associated with people who would so easily abandon him, his family, his coaches, and his student athletes in the face of unsubstantiated allegations and petty retribution from spiteful detractors. The whole relationship was becoming degrading.

In spite of all his successes and the positive national recognition of the basketball program, Shipley's coaching salary had been frozen at $15,800 for

3

three years. Technically his salary was listed at $16,800, but Beryl refused to acknowledge the extra $1,000 since he had raised the question as to why it was not more of an increase based on his national tournament successes. Shipley had been told by some who were privy to the administration's decision processes that the lack of raises and the insultingly small increase was because of his flaunting of the unwritten segregation rule. He and his family refused to accept the extra one thousand dollars.

Before the meeting concerning a letter of apology wrapped up, Beryl again raised the question of a potential salary increase. President Rougeau, who had previously promised an increase that never came, said he couldn't offer any information on a potential raise at this time. Beryl's facial expression was frozen as he said, "Doctor Rougeau, you get that information by Monday or there won't be any reason for a letter of apology."

True to his word, Beryl called the president early Monday morning on May 14. Rougeau told him that he didn't have any more information as to the status of a raise.

Shipley called two trusted friends who were also members of the Lafayette media. He asked J.C. Hatcher (now deceased), sportswriter for the *Lafayette Daily Advertiser* newspaper, and Ron Gomez, manager of KPEL radio and the play-by-play announcer for USL sports for the previous thirteen years, to set up a press conference for him for ten o'clock that morning.

Without preamble, Shipley calmly and with little show of emotion announced to the gathered reporters that he was resigning effective immediately as basketball coach at USL.

There was dead silence for several moments before a tumult of questions. Naturally several pointed to the NCAA investigation and asked if this was the reason for his leaving. Shipley, who honestly did not know the extent or context of the allegations, honestly answered no. He said he felt it was just time to move on to other, hopefully more rewarding challenges.

He was then asked if he intended to apologize to the Southland Conference as he had been ordered to. With a trace of a smile—some would describe it as a smirk—Beryl chuckled, "No. I won't apologize to the conference, but I damn sure will apologize to Mickey Mouse."

Needless to say, that remark made national headlines coast to coast the next morning.

Later Shipley would say, "You know, I thank God every day for Mickey Mouse's part in it. The Mickey Mouse comment was the vehicle that enabled me to remove myself from the degrading political environment that existed then."

It was the end of a sixteen-year roller coaster ride with great heights, great excitement, and abysmal lows. It was the "Shipley Era" of basketball in Acadiana.

But the story was just beginning.

Chapter Two

The Shipley Era

There was a time in southwest Louisiana, the area designated as Acadiana, when thousands of rabid fans would gather at tiny Earl K. Long Gym on the campus of the University of Southwestern Louisiana or Blackham Coliseum, just a mile or two down the road, to watch young athletes do wondrous things with a round leather ball.

They were taught and guided and cajoled and sometimes harassed into becoming better than they ever thought they could be by a red-headed task-master. He was in their face and on their backs (some would use a different anatomical description) and in their heads, and they became better because of him: better athletes, better students, better men.

It was a time of great passion, intense excitement, and the birth of basketball as a premier sport in Louisiana. But it didn't happen overnight.

"In the early days, recruiting was done from a station wagon," wrote Greg Lopez, staff columnist for the *Daily Iberian* newspaper, "and if Beryl threw a mattress in the back and slept on it three nights a week, he could get by on $10 per diem."

In Beryl Shipley's first year at Southwestern, game attendance ranged from 500 to 750 generally, but on big nights, as many as 1,000 to 2,000 would show up. In those days SLI played home games in Blackham Coliseum, unless some more important event had been scheduled. Bob Henderson, retired sports information director, writing freelance for the *Lafayette Advertiser*, wrote retrospectively in 1973, that more important activities were considered to be "a flower show, a rodeo, a crawfish boil, a travel lecture, or a dog show. When one of these events conflicted with basketball, Shipley and his crew had to move over on campus to the tiny men's gym." In those early years, obviously basketball was not considered very high in the scheme of things at the institute.

Beryl Shipley was a three-sport letterman (football, basketball, and baseball) at Dobyns-Bennett High School in his native Kingsport, Tennessee. After being discharged from the navy in 1946, he attended Hinds (Mississippi) Jr. College on a basketball scholarship, where he started for two seasons at guard. He completed his BS degree on a scholarship at Delta (Mississippi) State College, where he was a starter at guard for two years.

He began his coaching career at Morgan City (Mississippi) High School in 1951, teaching five social studies classes and coaching basketball, football, and baseball. His basketball team finished the season with nineteen wins, seven defeats.

In 1952 he became head basketball coach at Starkville (Mississippi) High School. In five seasons at Starkville, home of Mississippi State University, his teams won 111 games while losing only 26 and won three Little Ten Conference championships and two district titles. His Starkville club reached a peak during the 1956–57 season, winning twenty-seven and losing only two. During his service at Starkville, he acquired his master's in education at Mississippi State.

John Robert Bell was hired by SLI from Georgia Institute of Technology (Georgia Tech) as athletic director and football coach. A native of Shipley's hometown of Kingsport, Tennessee and graduate of the same high school, Bell had followed Beryl's outstanding high school coaching career. He wanted Shipley on his team. It was mutual admiration, as Beryl had a high regard for John's capability and looked forward to working with him and helping him build a good athletic organization. Shipley agreed to the princely salary of six thousand dollars per year.

After talking Bell out of a dual role of basketball and baseball head coach, Beryl coached basketball only. When Bell left after just one year, Shipley was given the additional task of athletic director, a job he enthusiastically relinquished with the hiring of A.G. "Whitey" Urban in 1961.

When the Bulldogs, as they were nicknamed then, were allowed to play their games in the rodeo arena known as Blackham Coliseum, it was on a removable floor. The floor had several warped areas that served to favor the home team because they knew where these were. The damaged parts of the floor caused the ball to have much less bounce. USL players could influence a driving opponent over one of these areas and, when the ball failed to bounce properly on the dribble, go for a steal. When they were sent back to Earl K. Long Gym, there were other problems. The place was so small the baselines of the basketball court were only three or four feet from the brick side walls of the building. Fast breaks and driving lay-ups were an invitation to hospitalization.

Beryl Shipley was a tough-talking, brash young coach with a GI haircut, a Smoky Mountain's accent, and a laugh as quick as his temper. He drove his players relentlessly because of his belief that physical conditioning was as important as raw talent. He also knew that his teams would not be very deep in quality substitutes, and the starters would have to be ready for iron-man duty.

He soon started winning over Cajun fans when he took a program that had suffered five straight losing seasons to a sixteen and eleven record in his first year. There would be only one losing season in Shipley's sixteen years, and that was by only one game. The turnaround impressed sports commentators and coaches enough that Beryl was named the Gulf States Conference's Coach of the Year. His fifteen and nine record in the 1958–59 season earned another Coach of the Year honor. Two more were to follow in the next eleven years spent in the old GSC. Beryl would end up the winningest coach in Gulf States Conference history. It was a harbinger of things to come.

In the early '60s, now coaching the renamed University of Southwestern Louisiana (USL), Shipley helped inaugurate the Bayou Classic, a Christmas holiday tournament held in Lafayette that grew to nationally recognized proportions. His early experiences with getting the Classic started should have warned him of future problems with the USL administration. He ran into stiff opposition from the president of his own university.

The inaugural tournament was planned for December 1959. Beryl was counting on the event to spur interest in the basketball program that was still not up to the coach's standards in spite of his early successes. Additionally it would bring wider publicity for the school by bringing in better-known opponents.

Beryl and his staff had three teams lined up for the tournament: Mississippi Southern, North Texas State, and Stetson University. These were all a step up in prestige from the previously scheduled opponents. The schools were guaranteed travel and accommodations as well as a banquet for participating teams and gifts for the coaches. The cost to USL was to be approximately eight hundred dollars, but it was expected that gate receipts would far exceed the cost. In the middle of November, with the tournament a month away, Beryl received a call from the school administration. He was told to cancel the tournament. The reason given: the event is too expensive.

The president of the university, Joel Fletcher, for whatever reasons, did not welcome the type of publicity the Bayou Classic would bring to the school, and the humiliation the cancellation would have brought didn't appear to bother him. In organizing the event, it should be noted, Coach Shipley had not breached his authority; he was solely responsible for the schedule of the basketball program.

Beryl, faced with this embarrassment, went to the community for a solution. Shipley's dynamic personality and coaching acumen had already won over many friends and personal supporters. The community came through. A group of supporters decided that the tournament was a good idea for the city of Lafayette as well as for the school, and interested organizations in the community financed the tournament and even sold the tickets. The principal backers were D.S. "Shine" Young Real Estate and Insurance, and Radio Station KPEL, which broadcast all USL football and basketball games. They were the initial sponsors, but help quickly came from many other sources.

The tournament was profitable from the outset and evolved to become one of the best in the country. It became a keystone event of the Christmas season and was recognized by coaches throughout the country as one of the tournaments to which they wanted to be invited.

The administration staunchly refused to get involved with the event at any time during its fourteen-year duration and shrugged off the proven record of profitability for each of those years. Community volunteers continued to raise the seed money, host the teams and their coaches, sell tickets and program ads, and generally run the tournament. The school reaped the profitability of the tournament, however, because the organizations that worked to produce it delivered all proceeds directly to the university's business office. It became obvious with time that cost had not been the factor for the initial canceling of the event; the administration's resentment of the success of the basketball program was becoming more obvious with each passing year.

The nickname of USL athletic teams had been slowly changed beginning in 1969 to "Ragin' Cajuns." Then Head Football Coach Russ Faulkinberry, speaking to a local Rotary Club, noted that the club had been split into two teams for a fundraising event. Sid Ory, a highly successful insurance salesman and raconteur, was the captain of one team that he named the Ragin' Cajuns. Faulkinberry liked the sound and told Sports Information Director Bob Henderson to start working it into all press releases. Ron Gomez, longtime play-by-play announcer for USL athletics, started using the new name in broadcasts. He remembers Dwight "Bo" Lamar, then a freshman, telling him on a bus trip to play Nicholls State University in Thibodeaux, Louisiana in February of 1970, "Ron, my girlfriend was listening to the game the other night and heard you call us the Ragin' Cajuns or something like that." Gomez told the future national scoring leader that was the new nickname being introduced. Lamar was mildly upset and said, "Man, I ain't no Ragin' Cajun, I'm from Columbus, Ohio." Gomez told him jokingly, "It could be worse, Bo, you could have gone to Georgetown where you'd be a Hoya or to Southern California and been a Trojan. Get used to it."

As envisioned, national publicity recognized SLI/USL's Bayou Classic.

In December 1971 an article written by colorful sportswriter William F. Reed appeared in *Sports Illustrated*:

Good Times Come to Cajun Country

The Cajuns operate out of Lafayette, La., the capital of the Bayou country, and for their mad followers they are a sort of Mardi Gras in sneakers. For the people who have to play them, another word with local flavor might be more descriptive: the word is pirates. The Cajuns throw up an intimidating front line, then send smallish guard Dwight Lamar running around it with the ball. He fires at will and, as the good folks say ... "Let the good times roll."

The good times rolled plenty last week when three other big, bad dudes — Long Beach State, Texas-El Paso, and Pan American — made the mistake of joining Southwestern in the 11th annual Bayou Classic ... Going into the tournament the three visiting clubs had one thing in common. They were all unbeaten. Southwestern, unaccountably, had lost its opener to Eastern Kentucky, 105–99 on the road. But that was only a small oversight. The Cajuns, playing as a major college for the first time this season, redeemed themselves on the Monday before the classic, ripping highly regarded Houston 97–88 at home. They led by as many as 18 points and Lamar gunned in 41. "Yeah," he said, "it was a bad night." Lamar, it seems, was not hitting the long, looping jumpers that he customarily makes from somewhere deep in the bleachers ...

On Friday against Pan American, Lamar came out with all guns blazing. Southwestern's first half offense, in fact, consisted of two plays: Lamar firing and, lamentably, missing from 30 feet while Roy Ebron, the Cajuns' superlative 6'9" sophomore center, quietly policed up the scene with his neat rebounds; and, play No. 2, one of the Cajuns' three big men—Ebron, 6'8" Wilbert Loftin or 6'7" Fred Saunders—getting a defensive rebound and firing a half-court pass to Lamar, who then soared off one of his sky-hanging, dipsy-doodle moves that end in easy baskets ... He almost never heads straight for the basket if there is a chance to double-pump or put the ball between his legs before letting fly. Every Cajun fan remembers the time last season when he went up, pirouetted 360 degrees in the air and hit a 20-foot jumper. The defensive man, according to the legend, ran off the floor and straight into the locker room.

USL won the tournament, but that was what was expected. Those were the years when a basketball game meant "Showtime at Blackham Coliseum," and maniacal crowds rocked the old building with every Lamar shot, every fast break, every Ebron block, every Jerry Bisbano assist, every Saunders steal. His sophomore, junior, and senior years, Lamar and his mates led USL to season records of 25–4, 25–4, and 24–5. Lamar ended his career with 3,493 career points and a 36.3 points per game average in a time when the long shots that he made counted for only two points, not the three points that they would count for today.

The elected officials of the City of Lafayette recognized the contributions of basketball early on. To celebrate the 1957–60 successes of the basketball program, Mayor J. Rayburn Bertrand proclaimed Saturday, February 18, 1961 Coach Beryl Shipley Day. The Bulldog mentor was to be honored during ceremonies preceding the USL-McNeese State cage feud in Blackham Coliseum.

The mayor's proclamation read:

> Shipley, a 34-year-old Kingsport, Tenn., native, came here in 1957 to become kennel master of the Bulldog hoopsters. Southwestern fans are already assured of enjoying a fourth consecutive winning season as the record now stands at 15–4.
>
> Under the expert leadership of this red headed strategist from the Eastern Tennessee mountain country, USL quintets have posted 65 wins in 98 games. Shipley's present edition appears to be on its way toward compiling possibly the best record in school history. In the latest small-college rating poll, USL is ranked No. 11 nationally. With four games remaining on the 1961 slate, the Canines hope to close shop with a 19–4 reading and maybe a spot among the top ten small-college clubs.
>
> Southwestern enters the McNeese battle with a regular home streak of 19 straight. This string dates back to the 1959–60 home opener, and if four more games played in the Bayou Holiday Classic were added to the list, USL can

boast a nigh perfect 22–1 mark in the friendly confines of the local arena.

A former cage star at Delta State (Miss.) the fiery but very modest Shipley will be recognized in ceremonies beginning at 7:45 p.m. Some 15 minutes later his USL crew will seek to upend McNeese State, the Gulf States Conference champion.

While building Southwestern basketball into a booming business, Shipley has twice been named GSC Coach-of-the-Year—first in his initial season, 1958, and again the following year.

In addition to enticing name schools to the Bayou Classic, Shipley also started peppering his schedule with teams never before engaged by Gulf States Conference programs—teams like Stetson, McMurray, and Kentucky Wesleyan; the University of Arkansas, Alabama, Western Kentucky, Tulsa; Mississippi State and Memphis State. If they were willing to play a relatively unknown team, Shipley was willing to take them on. Naturally, in those early days, most of the games against out-of-conference, big-name opponents were on the road. Why would they play an unknown like USL away from home?

The 1964–65 team made another breakthrough. Finishing seventeen and nine in the regular season, they qualified for the annual national tournament for National Association of Intercollegiate Athletics (NAIA) member schools to be held in Kansas City, Missouri. In those days this was among the most important basketball tournaments in the country, especially for mid-level programs such as USL. Regional tournaments were held at various sites, and the winners of these contests earned the right to compete in Kansas City.

When USL was notified that it qualified for a regional berth and a chance to host the playoff games, Beryl was elated but concerned about accepting the invitation to participate. If his team was to win the regional, the KC tournament would involve teams that included black athletes, and USL's policy, set by the State Board of Education at that time, did not permit its all-white team to compete against integrated teams. Athletic Director A.G. "Whitey" Urban emphatically assured Shipley that, if USL won the regional, the team would definitely be allowed to play. The university bid on and was awarded the right to host the regional tournament.

About two weeks prior to the tournament, Beryl, still concerned about the state board's policies, again asked Whitey to make sure that the politics were straight—that the team would be allowed to play in the KC tournament if USL won the regional. He didn't want to give his players false hope only to be dashed by disappointment. Whitey told Beryl, "You coach the basketball team; I'll handle the politics."

The March 2, 1965 issue of the *Lafayette Advertiser* ran a headline and story:

Going to Kansas City …
Kansas City, here I come!

These opening words of a popular song represent the ultimate goal of 32 basketball teams from throughout the nation which will soon form the field for the 28th annual NAIA National Collegiate Championship tournament. The 32-team field will represent an equal number of NAIA districts at this big tourney held every March at vast Municipal Auditorium in Kansas City, Mo.

One of these coveted 32 berths will be decided in Lafayette's Blackham Coliseum Tuesday night when the USL Bulldogs serve as host team for the NAIA District 27 playoff event. Southwestern will entertain three Alabama quintets—Athens College of Athens, Huntingdon College of Montgomery, and Troy State College of Troy. The Huntingdon Hawks are the defending district champs … winners of these first-round tests then clash … Wednesday for the title and an expense-paid trip to Kansas City for the national tournament March 8–13.

On March 3 an *Advertiser* story reported:

The Bulldogs bounced Athens College of Athens, Alabama, last night by a 71–58 score to advance to the championship game tonight at 8:00 in Blackham Coliseum against Huntingdon College of Montgomery, Alabama. Huntingdon reached the title game by knocking off Troy State of Troy, Alabama, by a 92–86 count.

Shipley's team rolled over Huntingdon College 78–69 in the regional championship game to win the District 27 NAIA Tournament and earn the right to represent the district in the NAIA Championship in Kansas City.

About six o'clock the next afternoon, Shipley and his assistant coach, Tom Colwell, were in the basketball office planning the practice sessions and the trip to Kansas City when a reporter phoned. He asked Beryl if he had heard the news. Beryl had no idea what he was talking about and asked, "What news?"

USL's president, Joel Fletcher, had informed the media that he had decided that the team could not participate in the Kansas City tournament after all. Fletcher did not acknowledge it, but obviously the state board, in its effort to stop USL's all-white team from possibly playing against a team with black players, had applied sufficient pressure on him to cause the turn-about.

Shipley was in shock. He started looking for the athletic director—the one who could "take care of the politics." He wasn't at the office and his home phone went unanswered. Beryl, on an impulse, jumped in his car and drove to Urban's home. He found him with his car packed, in the process of leaving town. It was obvious that Whitey knew what was going on. He told Shipley something had come up and he had to make a quick trip and said that Beryl should accept the situation; say nothing to the press or anybody else; don't make waves, just let it go.

Shipley was crushed, and he knew his team must have heard the news by now. He went directly to the dormitory. The players were gathered together, very upset, some of them crying. They wanted to know why. Beryl couldn't give them an answer. He explained that he had not been told of the decision beforehand and had received no word of explanation from the president or the administration. It was apparent that only the president could clarify the situation, so Beryl suggested that they form a group of students, visit the president's house, and ask him for an explanation.

Dean of Men Glynn Abel remembers the evening well. "About nine o'clock that night I got a call that said, 'Dean Abel, you better come with us; we're all going out to President Fletcher's house.' (Joel was living about a mile and a half off campus at that time.) 'We're gonna fight him because he won't let the team go to Kansas City.'

"A large crowd of kids had gathered, and I went with them out to Joel's house. When we arrived, they lined up all around his fence. We were there for some time, but Joel wouldn't come out to talk to them. I was concerned that there might be trouble, so I finally went through the gate, up to the house, and knocked on the door. He finally came to the door but opened it only a crack. I identified myself and told him, 'The kids want you to come out and talk to them.' He told me he would not come out. I couldn't convince him that he should, so I finally told him that I would get them to leave if he would promise to meet them at eight o'clock the next morning in front of Martin Hall (the campus administrative building) and talk to them. I told him that 'They feel like you ought to discuss it with them if you're going to make that kind of decision.' He said okay, he'd see them in the morning."

The next morning at eight o'clock, Fletcher was out in front of Martin Hall. The local paper reported:

> Fletcher's first words [to the students] were, 'are you from Moscow?' His next words were, 'I do not deal with mobs; I'll deal with your leaders. Now go on to your classes.' There was an uneasy silence from the crowd and a slight movement toward breaking up. This halted, however, when a voice shouted, 'We're not going to leave until we find out why we can't go to Kansas City.' Fletcher replied, 'There'll be no negotiations until you disperse.' A student in the crowd hollered back, 'We want to know why, that's all.'
>
> Fletcher made a move as if to go back to his office and then turned to the students. 'If I had known this action would develop I would not have made the telephone call I did an hour ago. At that time, I called the state board and told them I'm assuming full responsibility for sending the team to Kansas City. They're going.'

This ended a thirteen-hour interval of mass confusion for 350 to 400 students. The day before, at about 6:00 p.m., Fletcher had told Whitey Urban that W.E. Whetstone of Monroe, chairman of the State Board of Education, had informed him (Fletcher) that it was against the state board's policy to play in an integrated event. (Whitey, who said he would take care of the politics, evidently didn't have the nerve to tell the coach what the president had decided.)

The *Advertiser* contacted Whetstone, who promptly denied that he had told Fletcher that the team couldn't play in the tournament. He said that two board members, one from Lake Charles, the other from Pineville, had expressed concern over Southwestern's apparent participation, and he had merely called Fletcher to determine Southwestern's intentions. (The chairman and the two state board members who were concerned were associated with three different Gulf Coast colleges that were athletically competitive with Southwestern.)

The newspaper reported:

> Whetstone, when contacted by the Advertiser this morning said that he told Fletcher [during the six o'clock phone call] that he agreed with [Fletcher's] decision and was "behind him 10,000 per cent." Whetstone said that he did not realize that there was that much interest in the USL team

competing in the tournament. "I think it would have been detrimental to the state not to let USL play in the tournament," said Whetstone.

Several faculty members who were present during the confrontation with Joel Fletcher felt that the students were rightfully asking questions and disagreed with Fletcher's description of the student crowd as a "mob." One said, "This was no mob. Last night, between four and five hundred gathered at the president's house and were as orderly as could be. It was an appeal group—not a mob. They were puzzled youngsters seeking advice and counsel. They were quiet. Actually, I'm proud of our student body for the manner in which they acted during this time of crisis."

Whetstone told the *Advertiser* that he didn't think Fletcher would face any action from the board because of his decision.

About an hour after Fletcher agreed to allow the team to go to Kansas City, Dean Abel got a call from a friend in the business office. He was told President Fletcher had removed all of the money for him and the dean of women's travel from their budgets. Abel explained, "Joel thought I had organized the visit to his house, and that the dean of women and I had got all the students together. I went down to his office and said, 'Fletcher, why did you take my travel money out of my budget?' And he said, 'You caused this.' So I told him that 'I did not. I heard about the students' intentions and I went out there to save your life. If you think otherwise, you ought to fire me right now.' Then I turned around and walked out of his office. About an hour later he called me and said, 'We put the money back in your budget.'"

The events of those two days spoke volumes about the managerial style and effectiveness of President Joel Fletcher.

It was obvious from reports of events from various sources that the state board and school administration were in some disarray. They had their privately held views of the politics of athletic program integration but didn't wish to express them publicly. To the outside world, they attempted to exhibit a favorable attitude.

Three days later USL played Southern Colorado in its first game of the tourney at the 16,000-plus seat Municipal Auditorium Arena in downtown Kansas City. *Advertiser* Sports Editor Charles Lenox wrote:

> Southwestern's Bulldogs, a team that has battled the odds all year, came up with another clutch performance last night, and advanced to the second round of the 28th annual

National Intercollegiate Championship basketball tournament with a 66–59 decision over Southern Colorado.

Southern Colorado seeded second in the tournament and sporting an 11-game winning streak, went into the game a heavy favorite to knock off the upstart USL team. But Coach Beryl Shipley's team showed Kansas City its best basketball exhibition of the day and immediately became the surprise team in the tourney.

The Canines were some 850 miles from Lafayette, but it seemed as if the student body and band were right on the court as the "hot line" set up by Gene Martin of Sound Services and financed by the Southwestern student government came through loud and clear.

Martin had arranged with the USL play-by-play station, KPEL, to set up speakers in the Student Center so the students could hear the broadcast. He then piped the band and students cheering to speakers courtside at the Kansas City arena.

On the team's night off, Lenox wrote:

> Yours truly has known for some time that Southwestern basketball coach Beryl Shipley and his assistant Tom Colwell do a top notch job of coaching, but never did it show more plainly than Monday night against Southern Colorado.
>
> Many people said that the Canine's game was dull, but for people who knew the game of basketball it was a fine exhibition of the finer points of the game. One of the Southern Colorado players told me after the game he had never seen a team that played defense the way that USL did or had a greater desire to win. Several coaches had comments about the brand of defense that the Bulldogs exhibited, and it was clear that these coaches wouldn't like to tangle with the Canines.
>
> USL has received more publicity than any team in the tournament with the possible exception of the St. Benedict Ravens of nearby Atchison, Kansas. The Bulldogs had a front-page story in the Kansas City Times Monday morning and sports publicity director Bob Henderson appeared on television Monday afternoon.

It was a promising beginning, but USL lost in the second round. Lenox filed this report:

> To most casual observers the score Oklahoma Baptist 95, Southwestern Louisiana 82 meant only that another team had been eliminated from the second round of the NAIA basketball tournament here Wednesday. But to the fans in Lafayette and throughout the state of Louisiana it meant a lot more. They knew that this was a team that had battled all the odds and had become the first Gulf States conference team to compete in the NAIA tournament since NcNeese in 1956.
>
> The fact that the Bulldogs got beat wasn't really the important thing, although no one likes to lose. The important thing was that the Bulldogs got to come because of the finest student and town support in the history of the institution. This marked the first time that Lafayette and the Southwestern students really ever got behind a USL team.
>
> The flood of telegrams and the "hot line" that was set up in the Southwestern Student Center were deeply appreciated by the Bulldogs and coaches Beryl Shipley and Tom Colwell and served to spark the team.

USL's basketball team had now broken the Deep South's and State of Louisiana's "unwritten law." Its all-white team had played against two teams, Southern Colorado and Oklahoma Baptist, which each included black players. This action stirred the pot and initiated fireworks.

To those familiar with Louisiana politics, it was obvious someone would have to pay; no one, under any circumstance, was allowed to defy a policy mandate of the State Board of Education. The state board, the administration, some sportswriters, coaches of other Gulf States Conference teams, and political associates of the board members quietly seethed. The administration knew, despite Whetstone's comments to the contrary, that the state board was incensed and would initiate action to punish those who had apparently forced Joel Fletcher's hand.

Regardless of the undercurrent of emotions and the harbingers of things to come, that was the watermark year. In the next eight seasons, Beryl Shipley's University of Southwestern Louisiana team averaged almost twenty-one wins per season.

The '65–66 team repeated as Gulf States Conference champions and again qualified for the NAIA regional tournament. This time they lost in overtime in the opening game of the regional tournament to Athens State of Alabama.

In 1966 Coach Shipley, feeling he had the go-ahead of the president of the university, started the move toward national recognition. Playing major competition was one thing, but doing it without all the ammunition you could muster was another. He and his assistant coach, Tom Cox, arrived at a decision that would prove historical, produce incredibly exciting basketball, and sadly lead to the destruction of the basketball program seven years later by the NCAA.

USL President Joel Fletcher unexpectedly retired shortly after the Kansas City confrontation. No one can say for sure if the timing of his leaving the university was the result of those events. Dr. Clyde Rougeau succeeded him and, as related later, was the president who approved Shipley's recruiting of black athletes. The state board, however, had other ideas, and upon finding out the black players were signed up, notified the university that scholarship funds would not be available for them.

When Shipley was advised of that decision, he went to a number of solid supporters and the Lafayette black community. They raised separate funds for scholarships for black athletes, a practice later deemed to constitute an NCAA recruiting violation. Details of this episode will be covered in a later chapter. Shipley and Cox didn't sign just one token player. They signed four top-flight black athletes. Three reported for the start of the 1966 season. They were Elvin Ivory from Birmingham, Alabama, a 6'7" super-athlete with great leaping ability; Marvin Winkler, a hot shooting guard from Washington High School in Indianapolis, who had broken the fabled "Big O," Oscar Robertson's, high school scoring records; and Leslie Scott, another quick guard from McKinley High School in Baton Rouge. The fourth signee, Jessie Marshall from the Shreveport area, went to Grambling State University on a football scholarship.

The first integrated college team in the history of Louisiana—in fact, in the entire Deep South—opened the season with the most ambitious schedule ever seen in these parts.

Beryl described events that occurred early on. "On the first road trip as an integrated team, 1966–1967 season, the black players were freshmen. We started the season with eight games, all played away from home, and we played them in fifteen days: North Texas State, University of Tennessee, Vanderbilt, University of Louisville, University of Houston, Auburn University, Northeast Louisiana State, and Baylor University. We played the first game on December 1, played the last on December 15, and lost every game except one, Northeast Louisiana. We arrived back in Lafayette and played Lamar Tech [now Lamar University] on the seventeenth.

"Before we made that trip our guys had begun to feel that we were pretty good. I had some reservations about how good we were, and I had scheduled those eight games for two reasons. First, I wanted to play some well-known, successful schools that we had never played before, and in order to do so, we had to go to their place; they had no reason or desire to come to ours. Second, I wanted to determine how good we really were. Well, we found out. After we got back, I told the guys, along with a few other choice things, that we had a lot of work to do. And there wasn't any argument.

"These were tense times for the three black team members; they didn't know what to expect. On that first road trip, playing Auburn University, we started the pre-game with our usual huddle and a prayer, generally the Lord's Prayer. The attitude of the crowd had been unusually loud and unruly. But this differed from that at the Louisiana schools—this was a typical college crowd, giving the visiting team hell. They were noisy but not mean, and the three black players were the first that had ever played at Auburn. Naturally, our black guys were concerned. Just out of high school, they weren't used to the noisy, college-style harassment and it affected them. The team had finished its prayer before the game when Marvin Winkler noticed some activity and registered concern. He said, 'Coach, I think we better say that [prayer] again. I think I saw somebody in the rafters with a rifle.'" Winkler was always such a kidder.

Travel arrangements for the team were modified as the season progressed. When playing Northeast Louisiana State in Monroe, Louisiana, Southeastern Louisiana College in Hammond, Louisiana Tech in Ruston, or McNeese State College in Lake Charles, the team arrived, played the game, and left immediately thereafter. They didn't linger for a shower. They donned their warm-up apparel, climbed back on the bus, and departed. A police escort was necessary from the point of arrival to the gym or building in which the game was to be played and from the building to the bus on departure. After the game, on the way back to Lafayette, sandwiches were served on the bus, or the plane, when longer trips were involved. If the trip was short, the team delayed the meal until its arrival in Lafayette.

Most of the murderers-row opening eight road games were played before relatively peaceful audiences. The next four games were in friendly Blackham Coliseum. Then they were on the road again, but this time within Louisiana.

The January 7 game at Nicholls State in south Louisiana included jeers and some racial taunting from the crowd but was relatively well-controlled. This was still Cajun country.

However, the next trip, north to Louisiana College in Pineville, was frighteningly memorable. Traveling by bus, the team pulled up to the small gym on the piney-woods campus of the predominately Baptist college. They were greeted in a decidedly unchristian-like manner. The sidewalk leading to the dressing rooms on the side of the arena was lined with students four and five deep. They were chanting, "Gator bait, gator bait," at the dozen USL players. Three of them, black, got off the bus. They all knew that the Louisiana College nickname was not Gators. Somewhat in shock, the players anxiously trotted into the building. Shipley admonished them in the dressing room to not, under any circumstances, react to the crowd. "Just play your game. Show 'em what you can do with a basketball."

When the Bulldogs came out on the court for pre-game warm-up, the chanting erupted again and the Wildcat band started playing "Dixie." That was to be the scene throughout the entire game: the band played "Dixie" and the crowd chanted, "Gator bait," over and over again for two hours. To their credit, the team, the three minority members, and the coaching staff kept cool heads. Elvin Ivory put on a slam-dunk* exhibition whenever he had the opportunity, and the Bulldogs prevailed 89 to 80. Shipley ordered them into the dressing room immediately at the sounding of the final buzzer and told them to forego showers. They donned their warm-ups and immediately boarded the bus for the two-hour ride home.

Three weeks later, after lifting their record to ten and eight, the team traveled to Ruston in north central Louisiana to try to avenge an earlier loss to archrival Louisiana Tech. Coach Scotty Robertson's Tech, also nicknamed "Bulldogs," had beaten USL 72–66 in early January.

The scene the team had encountered in Pineville was virtually reenacted. Law enforcement officers had been called out when the crowds started gathering early in the afternoon on the Tech campus.

Police cars, lights flashing, greeted the team bus on the outskirts of Ruston and escorted it to the campus. Armed, blue-uniformed officers lined the walkway into the field house to protect the USL team as it disembarked from the Greyhound bus. Play-by-play announcer Ron Gomez remembered, "It was a scary scene. There was real hatred in the air. Not only did the police escort Shipley, his assistant coach, trainer, and the team to the dressing room, one officer was assigned to walk me to my broadcast position above

---

*The "dunk" was still allowed in college basketball in 1966. The NCAA banned it beginning in the 1967 season, and it was reinstated in 1976. Many felt that Adolph Rupp had influenced the decision to outlaw the dunk when his all-white Kentucky team was defeated by Don Haskins' all-black five from Texas Western for the national championship in 1966. The Miners' first offensive fast break was culminated with an intimidating, backboard-rattling slam dunk. Others think the new rule was in response to UCLA's signing of seven-foot Lew Alcindor (later Kareem Abdul Jabar).

the ground-level bleachers and sit beside me during the entire game." Tech won the game in a thrilling and somewhat controversially officiated game, 80–78. The black USL players were subjected to a physically punishing game and constant hissing, booing, and taunting. After the game Beryl praised his team for their courage, pride, and bravery and vowed that better times were on the way. It was the last time any team would beat a Shipley-coached USL team twice in one season.

The experience of that eight-game road trip opening the season paid off. Through the rest of the season, the team won nineteen games and lost only four. That fourth loss came in the third round of the NAIA National Tournament, again to Oklahoma Baptist, but this time by only one point.

The addition of the black athletes pulled Lafayette and Southwest Louisiana together like nothing before or since. Always a tolerant people, Acadiana fans, black and white, now stood and cheered together, hugged each other in consolation on the rare defeats, and filled chartered buses and airliners when the team traveled to take on the nation's elite. Home games were sold out, with standing room only, and a growing contingency of fans regularly followed the team on the road.

Shipley and his troops closed out their dominance of the Gulf States Conference in their last two years as members, winning championships in 1967–68 and 1968–69. That last year saw the team post its best ever season to date, with twenty wins against seven losses. Notably five of those losses came on the road against Michigan State, TCU, West Texas State, Texas El Paso, and Hawaii. But the big boys on the schedule were beginning to pay a price, too. USL beat Nevada, Las Vegas 84–82 on the Running Rebels' home court. USL also whipped Auburn 80–76 and Arizona State on the road and Mississippi State and Baylor in the Bayou Classic in Lafayette. They were beginning to get some respect.

The 1969–70 season was again an ambitious mix. An opening road trip to Houston, St. Louis, and DePaul left the Cajuns winless before they came home to beat TCU, Arkansas, and SMU. Two wins in Hawaii helped finish the season with sixteen wins and eleven losses.

In Coach Shipley's final three years, the team won seventy-four games, losing only thirteen. The '70–71 year saw the Ragin' Cajuns live up to their new nickname as they reeled off eleven straight wins to open the season, including big victories over nationally ranked Oral Roberts, Yale, Oklahoma State, and two giant decisions over Don Haskins' Texas, El Paso (formerly Texas Western) team in El Paso.

It was Beryl Shipley's flying circus. One of the coach's formulas for success was the fact that he could fit his coaching strategy to the talent at hand. In the early days at SLI, with a crew of relatively slow and small players, Shipley successfully used the "shuffle" offense, a scheme of many passes and quick interchange of positions by players. As his recruiting produced faster and more talented players, he opted for the fast-break offense. Now using the fast break and a "trap zone" defense, the Cajuns were scoring at unbelievable levels. They scored 124 against fast-breaking Oral Roberts, 115 against Southern University, and 119 against Eastern Michigan.

By the time they bused into Natchitoches, Louisiana to play Northwestern Louisiana College in late February, they were sporting a sensational eighteen and three record and averaging ninety-three points per game. The Demons' head coach, Tynes Hildebrand, was determined to put an end to the Cajuns' scoring machine. Hildebrand was an open and heated critic of Shipley's recruiting of black players, and there was no love lost in their rivalry. (Ironically, several years later, the majority of Coach Hildebrand's Demon basketball players were black.) Still fielding an all-white team, Hildebrand decided to let the air out of the ball. It was obvious from the beginning what the strategy would be. There was no shot clock in college basketball at the time, and little could be done to force a team to move the ball or shoot. Hildebrand instructed his players to simply cross the midline when they got possession and then stand and hold the ball.

At first Shipley's team reacted by aggressively going after the ball and was immediately called for fouls. Shipley called time out and devised a wait-them-out strategy. Play-by-play announcer Gomez was calling the game from a booth high above the Northwestern arena. "What do you do as a play-by-play announcer when there is no play? By halftime the score was something like eight to seven. The Demon fans were having a great time jeering at the USL players. After describing the interior of the Demon arena and everything else in sight in great detail, I was reading items from the program and the Natchitoches newspaper to the radio audience.

"One of the oddest incidents I had ever seen occurred during the game. As we got into the second half, the always-volatile Coach Shipley was roaming the sidelines, yelling instructions. One of the referees decided to caution him about his actions. Suddenly, the referee blew his whistle and signaled a technical foul. Naturally, I thought Shipley had responded to the official with an expletive. But no. The foul was called on the scorer's table. *Lafayette Advertiser* sportswriter, J.C. Hatcher, almost as short-tempered as Shipley at times, had said something the official didn't like and was called for a technical foul, giving the Demons another trip to the foul line. It's the only time in nineteen years of calling college basketball I ever saw a foul called on a sportswriter. To this day I wonder how the official justified charging the foul to USL. After all, sportswriters are supposed to be neutral, right?"

The Cajuns finally had to resort to fouling and forcing Northwestern to the free throw circle in hopes they would miss and give up the rebound. The strategy worked and USL came away with a very unsatisfying 25–21 victory.

In this, their last season in the NCAA College Division, the Cajuns staged an unforgettable South Regional Tournament at Blackham Coliseum, beating two nationally ranked college division teams, LSU-New Orleans and Tennessee State by five and four points respectively in two classic battles. The fire marshals were pulling out their hair as over 11,000 screaming fans jammed into the 8,500-seat coliseum for these barnburners. The Cajuns finished the season placing third in the NCAA College Division National Championship in Evansville, Indiana, winning two games but losing to eventual champion Evansville.

Now it was time to step up to the big leagues: Division I, NCAA. In 1971–72 the Cajuns repeated their best ever win-loss record of twenty-five wins and only four losses. This was accomplished taking on the best the country could put on the floor in their first year in the top tier.

Wins came on the road against Western Kentucky and Dayton. Perennial top-ten Houston paid off a debt for USL's previous trips to their arena when Guy Lewis brought his cocky squad to Lafayette. They were greeted by a rocking Blackham Coliseum packed to the rafters with raucous fans as the Cajuns triumphed 97–88. Nationally ranked Long Beach State arrived with their legendary coach, Jerry "Tark the Shark" Tarkanian, who showed up for his coaching lesson from Shipley. In an especially spectacular Bayou Classic, the Cajuns walloped Abe Lemon's Pan American Broncos 102–83. Then, with All-American candidate and former Bo Lamar high school teammate, 6'6" Eddie Ratleff, headlining the 49ers, Long Beach fell 90–83.

A titanic battle loomed against Louisiana Tech. Tech, still playing in the college division, was ranked number one in the nation in that division and carried a fifteen-game winning streak. The rivalry between the two schools was classic, and the head-to-head battles on and off the court between Shipley and Tech's Head Coach Scotty Robertson were legendary. USL had a not-too-shabby eleven-game winning streak going, and extended it to twelve with a 107–86 walloping of the upstate Bulldogs in a sound storm at Blackham Coliseum. The Cajuns would hammer Tech again 111–101 three weeks later in Ruston.

The Cajuns ended their first season in Division I losing by four to Louisville in the NCAA Midwest Regional in Ames, Iowa and then crushing the University of Texas by thirty points in a consolation match to finish eighth in the nation.

In Shipley's final campaign, the Cajuns were again undefeated as Southland Conference champions and ended a twenty-four and five season in the NCAA Midwest Regional in Houston. Along the way they had whipped nationally ranked Nevada, Las Vegas; Marshall; Mercer; Oral Roberts; and Houston, among others. Both wire services ranked USL as high as seventh during the year.

That season also wrapped up the college career of reed-thin, 6'1" scoring sensation Dwight "Bo" Lamar, who is the only player to lead the nation in scoring in both the college division and Division I of the NCAA.

Former USL sports information director Dan McDonald, writing for the *Lafayette Advertiser*, recounted the Lamar history in 2005:

> Few people can really claim to be legends in their own time. But nobody disputes the fact that Dwight "Bo" Lamar is one. When longtime Ragin' Cajun basketball fans drive down Johnston Street and pass by Blackham Coliseum, they collectively see one mind's-eye image.
>
> They see that No. 10 jersey and the big Afro on top, elevating higher than most people thought possible on his jump shot, firing off rainbows that threatened the lights in the venerable building. As the years have passed, the distances on those shots have grown. So have the stories. That's what being a legend is all about.
>
> But the facts and the record books don't lie. In the storied history of USL/UL basketball, even in the current era of the 3-point basket, nobody shot it like Bo ... never before, and almost certainly never will again.
>
> "He had as much confidence shooting as anybody that ever played the game," said longtime coach Beryl Shipley, the architect of the school's greatest basketball era. "He felt like he could hit from anywhere." A lot of times, he did.
>
> Lamar led the nation in scoring twice—once in 1970–71 (36.0 points per game) in USL's final year as a college-division team, and again in 1971–72 (36.3) in the Cajuns' first year in what was then called the NCAA's University Division. He remains the only player ever to lead both. At the same time he and his teammates—and in no small role, the Cajun fans—made Blackham one of the nation's college basketball hotbeds. "The crowd is your home-court advantage," Lamar said. "The basket's 10 feet high everywhere. It's what the crowd did that made it special. The fans fed off the

team, and the team fed off the fans. It worked both ways. We had a good team and we had a heck of a crowd."

Standing-room-only crowds weren't unusual in those early-1970s' seasons when USL played big games, and it helped that the Cajuns lost only one home game (Baylor, 93–90, in Lamar's sophomore year) during his final three seasons. USL went 25–4, 25–4 and 24–5 those years, going deep into the NCAA college division national tournament the first year and winning NCAA Tournament games each of the following two years when the tournament field was only 24 teams.

The fans came to see the Cajuns win, but they also came to see Bo. "It was home for me," Lamar said. "I don't know of any other place I would have wanted to play. You could talk to the people in the crowd and get to know them because you knew where they sat all the time. It was crazy, fun for us but terrible for the visiting team." Lamar finished his career with 3,493 points, a lot of them from long range.

"What separated Bo from most guards was he had tremendous jumping ability," said Tom Cox, a USL assistant coach at the time and the man that recruited Lamar. "When you shoot a jump shot, you have to have power in your legs. He could shoot it 30 feet because he could jump so high." "He'd scare you at times when his shots were dropping," Shipley said.

Beryl Shipley, the man from Dobyns-Bennett High School in Kingsport, Tennessee, had come to Cajun country by way of Starkville, Mississippi High School to change forever the athletic history of what is now the University of Louisiana at Lafayette. Along the way he had produced All-Americans, had been named Coach of the Year in Louisiana and the Southland Conference, and made his adopted home a better place in which to live. His players have become leaders in a range of professions. Many have had great positive effects on other young lives by their example and hands-on coaching or encouragement.

His 296 wins still stand as the university's best, as does his nearly 70 percent winning percentage.

But on August 4, 1973, all of this glory was tainted with a pall of doubt and denunciation. The National Collegiate Athletic Association chose to ignore hours of testimony and hundreds of pages of documentation in favor of allegations of violations of NCAA rules from a couple of bitter, discredited former associates and a handful of other questionable witnesses. The program was given the "death penalty," the elimination of the basketball program at USL for two years.

Chapter Three

Integration of the South

To the Lafayette community and most of Acadiana, the recruitment of three black basketball players was not earthshaking. But outside of this relatively quiet area of coexistence and acceptance, the story was quite different.

Even in the mid-1960s, in defiance of the U.S. Supreme Court, the racial divide in communities, social gatherings, and public places extended into the schools, colleges, and universities. Louisiana schools of all levels did not mix the races, period. There were so-called "separate but equal" facilities. In Louisiana this was set in law after the Civil War reconstruction effort was eliminated from the state. The U.S. Supreme Court upheld that law in 1896.

In 1954 the law was overturned. Individual court cases were filed throughout the South to force compliance with the new Supreme Court ruling that "separate but equal" school facilities were no longer legal. In Lafayette such a case was adjudicated and mandated that SLI President Joel Fletcher and his registrar, James Bonnet, could not deny the admittance of the four black applicants named in the suit, "or any other Negro citizen of the state and similarly qualified and situated, on the basis of race or color."

Fletcher and his staff and faculty fully complied immediately. In fact, not four but 114 black students were admitted to the university in the fall semester of 1954, and the number grew exponentially year by year.

This was not happening in the rest of the South. As late as 1962, eight years after the peaceful integration of SLI, a crowd of two thousand angry whites battled federal marshals on the campus of the University of Mississippi at Oxford to prevent the admission of James Meredith, a black high school graduate. Two people were killed and 160 U.S. marshals were injured (28 were shot) in the chaos that erupted.

In June 1963 Alabama Governor George Wallace stood in the doorway of an Alabama schoolhouse to physically block its integration.

Suits were filed against other Louisiana universities but were tied up in litigation for years without successful conclusions.

With noncompliance the rule rather than the exception, the United States Congress attempted to reinforce the 1954 Supreme Court ruling by passing the Civil Rights Act of 1964. While SLI and Lafayette, Louisiana quietly went about interracial business, the rest of the South became a battleground.

Thousands of northern college students and other demonstrators traveled to Mississippi in 1964 to participate in "Freedom Summer" in efforts to assist voting registration of black citizens.

Thirty-seven black churches and thirty black homes and businesses were firebombed or burned during that summer. Most of the cases went unsolved. More than one thousand black and white volunteers were arrested, at least eighty were beaten by mobs or police officers. Culminating the violence was the murder of three young civil rights workers, James Chaney, a black volunteer, and two white coworkers, Andrew Goodman and Michael Schwermer. The three young men disappeared after being released from jail, where they had been held several hours for a minor traffic violation. Their decomposed bodies were found six weeks later under a nearby dam near Philadelphia, Mississippi. The two white men had been shot, and Chaney had died from a savage beating.

In 1965 a peaceful demonstration in Selma, Alabama was interrupted by violence when local white residents and police disrupted the march. One young black man was shot and killed. The Reverend Martin Luther King went to Selma to attend the young man's funeral and subsequently organized a massive march from Selma to Montgomery. Governor George Wallace again intervened, ordering state troopers to halt the march. White vigilantes joined the police. The force moved on the marchers with dogs, tear gas, and billy clubs. It was all caught on film and shown to the American public on national television. Public opinion began to change what courts could not. Slowly and inevitably the segregation barriers came down in elementary schools, high schools, and universities in the Deep South.

Across the Atchafalaya swamp from integrated SLI, the "flagship" university of the state, Louisiana State University, admitted its first black student in 1960. It would be more than a decade later when a black athlete wore the purple and gold of the "Ole War Skule." Collis Temple became the first black basketball player at LSU in 1971. The University of Georgia and Clemson

University in South Carolina were two of the major universities to allow admission of black students in 1961.

It is ironic that Glynn Abel, the dean of men at SLI, was called upon by the university's president, Joel Fletcher, to take charge of the integration process on the campus. Abel would hold off a student uprising at Fletcher's home in 1965 when the president tried to stop the basketball team from participating in the post-season NAIA Tournament in Kansas City, Missouri because some of the universities in the field were integrated.

Abel, one of the most honored athletes in the school's history, later recalled, "He [Fletcher] told me that I was to be totally in charge of integration at the institute. I was to be responsible to make the transition work. After I made sure I would be in *complete* charge, I said, 'Okay I'll do it.' I knew that most of the people in Acadiana were used to the coexistence of the cultures and were more accepting of integration than people in my home state [Mississippi] and other areas and that should help us."

The dean's handling of the media was inherently brilliant and would have been absolutely impossible in today's atmosphere. "As the day for registration approached, I talked to the *Daily Advertiser*, our local paper," Abel said. "I told them I didn't want them to take pictures of the students in the registration line. There'd be, at various times, one hundred to four hundred students lined up before they got in to register. I knew too much publicity, with pictures in the paper, would upset some of the people in town. The *Advertiser* people accommodated me and acted entirely responsibly. A *Life* magazine reporter came in with a camera and I told him not to take any pictures and to get off the campus. I knew that national attention would attract the more radical elements from the outside that opposed integration. The reporter told me he had a right to report on the event. When I repeated that he couldn't, he said he'd sue. I told him he didn't have a right to upset our community, I was in charge of security and everything else associated with the event, and he'd have to get off the campus immediately. And he left—unhappy—but he left."

Because of the dean's banning of media, there is no pictorial evidence or news accounts of this historic event.

"The first day of class, I had a meeting with all 114 of the black students," Abel related. "I told them that this is going to be different for all of you and different for all of us—but I wanted to do everything possible to make it work. And to make it work, we would all have to work together. With that, a big black guy in the back stood up and said he'd take care of any black problems if I'd take care of white ones. I said, 'Okay, I'll tell you what. You pick two of your buddies and come into my office Monday morning at nine o'clock and let's talk about that.' I picked three white student council members to meet with us, to make a total of six students, white and black, to take care of things.

"Before we concluded the first meeting, I asked them if any of the students had noticed anything that didn't seem right. One of them spoke up and complained that teacher so-and-so is putting the black students in the back of the class and white students up in front. I knew exactly who teacher so-and-so's boss was and I left the meeting to tell the boss what the kids had said. In response, he told me to tell the black students that ten minutes from now, that problem will be resolved. I told them what he had said and at the next meeting, when I asked the committee if it had been resolved, I was told, 'Yes, sir.'

"During that second meeting, I asked if anything else had happened that I should know about and one of them said yes, a black girl wants to go out for cheerleading. I told them it was too early in the process; she shouldn't go out. It will upset the other students and cause unneeded trouble for everybody. Let's agree that she will not go out and you won't have to worry about troubles. They agreed. Just like that, and it had nothing to do with legality. The committee knew that if she showed up for cheerleading, it would just raise a ruckus and cause trouble for all, for the black students and the whites. Just like that they elected for civility and another problem was resolved."

In the atmosphere of today's politically correct and super-sensitive racial relations, Abel's actions seem arbitrary and discriminatory. In retrospect, it was just such tough decisions that ensured the uneventful integration of the university.

According to Dean Abel's memory of the events, there was definitely one problem that was not resolved legally. "We decided that for the first semester black students shouldn't get into the dormitories. It would upset other students too much. Everybody agreed except one little black guy. He didn't agree. We brought him in and talked to him, talked to him, talked to him—but he still wouldn't agree. He said he knew what the rule was and he could get in. We told him that we agreed that he could get in, but we thought he ought to do what was best for himself and others. We told him, 'If you do get into the dormitory, it's going to hurt you and it will be upsetting for others. Let's wait just a little while.' He wouldn't budge. He was going to get in. Finally, I asked him, 'Are you a good, religious student?' He said he was, that he was a good Catholic. So I called Father Alexander Sigur, a chaplain on the campus. I asked to see him and he said to come on. I went to see him and took the young black man with me. I told Father Sigur what the committee had decided, that the kid could get his way because it was legal, and explained why we had made the decision. Father Sigur talked to the young man for three minutes, maybe five, and the kid told him, 'Okay, I agree to wait.'"

32

Abel continued, "We had a lot of little bitty things like these come up and we settled them right away. The committee's objective, and mine, was to make progress, a little at a time, and to do it quietly, without publicity."

And successful they were. Even in ensuing crises, cool heads and responsible university, media, and local political leaders prevailed.

When Martin Luther King was assassinated in 1968, black students were distraught, angry, frustrated, and wanting to vent their emotions. Dean Abel immediately had the American flag flying in the school's quadrangle lowered to half-staff. He then joined the three hundred or so students in marching the half-mile or so to downtown Lafayette and the federal courthouse. Before leaving the campus, Abel phoned Lafayette Mayor Rayburn Bertrand to let him know what was happening and asked that the city hall and courthouse flags be lowered as well. The mayor immediately complied. When the marchers arrived downtown, they were satisfied that respect was being shown for their fallen leader and peacefully returned to campus. There was no media coverage of the march.

When lunch counter sit-ins became a popular form of protest around the nation, a local group of black citizens decided to emulate. The word was passed that the Morgan and Lindsay store's lunch counter would be the target. The news media was alerted and studiously stayed away from the scene. A dozen or so marchers showed up, ordered, were served, ate, and left. That was the extent of "demonstrations" in Lafayette, Louisiana.

When word got out in the fall of 1966 that three black basketball players were enrolled at the university, there were mixed feelings in the community. Naturally the black population was elated. Many of their leaders were instrumental in providing the money for the scholarships the athletes would use. Most of the basketball fans were excited or at least anxiously curious at the prospect. The face of college basketball had changed forever on March 19, 1966, when Coach Don Haskins of Texas Western (now named Texas, El Paso) won the national championship with an all-black starting lineup over Adolph Rupp's all-white Kentucky Wildcats. The avid Shipley and USL fans were ready for the great experiment. But it was not, by far, a unanimous welcoming in and around Lafayette. However, the mostly positive experiences of the previous twelve years of integration on the campus had dampened the opposition and softened the resistance.

The enrollment of the black athletes took the rest of the state by surprise, and resentment ran high in athletic circles at the other state schools and in the State Board of Education, the governing board of USL. The board's commissioner of athletics, Stanley Galloway, was retired as the highly successful head football coach at Southeastern Louisiana College in Hammond and had once been rejected by USL when he applied for the same position at the

Lafayette school. Many felt that he carried animosity against USL because of that rejection.

Chapter Four

"Go get 'em, hoss"

In 1966 Dr. Clyde Rougeau was selected as president of USL to succeed the retiring Joel Fletcher. Fletcher had been with the university forty-five years, twenty in the College of Agriculture and twenty-five as president. Though he had reached retirement age, there had been little warning that he would elect to retire. Some felt the NAIA/Kansas City debacle was a contributing factor to his decision.

Seeking the presidency, Rougeau asked for Beryl's assistance. He recognized Beryl's growing influence in the community as a result of his coaching successes and his dynamic personality. Beryl contacted some friends and supporters on Dr. Rougeau's behalf.

The State Board of Education soon appointed Clyde Rougeau as president of USL. Shortly afterward the president unexpectedly showed up to watch a basketball practice. Beryl took the opportunity to tell Dr. Rougeau that he had been approached by several black students who wanted to try out for the team and that several leaders in the black community had offered to help recruit black athletes. Beryl said he was beginning to get uncomfortable about turning down these requests in light of the court and legislative mandates in place concerning integration. He had personally been turning down black recruits since he arrived on the integrated campus in 1957. He suggested that he thought he ought to refer all black student requests of this nature to the administration. Maybe someone with more authority should explain school policy. It was a clever ploy on Shipley's part.

As might be expected, Dr. Rougeau cringed at the thought of handling such an unsavory and possibly illegal task. Rougeau thought about Beryl's suggestion for a few seconds before opening the door to the subsequent historical events. He slapped Beryl on the knee and said, "Go get 'em, hoss." "Hoss" was the president's favorite nickname for everyone.

According to Shipley, *Advertiser* sportswriter Charles Lenox was present during the conversation.

Shipley still insists that Dr. Rougeau should be recognized as the individual most responsible for integrating the first Deep South athletic program, though he staunchly refused to take credit (or blame) for the events.

Beryl had the mandate he wanted from his president.

Assistant Coach Tom Cox was chomping at the bit. He had already compiled information on potential black recruits gleaned from a network of friends of USL and published reports on high school athletes and friendly high school coaches, especially in the hotbed states of Indiana and Ohio, where Cox had grown up. Within weeks Cox and Shipley managed to locate and sign four outstanding black players for the 1966–67 season: Elvin Ivory from Birmingham, Marvin Winkler from Indianapolis, Leslie Scott from Baton Rouge, and Jessie Marshall from Princeton, Louisiana, a small town just outside of Shreveport. State board Athletic Commissioner Stanley Galloway later declared Marshall's USL signing void, declaring that he also signed a football scholarship to attend Grambling University. The dating of the Grambling agreement and the ruling by the commissioner were highly questionable, but the coaches chose to drop the subject. All of the new recruits signed the standard forms that USL and all other schools in the Gulf States Conference were using and had been using for more than ten years. The first steps had been taken for USL to become the first state-supported school in the Deep South to officially integrate its athletic program.

It didn't take long for the news of the three black athletes to get out. Now Shipley and USL had really done it. Not only had they traveled to Kansas City and participated in athletic contests with integrated teams, now they had actually signed "Negro" players to wear their uniform and be a part of the team. The seething that had boiled over when the "unwritten law" had first been breeched now turned to rage.

From this time on, the basketball program was to be subjected to unending criticism, constant surveillance, and innuendos, rumors, allegations, and distortions of fact. Not only were Shipley, his team, and his program the target of outright bigots and defenders of segregation, but these were also joined by the State Board of Education, coaching peers, a large group of sportswriters, and, unfortunately, many within the USL administration. Soon this group would also be joined and abetted by the NCAA.

To put it mildly, the state board didn't like the news that USL had signed three black athletes. They quickly arranged a meeting, held at a Lafayette motel. A.D. Smith, president of the state board; Fred Tannehill, board member; Dr. Rougeau, president of USL; Whitey Urban, athletic director; Stanley Galloway, the state board's commissioner of athletics; and Beryl Shipley were in attendance. The first subject was establishing how the black players got to USL. Beryl decided the truth would put Dr. Rougeau in a dangerous situation with the board, possibly leading to dismissal. So he told them a big *white* lie. He said he figured the National Association for the Advancement of Colored People (NAACP) had sent them. The discussion quickly turned to how to get rid of them.

Two important suggestions were explored. With all present as witnesses, Galloway said to Dr. Rougeau, "You're the president; flunk the black students on entrance requirements." Rougeau told him he couldn't do that. He said they were already registered and in school and they were qualified, with high school diplomas. At the time USL had no entrance examination; only a legitimate high school diploma was required. Galloway then suggested that Beryl start practice a week early and to make sure that the black athletes were not good enough to play.

NCAA rules mandated that member basketball teams could not hold organized or supervised practices prior to October 15. Tom Cox, assistant basketball coach, remembered, "The board's commissioner of athletics [Galloway] and our athletic director [Urban] forced us to close the doors on October 7, start practice early—and make sure that the black athletes were not good enough to play."

Since the board, its athletic commissioner, and his athletic director ordered it, Shipley complied with the early practice. But he knew he couldn't dump the black athletes; there was no way that he could convincingly maintain that they couldn't play well enough. They were all outstanding athletes, and two of them had been high school basketball All-Americans.

But that wasn't the only segregationist strategy practiced by the State Board of Education. The board informed USL that no scholarship funds would be available for the black athletes. This wasn't because there was a shortage of funds; the state board was refusing funds for these three athletes because they were black. (That was absolutely one of the rankest examples of pure racial discrimination, as was proven and rectified before the NCAA even began its investigation. Yet the NCAA, with full knowledge of these facts, closed its eyes to the matter.)

No arguments would sway the board's stance. Shipley and Cox focused on another way to fund the scholarships. They had the support of the Lafayette community, so Shipley appealed to his supporters and civic leaders who had supported him earlier in making the Bayou Classic tournament a success.

This time the leadership of the black community rose to the occasion. Carlton James—an outstanding black citizen and former educator, retired because of blindness—and two black businessmen, Fred Mouton and Denris Mouton, stepped forward. They agreed to raise the funds necessary and formed the Lafayette Business League for that purpose.

Rocke Roy, whose family owned a local automobile dealership, talked his father, George M., into donating a car to be given away in a raffle. It wasn't a top-of-the-line model. As a matter of fact, it was a used, older car, but it was a car and it was free.

The Black Business League took on the task of raffling off the automobile. The three founders of the business league enlisted the aid of other black leaders such as Robert Henderson, Dr. Ernest Kinchen, Dr. Jim Caillier, and Wallace "Wa Wa" Mouton. When the proceeds from the raffle came up short of the needed funding, the three founders of the league personally donated additional funds.

Within weeks of the beginning of the project, the business league delivered an amount of money exactly equivalent to the total of three state grant-in-aid athletic scholarships to the university. They did not deliver the money to Shipley, Cox, or the athletic department. Carlton James personally delivered the funds directly to the business office of the university. The funds were to pay for tuition, books, and other expenses normally covered by athletic scholarships for white athletes. But because of the state board's ruling, the funds were designated specifically for the benefit of the three black athletes.

Subsequently it was learned that this was contrary to NCAA rules. Scholarship funds were not allowed to be designated for specific athletes. In spite of the fact that these funds were raised only because of the denial of scholarships to the black athletes, this was deemed one of the major violations later cited by the NCAA in its first punishment of the program.

Jim Caillier, though younger than most of the principal players in the Black Business League, was a member of a prominent black family in Lafayette and got involved in the recruiting effort. Jim was a student in 1960 and later became a USL staff member, then a university vice president, and later president of a large technical school in New Orleans. Caillier remembers, "This school integrated its athletic program; the other Gulf States Conference schools didn't. So the others got together to chastise us because, they said, the agreement was for everyone to integrate at the same time. The idea, they said, was a smooth integration for all, with each school bringing in one black player. I heard this story around the state, but it was junk; it was merely a story cooked up to make it palatable for maintaining segregation.

"Some of the other coaches said, 'USL jumped ahead, and therefore, dominated the whole conference.' But this rationalization doesn't square with the facts. They forget that Coach Shipley was dominating the whole conference before the team integrated. He was a good coach before and a good coach after integration."

Caillier added, "When Beryl came to SLI all of the regional schools in the conference at that time were on equal par—designed to be a conference of Louisiana schools that would play within the state. But Beryl wanted to attract great players and compete with the best. He did that very well, despite limited resources. Even before he brought in the black players, before 1966, Beryl was recruiting athletes from out of the state. He brought in great white players from the outside, and they were a part of the successes. The other schools resented USL playing the big guys and gaining national attention. USL was moving too fast. USL was supposed to stay in the GSC, but times were a-changing, and if a coach at that time was to remain successful, he had to reach out."

Jim continued, "This school jumped the gun when President Rougeau said to go. But when his hand was called, he passed the buck to the coach, and the coach blamed the NAACP. And we know that if he'd said 'Clyde told me to do it,' Rougeau would have been fired on the spot. Clyde got pressure to resign later, because the board blamed him for not maintaining control and for not informing the board in time sufficient for it to prevent the action. All of this put pressure on Dr. Rougeau."

It didn't take long for Athletic Commissioner Stanley Galloway to enlist the aid of the NCAA in penalizing USL and Shipley for recruiting black athletes. It is revealed in an NCAA document dated December 20, 1967 that Galloway phoned the association's assistant executive director, Arthur J. Bergstrom, on October 18 and 21, 1966, within two weeks of the illegal practice. Galloway wanted to report NCAA violations on the part of USL, one of which was an early practice session—a session he had ordered!

With these allegations from the Louisiana athletic commissioner, Bergstrom assigned Warren Brown to begin an investigation. Brown, relishing his first assignment as an investigator, conducted interviews on November 17 and 18 in Louisiana. During those two days, Brown interviewed Galloway and USL officials: A.D. Urban; the university's chief financial officer, Ovey Hargrave, Jr.; Leo Herbert, chairman of the student financial aid committee; Dan Roy, assistant football and head baseball coach; Beryl Shipley; Tom Cox; and Billy Mistric, a USL student athlete.

Shipley remembers the interview held in his office: "We talked candidly about all of our activities that could have been violations and I explained to Warren precisely what had occurred in recruiting the three black athletes. I explained there was no way to provide scholarships without the help of the outside Lafayette Business League, because the state board had informed me that it would not provide the normal scholarship funds. The kids were in no financial condition to pay their own way, so another source for funding had to be found. I told him about the early practice and the reason for it: the state board had ordered it. I volunteered information on all activities that I thought might have been infringements of NCAA rules in providing for support of the basketball program's black athletes. For each activity I emphasized the reason that it had become necessary, and I pointed out that none of the violations involved poor sportsmanship or gave us recruiting advantages over our competitors. They were purely technical in nature and forced on us by the state board mandate." The proof of violations as poor sportsmanship and giving a school recruiting advantages were two criteria for NCAA sanctions.

Shipley concluded, "I showed the investigator that under the current set of NCAA rules, there was no way these highly competent, but educationally deprived black athletes of the '60s—children of black parents who had lived as second-class citizens all their lives—could have been able to attend USL or any other white school in the Deep South. I've often wondered what kind of training program Walter Byers set up when he hired Warren Brown and David Berst as NCAA investigators. They obviously knew very little about American history and the history of integration and segregation in the South."

During the meeting, Brown questioned the integration situation. He said to Beryl, "If the school didn't want you to integrate, why did you do it?" And Beryl explained that the university had been academically integrated since 1954. Still concerned that Dr. Rougeau would take the brunt of the blame, Shipley merely said the university administration was not the problem; the Louisiana State Board of Education was the principal source of the objections to integration.

There was another problem with the school administration that hadn't yet surfaced; the philosophy expressed by Rougeau's predecessor, USL President Joel Fletcher, still infused the leadership. He had told members of the athletic staff he didn't like too much activity on the "left side" in the athletic programs. His coarsely coded message referred to a win–loss column where wins are on the "left side." Fletcher had once told a coach that he liked seeing a sports page show the football team at Iowa State University, where he received his master's degree, had been badly beaten. "It tells me they're still keeping academics strong." He was now of the opinion that too much national attention was being focused on the popularity of the team and the basketball coaches.

The fact that the university was getting much favorable attention along with the basketball team was apparently inconsequential to those in the administration who felt their own personal importance was being diminished. In addition the success of the basketball program had upset other members of the Gulf States Conference, and Beryl didn't realize the extent to which they were seething. Little did anyone realize how these forces would come together to ultimately destroy the program.

Warren Brown's question—"Why did you integrate?"—is interesting in retrospect. Walter Byers, executive director of the NCAA, has quoted Bill Bell, a great black Ohio State lineman, as saying, "As a result of the quite unpublicized work of the NCAA, thousands of black Americans are enjoying richer and better lives which have accrued from black participation in college athletics." Bell, as noted by Byers, "graduated in 1931" and "devoted many hours to NCAA affairs." Evidently Bell didn't know Warren Brown, the NCAA investigator. Brown's question in 1966—"Why did you integrate?"—puts some doubt into the legitimacy of Bell's commendation. The entire NCAA organization, with subsequent actions against USL, actually impeded the progress of integration and delayed black students' participation in athletics in colleges and universities of the Deep South—by at least four years, maybe more.

The two principal investigators in the USL case, Warren Brown and David Berst, were both hired in 1966. Brown was a Kansas State graduate and former member of the Wildcats basketball team. He, in turn, recommended the hiring of Berst, another young recent graduate of McMurray College. The USL case was possibly the first opportunity for these two to earn their stripes. Their boss, Byers, obviously recognized their zealousness when he noted in his 1995 book, *Unsportsmanlike Conduct*, "For the most part, our investigators were young, and member colleges had begun complaining that the NCAA's 'Young Turks' were so eager to prove violations that they were manufacturing evidence to enhance their investigative reputations." The complaints voiced by others were obviously well-deserved and quite evident during USL's two investigations. Adding credence to Byers' concerns about the veracity of his investigative team is the fact that a seasoned investigator, former FBI Special Agent Hale McMenamin, was hired in 1975 to bring in some expertise and counter the voluminous criticisms.

Another factor probably influenced the NCAA and its operatives at the time. The sports media had recently been uncovering probable recruiting and aid violations at some of the major athletic programs, to which the NCAA had not reacted. There were rumblings that the association was a "paper tiger" incapable of controlling its big-time university athletic programs and indeed fearful of doing so, lest the majors chose to organize on their own and split from the national group.

One famous case that the media picked up on was that of Wilt Chamberlain and his recruitment by Kansas University. "Wilt the Stilt," an athletic seven-footer, chose the Jayhawks over dozens of other programs, including

41

the cream of the college programs in the East, near his home in Philadelphia. Wilt arrived on the Kansas University campus driving a 1950 Buick, but by May 1956 had graduated to a 1953 Oldsmobile supplied by a prominent Kansas City auto dealer. The dealer told NCAA officials Wilt was paying for the car in twenty-five-dollar-a-month increments. By the way, the payments were delivered in person, in cash—no checks, no paper trail. By 1957 the Stilt was driving a 1956 Oldsmobile convertible obtained from a Lawrence, Kansas dealership. When Wilt left the school, he drove away in a 1958 two-tone Oldsmobile 98 convertible. For these acts and other violations in football recruiting, KU eventually received a two-year probation—after Chamberlain had left the campus and had participated in two national championship games.

You'll note that as the USL alleged violations are unfolded several were for "loan of an automobile" for dates and small cash payments for purchase of gasoline. All-American Bo Lamar, the nation's leading scorer for two years, finished his USL basketball career driving an ancient, banged-up Toyota that he had purchased from an athletic department staff member for less than five hundred dollars.

As Brown and Berst started their investigative careers, many of the major universities, according to Byers, complained that, "The NCAA cops don't know what's going on in the real world" and "The Young Turks are out to get any and all." Thus, a bushel-load of allegations lodged against a mid-level newcomer such as USL was a great opportunity to quiet the critics and inflate the egos of the two new investigators, Brown and Berst.

Whether intentionally or not, the NCAA in fact cooperated completely with the Louisiana State Board of Education's desire to maintain athletic segregation. Their actions fully enhanced the state board's efforts to punish USL's athletic program for breaking the "unwritten law" by integrating its athletic program.

Stan Galloway, apparently acting on behalf of the Board of Education, conducted his own investigation of the situation. As reported in a column by J.C. Hatcher, an *Advertiser* sportswriter, Galloway had an intense dislike for USL and its administration. While he was football coach at Southeastern, the job as head coach at USL had opened up in 1961. Galloway applied for the job, but the school administration neither acknowledged his application nor granted him an interview. Russ Faulkinberry, a protégé of the legendary Paul "Bear" Bryant was hired instead. Hatcher surmised that Galloway was still bitter from that experience.

The sportswriter pointed out that Galloway was the individual who first contacted the NCAA to initiate the 1966 investigation. With help from other institutions, competitors of USL, he became the chief investigator for the State Board of Education. Hatcher said that Louisiana State University, the ordained top state university dating from Huey Long's reign as governor, resented USL's rise in national popularity, as did Grambling State University and Southern University, Louisiana's principal black schools, which feared for the future of their athletic programs.

Bill Carter, sports editor of the *Alexandria Town Talk* and a highly partisan critic of USL, reported in 1968:

> Trouble began almost two years ago [1966] when USL signed...Leslie Scott.... At, or about this time, Grambling and Southern reported that if wholesale recruiting of Negro athletes in Louisiana were allowed, their programs would be wrecked; that they would have to go out of state to recruit, or join the Gulf States Conference (GSC).
>
> This encouraged the 'gentlemen's agreement,' in which integrated athletics [would be] permissible, but that it be done gradually. When USL continued to recruit Negro athletes, the other GSC members complained that they were living up to the agreement, but that USL was not.

Since his arrival on campus in 1957 until 1971, when LSU granted its first scholarship to a black athlete, Shipley realized that other Louisiana schools frequently used the race card when competing with him for recruits. White high-school athletes were being told, "You know, of course, if you go to that school (USL), you will have to attend with Negroes; the school is integrated." This problem was unique to Southwestern, the only school in Louisiana and the Deep South that was academically integrated, and it prompted Beryl to seek potential athletes in areas outside of Louisiana. Even this recruiting practice engendered criticism. According to a memo sent to him by his superiors shortly after he took the job, he was supposed to stick with Louisiana students and not go looking for athletes in distant places. Beryl ignored the suggestion.

Obviously no plans were being pursued to integrate any of the athletic programs in the state in the near future. Shipley chafed at the hypocrisy. Even worse was the attitude of the black schools toward integration of Louisiana's university athletic programs.

Shipley recalled, "I had expected that all black people would welcome this obvious expansion of horizons for black student athletes. But I hadn't considered it from the perspective of the black schools and their coaches. And when I realized that, it became obvious that the opposition to athletic integration was almost universal in the Deep South. The only people who were excited and happy were USL's team members, USL students, alumni and fans from around the state. Some members of the university administration were unhappy, and many of them were actively engaged in seeking anything possible that might bring USL's basketball program down and to punish those responsible for ending segregation."

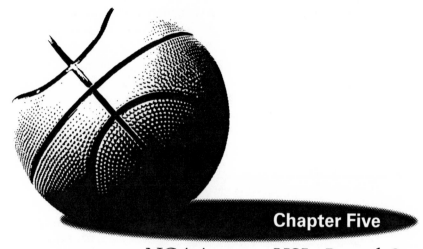

Chapter Five

NCAA versus USL, Round One

Louisiana Athletic Commissioner Stanley Galloway did his job well. On January 20, 1967, the NCAA issued a seven-page, fifty-eight-item official inquiry that required answers and explanations. Joel Fletcher's successor, USL President Clyde Rougeau, responded by letter dated March 3, 1967.

It is obvious to those familiar with the events involved in the allegations that Dr. Rougeau's intention was to appear to be defending the basketball program and the university while not revealing the underlying reasons for the problems: institutional racism.

For example, consider his response to the first question: "What agency or individual is responsible for the creation and establishment of USL's athletic policies and practices?" He answered, "The athletic committee of the Louisiana State Board of Education." There was no committee; only one individual was involved: Stanley Galloway. The NCAA was obviously participating in the subterfuge. Stanley Galloway at that point had been and still was the association's principal source of the allegations against USL.

It should be noted that Coach Shipley was never apprised of this "official inquiry." Dr. Rougeau's responses were formed without any input from anyone connected with the basketball program.

Also, in point eight, "It is alleged that USL's head basketball coach arranged for the Lafayette Business League to pay the educational expenses [of three athletes]." Rougeau did not respond with the facts leading to the fundraising efforts. Such a revelation may have highlighted the obvious racial framing of the entire list of allegations and ended the inquiry immediately. He didn't say that the state board, wholly in charge of USL activities, refused to fund the athletes because they were black (or, in terms of the day, Negroes), and other arrangements had to be made. He didn't say that the students had been placed on regular scholarship in December 1966, three months earlier, because the federal government had ruled that the rights of the black athletes had been violated. He didn't mention Beryl's trepidations, related to him in 1966, concerning turning black athletes down because of their race. Instead he replied without fully disclosing the orders of the state board:

> Since its integration in 1954, the University of South-western Louisiana had received several expressions of interest in having Negro students participate in varsity athletics. In the [*spring* crossed out and a handwritten insertion, *fall*, was written in to replace it] of 1965, the first Negro student (non-scholarship) participated in varsity athletics as a member of the track team.
>
> In an effort to secure funds to pay for the educational and other allowable expenses for Elvin Ivory, Leslie Scott, Marvin Winkler, <u>who could not be placed on regular University scholarships</u>, [Why couldn't they?] Coach Shipley and Coach Cox sought the help of Mr. Carlton James and other leaders of the Negro community. The Lafayette Business League was formed to raise the necessary funds for these Negro student-athletes and this organization did finance the scholarships afforded Ivory, Winkler and Scott until they were placed on regular university athletic scholarships.

Point eleven stated:

> Information made available to the Committee on Infractions indicates that the grant-in-aid or scholarship form utilized by the University of Southwestern Louisiana to notify student-athletes of awards made to them is not in conformity with NCAA requirements. Specifically it is reported that no provision is made on the form to indicate that the award has been approved, granted, and certified by the University's scholarship or grant-in-aid committee.
>
> (a) Please submit a copy of the form currently being utilized by the University to notify student-athletes of awards made to them.

Rougeau didn't say that *the form used was the only one USL was authorized to use by the Gulf States Conference at the time, and it was the only one that had been in use for over ten years.* And he didn't point out that the GSC had no such form, as described, until the NCAA noted in a December 20, 1966 memo that "the Gulf States Conference has modified the form used to describe the amount, duration, terms and conditions of awards made to student-athletes to bring it into conformity with the NCAA requirements." This was long after the athletes had been signed.

Rougeau's response was less than forceful:

> The Gulf States Conference adopted forms to be used by the scholarship Committee in December 1966. These forms, which comply with NCAA requirements, have been used at Southwestern since that date. Prior to joining the NCAA no such forms were used.
>
> Since becoming a member of the NCAA, the University of Southwestern Louisiana has endeavored to comply with all NCAA regulations. (A copy of the form now in use is enclosed.)

Rougeau, with this inane comment, did nothing to defend the university in any useful way.

Point twelve is another example of Dr. Rougeau's timid approach to defending the program:

> It has been alleged that coaches of the University of Southwestern Louisiana recruited Elvin Ivory and Marvin Winkler, then prospective student-athletes, encouraged their enrollment at the University by offers of institutional financial assistance and submitted to these young men pre-signed documents which described the aid available to them. It is further alleged that the University's scholarship or grants-in-aid committee was not called upon to take subsequent action on these pre-signed documents. Please indicate whether this information is substantially correct and submit all pertinent evidence.
>
> > (a) In the event the allegations described above are substantial, please indicate by whose authority the documents were pre-signed and by whose authority coaches and/or the department of athletics are

authorized to make awards of institutional financial
assistance. Also indicate whether the coaches' action
in this case represented the University's normal recruiting procedures.

Rougeau should have replied that the Louisiana State Board of Education had refused to fund the scholarships because the athletes were black, so
any action from a regular grants-in-aid committee would have been out of
the question. Also the federal government had since ruled that refusal of the
scholarship funds violated the athletes' civil rights and had forced the board
to put them on regular scholarships. The president could have also reported
that the coach had been told in a meeting with state board members that no
funds would be made available for black athletes and was told to get rid of
them with the early practice.

Instead Rougeau replied with this obfuscation:

The Athletic Department of the University was informed by the Athletic Committee [Stanley Galloway as a
committee of one] of the State Board of Education late in the
spring of 1966 that documents presented to Negro athletes
and signed by them could not be honored by the University.
Hence they were not presented to the University Scholarship
Committee until December, 1966, when the University was
informed it could honor the commitments of scholarships to
Ivory, Winkler and Scott.

At times the application forms have been pre-signed by
authority of the Athletic Director because some parents have
insisted on a copy of the application (completely signed) at
the time of the student-athlete's commitment (a copy in use
enclosed). No member of the coaching staff has the authority to make awards of institutional financial assistance. The
coaches' action in this case represents the University's normal recruiting procedures.

Dr. Rougeau was walking a tightrope between responding accurately
while protecting the state board. Today Coach Shipley still defends Clyde
Rougeau as a fundamentally honorable man, but the state board and its in-
tractable position against black athletes placed him in an untenable situation.
The only explanation for Dr. Rougeau's less-than-forceful responses is that he
feared for his career. The board had total control of the school, and it could
replace the school's president in a heartbeat if it so desired.

The NCAA's list of complaints, derived from its investigations of USL activities, generally led with a description of USL's irresponsible act of using an outside group to fund the scholarship of three black players, the form used to sign them that didn't incorporate enough information, the athletic staff making the decision to financially fund the black players, and other items related to the funding. Thus, the basketball program and its coaches were punished for: raising outside funds for black athletes when those athletes were denied aid because of their race; using an improper form, although the form used was the official document used by their conference for ten years; and holding an illegal practice, though that practice was ordered by the state board with orders to get rid of the black players.

Not many people know that all of these problems, with the exception of the early practice, had been resolved before the NCAA even began its investigation.

Carlton James, the brilliant, retired black educator and major contributor to the fund for the athletes, knew discrimination when he saw it. After arranging for the welfare of the three black athletes, he heard of the problems with the State Board of Education that Shipley and his program were enduring. James made a call to Washington, D.C. Shortly thereafter a young woman paid a visit to the USL campus and asked a lot of questions, and not long after that, in September, Dr. Rougeau was informed that the university was in violation of federal acts involving equal rights.

David S. Seely, assistant commissioner of the Equal Educational Opportunities Program, using information supplied by the young woman, ruled that the "Negro athletes in question had been discriminated against and that there was an apparent violation of the Civil Rights Act. As a result of the investigation and conclusion, the three Negro athletes have since been placed on regular scholarship."

The funding matter had been concluded, and the athletes were placed on regular scholarships before the end of September 1966. The first letter from the NCAA was dated January 20, 1967, long after the funding problem had been put to bed. The NCAA was beating a dead horse and knew it. But how would it look for the association to admit that this entire investigation had been instigated by a segregation-inspired governmental entity?

Another important impropriety, according to the NCAA, involved starting practice early. The NCAA, from the Warren Brown investigation, knew that the State of Louisiana, in the form of the Louisiana State Board of Education's commissioner of athletics, Stanley Galloway, had ordered that done, and the state board was the ultimate authority in university affairs. Practically speaking, there was nothing the coach or the school could have done without expecting punishment. Yet the NCAA, with full knowledge of these facts, proceeded with the allegation against the basketball program and the university.

It is obvious that the NCAA had an agenda to prove it had the ability to punish member schools. In doing so it joined the racially motivated Deep South segregationists who had decided to discipline Beryl Shipley and his basketball program for integrating his team. It is hard to believe this battle to integrate athletics was occurring in 1967, yet the school had integrated its student body thirteen years earlier, in 1954.

USL's response is dated March 3, 1967, but an NCAA confirmation of receipt cannot be found. Since much of the rebuttal evidence seems to have been totally ignored, some have wondered if Rougeau's response letter was actually mailed or received by the NCAA.

The next record, a letter from NCAA executive assistant Arthur Bergstrom to Rougeau dated June 2 (with copies to Galloway, Lewis, Urban, and the NCAA Committee on Infractions) sets up a meeting date. It suggests that Rougeau select USL representatives with which "the Committee will review the case involving your institution and would like to meet with representatives of the University in order that full facts may be developed."

Rougeau acknowledged the letter and appointed Dr. Ray Authement, W.D. Lewis, and A.G. Urban as USL representatives. Authement and Lewis were needed for the general university allegations, and Urban for those involving basketball. Two individuals, Beryl Shipley and Tom Cox, had the most broad-based and extensive knowledge of all areas, yet USL did not find it necessary to include them in the meeting or even inform them that the meeting was being held. The NCAA invited Stanley Galloway to the meeting, and he had free reign with his allegations. According to observers of the meeting, Dr. Rougeau's selection of attendees didn't have the fortitude with which to rebut Galloway, the undisputed source of most of the allegations.

The entire exercise appeared to be a prearranged farce. In spite of multiple items evidencing the blatant racial undertones of the entire matter, the NCAA led the way for the board and the university to conceal its segregationist policies.

At that time, all of the state universities other than the Louisiana State University System and the two predominately black schools, Southern University and Grambling University, were governed by the State Board of Education. In 1966, some twelve years after Southwestern integrated its student body with 114 black students, there were fewer attending all of the other seven schools combined.

Coach Shipley's meticulous explanation of the whole situation to the NCAA investigator, Warren Brown, during the November 18, 1966 meeting held in Beryl's office was never acknowledged by the association.

On September 13, 1967, Arthur Bergstrom wrote Clyde Rougeau a letter in which additional charges of violations were presented. A Supplemental Official Inquiry was attached. It was five pages long and involved about thirty-nine questions requiring responses. Marked for copies were Stanley Galloway; W.D. Lewis; Earl M. Ramer, VP NCAA Third District; A.G. Urban; and the NCAA Committee on Infractions.

The NCAA asked for copies of all correspondence or records of phone calls between university officials and a high school athlete, Larry Highbaugh, or his parents. Highbaugh was a highly recruited football player. The allegations appear to have been triggered by a fishing expedition conducted by Jim Angelopolous, a sportswriter in Indianapolis who questioned an alleged offer of money, a car, and a guaranteed six-year scholarship supposedly offered Highbaugh by Southwestern coaches. It was ridiculous, of course, but the university had to respond. The coaches had no way to pay for the car, and a six-year scholarship was way beyond anyone's ability to guarantee. Ultimately the NCAA dropped the allegation because of lack of corroboration, but it remained part of the record reported by the media.

In December 1967 Arthur Bergstrom dispatched a letter to Dr. Clyde Rougeau marked confidential, with an attachment headed Confidential Report No. 49, with which was another attachment headed Case No. 252. The latter attachment presented NCAA conclusions concerning USL's alleged violations: the last step before punishment was to be handed down. The letter is of extreme interest because it stated NCAA policy concerning the allegations presented in the Case 252 attachment: "The report of the Committee, less its recommendations, if such are made, shall be made available to the member involved and *it shall be notified that it is entitled to appear before the Council to challenge the findings of fact and the evidence upon which the report is based, to produce additional evidence and to argue such matters of Association law as may be involved. The Council shall not act upon the report of the Committee until the report has been forwarded to the member involved and the member has had an opportunity to appear before the Council"* (italics authors' emphasis).

USL's archive records, notwithstanding the above invitation, reveal no reply to the NCAA's December 20 letter from the university. Shipley did not receive a copy of the letter with the statement of policy; he was only belatedly given access to a copy of the attachment that detailed the alleged violations.

USL made no real effort to argue the case. Regardless of news reports to the contrary, the school was in no position to argue. Its administration was under the thumb of the Board of Education. The board wanted punishment to be administered to the basketball program and coaches primarily and to the university secondarily for allowing the problem to develop. The objectives of USL's administration were to satisfy the board, make no waves, and do anything possible to keep their jobs secure.

With the arrival of Bergstrom's letter and attachment, Case 252, the identity of the principal USL accuser, Louisiana Athletic Commissioner Stanley Galloway, was officially revealed for the first time.

Now it was USL's last chance to rebut the allegations. The Case 252 document started with Part I, Origin of the Case: "On August 29, 1966, the secretary of the Committee on Infractions [Arthur Bergstrom] received information which charged the violation of NCAA legislation on the part of the University of Southwestern Louisiana. During the preliminary checking of the charge, allegations of additional violations were submitted to the Committee."

The section headed Part II, Information Examined by Committee was most interesting. It itemized information acquired during the investigative stages and provided the sources and dates. The initial complaint, made on August 29, 1966, the second (September 1), and the third (September 23) involved only USL Head Football Coach Russ Faulkinberry. None of these allegations were deemed important to the media and went virtually unreported.

The basketball program didn't get any attention until October 18 and 21, when the NCAA's Bergstrom had telephone conversations with Stanley Galloway. The commissioner—whose responsibility should have been to the universities he represented, the board he served, and the athletic conference of which USL was a member—chose instead to bypass them all and go directly to the NCAA.

The letter dated December 20 was the first clue to the fact that the Louisiana State Board of Education, in its illegal and discriminatory effort to maintain racial segregation of athletics, asked the NCAA to get involved. With that action it seemed obvious that Galloway had begun his trek to get even with USL for ignoring his application (there were actually two) for its head football coach position.

Part III of the document listed Violations of NCAA requirements or questionable practices in light of NCAA requirements as determined by Committee. The first allegation read:

> 1. At the beginning of the 1966–67 college year, the University of Southwestern Louisiana permitted an outside organization to pay the educational expenses of three student athletes at the University. Inasmuch as members of the University's athletic staff promised

> financial assistance to the three young men and it was
> ultimately forthcoming, the Committee holds that
> the three student-athletes involved were not cogni-
> zant that the assistance provided to them originated
> from a source other than the University.

The facts were: USL was not responsible. The State Board of Education violated the three student-athletes' civil rights by refusing to fund their scholarships because they were black. The federal government had informed the university in September 1966 that the athletes' civil rights had been violated and directed it to put them on regular scholarships—**before Galloway and the NCAA began the investigation.**

In addition, no athlete, white or black, was cognizant of the source of their funds. The school knew, but not the athletes. All any student athlete knew was that the funding came from the university, and this was entirely true also for the three black athletes. From the very beginning, the school delivered and controlled the funding for the black athletes.

Shipley decided to personally respond to the allegations presented in Case No. 252. He wrote a letter to Walter Byers, executive director of the NCAA, and presented his arguments for his and the school's position. He addressed his appeal to Byers because he had already explained the circumstances to Warren Brown, his own university administration, and Bergstrom to no avail.

Beryl's letter, dated January 4, 1968—two weeks after the date of Berg-strom's confidential letter to Clyde Rougeau—strongly presented the case for the university. He and the university had been placed in an untenable position by the conflicting demands of the NCAA, the Gulf Coast Conference, the Louisiana State Board of Education, and United States law, the Civil Rights Act of 1964.

January 4, 1968
Mr. Walter Byers
Executive Director
National Collegiate Athletic Association
Midland Building
Kansas City, Missouri 64105

Re:
Alleged Violation of NCAA Legislation
by the University of Southwestern Louisiana

Lafayette, Louisiana
Case Number: 252

Dear Mr. Byers,

As head basketball coach at the University of Southwestern Louisiana, at Lafayette, Louisiana, I have recently received a memorandum pertaining to the captioned matter, to which I would appreciate making formal reply, since the bulk of the charges contained in said memorandum seem to be directed to me.

The aforementioned memorandum, in Paragraph III, alleges that there have been violations of the principles governing the award of financial assistance to student-athletes (NCAA Constitution 3, 4 (a) and (c)), in that members of the Athletic Staff of the University permitted an outside organization to pay the educational expenses for student-athletes at the University and that the Staff promised such financial assistance to three young men without these students' knowledge. It is further contended that the decision to assist these three students financially was made by the University's athletic staff rather than the "Institution's regular committee on scholarships and grant in aids" and the recipients were not "provided with a proper written statement describing the amount, duration, conditions and terms of the award." It was found therefore that the procedures followed in these instances placed the University's Athletic Department in administrative control of the financial assistance awarded to the three student-athletes.

It was further alleged in said memorandum that the University of Southwestern conducted several practice sessions in basketball beginning on or about October 10, 1966, in order to evaluate the skills of certain candidates and to determine the personnel to make up the University's 1966–67 basketball squad.

While I do not deny, in retrospect, that the afore described actions may have been technical violations of NCAA rules, I do emphatically insist that the actions taken by the University of Southwestern Louisiana, and particularly, by myself, were as a direct result of:

a) the arbitrary and obviously discriminatory rules and instructions placed upon the University and myself by the Louisiana Board of Education which is the State governing body for all State Universities excluding Louisiana State University and/or;

b) because of the instructions and mandates issued to and placed upon the University and myself by Mr. Stanley Galloway, the Commissioner of the Gulf States Conference, who was appointed by the aforementioned State Board of Education.

It seems quite obvious to the writer that since all activities of the University of Southwestern Louisiana, including the operating budget of the entire University and the employment of all school personnel, is under the specific control of the Louisiana Board of Education, and further, since the Commissioner of the Gulf States Conference has unlimited control and authority over the athletic programs for the member schools of the Gulf States Conference, that the University of Southwestern Louisiana and I were compelled to follow their instructions.

In order to place the entire history of this matter on record, I would like to inform the Committee of the following facts. The University of Southwestern Louisiana was the first school of higher learning in the State of Louisiana to become integrated. For many years, Negro students have been permitted to attend the University, and the relationship between Negro and White students and faculty has always been good. Apparently, for this reason the University of Southwestern Louisiana was placed into the position of having various Negro athletes inquire into the possibility of their participating in athletics at our school. For many years, it was the written rule of the State Board of Education that Negroes could not participate in athletics within the State, and certainly could not be placed upon scholarship by any of its member schools. However, after many court decisions made it obvious that this State Board of Education rule was unconstitutional, this written rule was dropped; however, a tacit understanding clearly remained between the Board and coaches throughout the State of Louisiana that Negro athletes were not desired. Nevertheless, prior to the 1966–67 season, I came to the view that it was unfair to Negro students who earnestly desired to attend our University and participate in athletics as well as to the student body of our University and the citizens of this Community, not to permit and in fact, recruit qualified Negro athletes. Accordingly, I did offer a basketball scholarship to one Jessie Marshall, of Princeton, Louisiana, after he visited our campus and indicated that he was most desirous of attending our University. Immediately after signing Marshall we were reported by other schools in the Gulf States Conference to the Louisiana Board of Education and were immediately instructed by said Board of Education that we must release Marshall from his signed commitment in view of the fact that he had allegedly previously signed a football grant with Grambling College of Louisiana, a colored institution.

During the conferences and discussions which were held with regard to this episode, it was made abundantly clear that the Louisiana Board of Education was still not willing to yield to political pressure or otherwise in allowing Negroes to participate in college athletics.

It was further made clear that regular scholarship monies could not be used for Negro athletes.

Up to this time, it must be pointed out that as a former athletic director of the University of Southwestern Louisiana, and as Head Basketball Coach of that University, neither I nor any other coach at the University, to my knowledge, knew of or used a "regular committee on scholarship and grants in aid" which is referred to in the memorandum of alleged violations. Up to that time, whether it be in technical violation of the NCAA rules or not, a scholarship committee at the University of Southwestern Louisiana did not exist, to my knowledge.

Nevertheless, the Louisiana Board of Education's actions and instructions, during and following the "Jessie Marshall" episode, [makes it] obvious that it would be impossible to grant a scholarship to a Negro athlete, if a "regular scholarship and grants in aid scholarship committee" was used, even if it did in fact exist.

Because of my deep conviction that the actions of the Louisiana Board of Education and Mr. Stanley Galloway, GSC Commissioner, were most arbitrary and obviously discriminatory against colored athletes, I then agreed that scholarships for these students would be paid for by organizations outside of the University; however, all monies used in financing the scholarships were run through the University's Administrative Office, and the Athletic Staff nor any outside persons had any actual control over these monies. My action in this regard was not with the intent of violating any rule of the NCAA, but was rather for the purpose of avoiding the discriminatory rules of the Louisiana Board of Education.

As set forth in the memorandum of December 20th, the students involved had no knowledge of these facts, and as far as they were concerned, the scholarships did come from the University directly. This was, in fact, true even though the monies used to pay for the scholarships were contributed by outside organizations.

For these reasons, I feel that the conclusion that the University's Athletic Department administered control of the financial assistance awarded to the three student-athletes is unfounded, for, in fact, the University through its Administrative Office did administer the control over these scholarship funds.

Subsequent to the admission of these students to the University, and subsequent to the investigations made by the NCAA and Louisiana Board of Education, the scholarship assistance to these students was seriously impaired, and for that reason the Federal Department of Health, Education, and Welfare made an extensive investigation into this entire matter. As a result of their investigation, Mr. David S. Sealy, Assistant Commissioner of the "Equal Educational Opportunities Program" concluded that the Negro athletes in question had been discriminated against and that there was an apparent violation of the Civil Rights Act. As a result of that investigation and conclusion, Negro athletes have since been placed on regular scholarship—which action I would have taken at the outset had it not been for the actions of the Louisiana Board of Education and the Gulf States Conference Commissioner.

Insofar as the forms which were used to notify recipients of the awards made to them, which forms the NCAA indicates did not comply with NCAA requirements—they were the forms prepared by the Gulf States Conference Com-

missioner, Mr. Galloway. Not to have used that form would
have been a violation of the Gulf States Conference rules and
it was assumed by me that that form satisfied all interested
persons. NCAA apparently recognizes that this form was
drafted by the Gulf States Conference, for in Paragraph
IV, Subsection (b) of the December 20th memorandum, it
points out that "the Gulf States Conference has modified
the form used to describe the amount, duration, terms and
conditions of awards made to student-athletes to bring it
into conformity with the NCAA requirements." Accordingly, since there was every reason to believe that the form
in question had the sanction of the NCAA as it was drafted
by the Commissioner of the Gulf States Conference, it seems
unfair that I, or the University of Southwestern Louisiana,
should be criticized or penalized in this regard.

The third complaint made against me and the University is that an early practice was held. First, let me point out
that the information with regard to this early practice was
volunteered by me to Mr. Brown, the NCAA investigator
which should make it apparent that I was in good faith
insofar as the practice was concerned and did not attempt
to conceal that information from the NCAA. As I have attempted to explain before, the early practice was called at the
instructions of the Gulf States Conference Commissioner.
He insisted that the practice be held prior to the beginning of the season, and that any Negro athletes interested
in trying out for the USL squad should be asked to attend
and that following that early practice, I should then refuse
any of these athletes for scholarship—either on the ground
that they had failed to pass the NCAA approved examination, or that they were not good enough to make the team.
I specifically informed Mr. Galloway that I knew this was
a violation of the NCAA rules but he in turn stated that it
was O.K. and that he would accept full responsibility for
the early workouts. Again, I had no alternative but to hold
the practice.

The irony of this entire controversy is that the Conference Commissioner and members of the Louisiana Board
of Education were primarily responsible for the instant investigation even though I consider that these officials were
the sole cause of any infractions, technical or otherwise,

which may have been committed. It must be realized that as a coach of a state university completely governed by the State Board of Education and by Mr. Galloway as Commissioner of Athletics, I had no alternative but to follow their instructions. Every effort was made to comply with their instructions, while at the same time not violate any NCAA regulations, nor discriminate against any Negroes or other qualified students who were interested in attending the University of Southwestern Louisiana and participating in our athletic programs. To have done this would possibly have been a violation of the Civil Rights Act and subject to criminal penalties and/or sanction from the Federal Department of Health, Education, and Welfare.

Evidence of the attitude of the State Board of Education and the Conference Commissioner toward me as a result of my sincere feeling that Negroes were entitled to attend USL and participate in the Athletic Programs if they were qualified, is the fact that my salary was ordered frozen by the Board of Education and a salary increase which had been suggested for me by University Officials was not granted.

In summary, I respectfully submit that the political overtones surrounding this case which cannot be fully discussed in this letter, have brought about this unfortunate state of affairs and I am being used as the "whipping boy." It is my sincere hope that the NCAA, for which I have great respect and confidence, will take what I have said into consideration in rendering a decision in this unusual case. I have attempted to be very frank and honest in the foregoing and have full realization of the consequences which may result, not only from the ruling of this body, but from the action which may come from the State Board of Education and/or the Conference Commissioner when my position is made known. Nevertheless, I cannot in good conscience permit my personal welfare or future in athletics to deter me from making my position crystal clear to NCAA officials, or others who are interested in knowing the true facts surrounding the charges in question.

I think it must be admitted that, assuming there has been a violation of any NCAA regulations, these violations did not result in the University of Southwestern Louisiana, or [me], realizing any unfair advantage over other NCAA affiliates or members.

Furthermore, the record shows that the acceptance of Negro athletes at USL has set a precedent within the State of Louisiana and the illegal and immoral segregation line has been finally broken within our State. While the NCAA is perhaps not personally concerned from that standpoint, again I feel that these results should be taken into consideration by the Committee in making its ruling on the charges at hand.

Should there be any further information you desire of me, or should any further explanation of what I have said be thought important, I certainly welcome your inquiry.

Respectfully,
Beryl Shipley,
Basketball Coach
University of Southwestern Louisiana
Lafayette, Louisiana

Shipley's impassioned and obviously heartfelt but belated appeal was ignored. The decision to punish USL and the basketball program had already been made, and the document, the resolution, had been written and was dated January 6, 1968. The university was notified of the NCAA's decision by telegram from Marcus L. Plant, president of the NCAA, dated January 7, 1968. The university's athletic teams would be placed on two years of probation and not allowed to participate in any post-season activities. In addition no USL team could appear on television broadcasts for the probationary period.

It is obvious that the decision had already been made because the December 20 letter stated that the report on the case would be presented to the Association's Council during its meeting on January 6, 1968. The Council's Resolution of the problem was dated January 6—the same day in which the case was presented to it. Amazingly the council heard the report, evaluated it, ruled, and wrote the Resolution all on the same day. It is obvious that the resolution had been decided, drafted, and delivered to the meeting. The whole procedure was a farce.

It is hard to believe that anyone in authority in a national association could receive a fact-filled, emotional letter from a member head coach and not respond. Walter Byers never replied to Beryl's letter. Not only that, the NCAA even neglected to send an official copy of the resolution to USL.

More than a month later, on February 9, 1968, Mr. Byers wrote President Rougeau: "In checking our files I find that we have not forwarded to you a copy of the Resolution adopted by the NCAA Council, January 6, 1968, and made a part of that group's official minutes. Enclosed is a copy of the statement for your records." Obviously just a minor oversight.

The NCAA had made sure that the national media had received information on the infamous resolution but had neglected to send a copy to USL, the alleged university culprit.

Just seventeen days after Bergstrom's December 20 letter to Rougeau, the die was cast and USL was put on probation. It is obvious, from university records of this period, USL's administration made no concerted effort to argue its case. The only explanation is that USL administrators had too much to lose politically. The board's objectives were being met by NCAA actions. Shipley and his program were being pilloried, and USL had to bow and suffer with him. Some were bowing and snickering.

The Board of Education and Galloway were obviously vindicated and empowered. Their previous activities having been ratified by the NCAA, they could now enhance their position. Obviously they would receive no obstructions from the USL administration.

It is interesting to note that in university records of this period, there were many letters and documents of transmittal, and copies were designated for various members of the president's staff and to Urban, Galloway of the state board, and the NCAA, but not a single letter of transmittal in the records, from anyone, shows a copy designated for the coaches or anyone officially involved in the basketball program.

After Coach Shipley received a copy of the resolution from the administration, his connections with its members were totally severed. Phone calls went unanswered or never returned. Anything he learned about activities being conducted by the state board, Gulf States Conference, (later) Southland Conference, or USL administration came from outside sources. Stan Galloway, obviously emboldened, continued, even escalated, his attacks on his favorite target.

Beryl's personal analysis of the violations of which the program was accused, even considering the distortions, had been that they were insufficiently serious for the NCAA to exact stringent penalties on the basketball program—particularly if the real story became public. Amazingly the sordid story of racist influences on an NCAA investigation were never heard outside of Acadiana.

The *Advertiser* commented on this: "When you consider the entire USL case it is easy to see that only [a couple of] cases would have been considered by the NCAA if it had not been for the State Board of Education's unwritten rule on giving Negro athletes scholarships. [And these] cases would have seemed minor and probably would have drawn no more than a reprimand." The NCAA, as the *Advertiser* pointed out later, stated that the two cases referred to, both involving football, were minor and had no effect in its final decisions.

Four days after the NCAA's document of resolution was dated, the following letter was sent to J. Marshall Brown, a former state representative, close ally of the sitting governor, John McKeithen, and a member of the Democratic National Committee from Louisiana. The Shipley forces were pulling out all the stops while fighting for survival.

DOMENGEAUX, WRIGHT & BIENVENU

Attorneys at Law
320 West Main Street
Post Office Box 3668
Lafayette, Louisiana 70501
January 10, 1968
James Domengeaux Telephone 234-7478
Bob F. Wright
Mark Bienvenu
W. Paul Hawley
Fred M. Smith

Mr. J. Marshall Brown
Marshall Brown Insurance Agency
225 Baronne Street
New Orleans, Louisiana

Dear Marshall:
    The recent action of the NCAA placing the University of Southwestern Louisiana on a two-year probation, banning it from post-season activities resulted in a very explosive and delicate situation which could easily develop into a major controversy of racial nature, attracting nation wide attention.
    The person who could be most injured by this, in my opinion, is Governor McKeithen.
    The Negroes that I have spoken to feel there was a serious discrimination of the three Negroes in question due to

the unofficial instructions of the state Board of Education to deny athletic scholarships to Negroes.

Likewise, it seems to me that the entire community is behind Coach Shipley and resents the unofficial action of the State Board which caused him to circumvent the NCAA law, resulting in the disciplinary action.

The TV news media and the newspapers are very critical of the University authorities. Much of the resentment comes from the belief that the authorities made no defense of the scholarship charges for fear of bringing down the displeasure of the State Board of Education.

I am enclosing to you a clipping from the sports editor of the Lafayette Advertiser, which pretty well brings out this whole situation.

Coach Shipley was contacted by the Equal Educational Opportunity Program of the Department of Health and Welfare, to obtain his co-operation in the filing of a civil rights suit to nullify the action of the NCAA based on the discriminatory policy of the State Board of Education.

We have learned that an appeal or review can be filed by the authorities of the University to the NCAA to request reconsideration. This appeal can only be made by the authorities of the University and not by Coach Shipley.

I suggest that the State Board of Education instruct President Rougeau to undertake this appeal. If this is done and you are able to prevail on the Board as suggested in our telephone conversation, I am confident that the NCAA would at least modify and reduce the penalty. I believe that this should be attended to immediately because this situation can explode at any time.

I would further strongly recommend that you do everything possible to see that the State Board does not attempt to persecute Shipley or the University even though certain members may be displeased with Shipley. Also, Commissioner Galloway should be instructed to further not involve himself in the matter and attempt other disciplinary action. Either one of these actions would really bring about the explosion which we hope for everyone's sake could be avoided.

I have not discussed this with the Governor as I believe it would be best for you to do so if you see fit.

Very truly yours,
James Domengeaux

Mr. Domengeaux, prominent attorney and former congressman, soon found out how much influence *former* congressmen have. No action was taken as a result of his letter.

On March 3, 1968 the *Daily Advertiser*, Lafayette, weighed in. Its staff had knowledge of events surrounding the conduct of the basketball program and had added to it by specific investigations into the substance of the allegations presented in the NCAA's Resolution. On that date, it made them known clearly and pointedly. The following is the entire text of the feature article. Additional comments by this book's authors have been added in bold text.

Facts Behind USL
Suspension Are Explained

Since the University of Southwestern Louisiana basketball team was put on a two-year probation by the National Collegiate Athletic Association for technical violations of recruiting rules, charges, countercharges, and half-truths concerning the violations have been heard and read publicly and privately.

To clarify the situation and to spell out exactly what happened to bring on the action by the NCAA, why it happened and just what action was taken, The Advertiser today prints the complete text of the NCAA resolution, with an explanation of each section.

The Advertiser hopes that with this publication, the misinformation, half-truths, insinuations, and outright falsehoods concerning the issue will cease, and Southwestern's backers can once again back the university to the hilt as she moves toward academic and athletic greatness.

Interested persons are urged to study the complete text and find their own conclusions about the incidents.

True Facts Revealed About USL-NCAA Case

The National Collegiate Athletic Association (NCAA) recently released a resolution charging the University of Southwestern Louisiana with eight violations of NCAA regulations.

The NCAA then placed Southwestern on two years probation and said that during the probation that USL's basketball team would not be permitted to participate in any post-season competition.

There have been many half-truths printed by misinformed persons claiming to be authorities on the subject. The Advertiser feels that its readers—the supporters of USL—deserve the whole truth.

Printed below you will find each NCAA charge with the facts following. Every person interested in USL is urged to read the entire text.

WHEREAS, the NCAA Committee on Infractions has investigated alleged violations of NCAA legislation on the part of the University of Southwestern Louisiana, and has reported its findings to the Council;

WHEREAS, the Council has found the University of Southwestern Louisiana to have violated the principle governing financial assistance to student-athletes (NCAA Constitution 3-4-(a) and (c)), in that:

NCAA CHARGE

1. At the beginning of the 1966–67 college year, the University permitted an outside organization to pay the educational expenses of three student athletes to attend the institution. Inasmuch as University athletic department personnel promised financial assistance to the three young men and such aid was ultimately provided, it is held that the student athletes involved were unaware that the assistance came from an outside source.

THE FACTS

In 1966 the University of Southwestern offered a basketball scholarship to Jessie Marshall of Princeton, La., a Negro youth, but the athletic committee of the State Board of Education, Frederick Tannehill of Pineville, V.J. Scogin of Slidell and Angus D. Smith of New Orleans, along with Gulf States Conference Commissioner Stanley Galloway, said that USL could not offer Marshall a scholarship because he had signed a football grant-in-aid with Grambling.

There was no rule on the books that said that Southwestern had to honor a Grambling signee, but the athletic committee came up with one and made it clear to all concerned that they did not want Southwestern recruiting Negro athletes.

When three Negro athletes indicated to USL basketball coach Beryl Shipley that they would like to attend USL he agreed to let the Lafayette Business League pay the educational expenses of the athletes since it was clear they could not be put on a regular Gulf States Conference grant-in-aid.

[The paper's information is somewhat understated. Beryl had been specifically told by the State Board of Education that it would not provide funding for the three black athletes, and the denial of funding was because the athletes were black.]

All monies used in financing the scholarships were run through the university's Administrative Office and neither the Athletic Staff, nor any outside persons had any actual control over these monies.

After the students were admitted to the University, an investigation by Mr. David S. Sealy, Assistant Commissioner of the Equal Educational Opportunities Program, concluded that the Negro athletes in question had been discriminated against and that there was an apparent violation of the Civil Rights Act. As a result of the investigation and conclusion, the three Negro athletes have since been placed on regular scholarship.

The actual rule violation was not that the outside organization raised the monies for the scholarship but that they specified which athletes were to receive the monies.

[This was a protection the league was required to take because of the circumstances introduced by the board.]

There is no denying that Southwestern broke a rule. But it was not intentional and would not have even come up if the athletic committee of the State Board of Education had allowed the athletes to be placed on regular scholarships.

NCAA CHARGE

2. Inasmuch as the decision to financially assist the three young men was made by members of the University's athletic staff rather than the institution's regular committee on scholarships and grants in aid, the recipients weren't provided with a proper written statement describing the amount, duration, terms and conditions of the award. Further the procedures followed in making these awards placed the University's department of athletics in administrative control of the financial assistance awarded to the three student athletes.

3. The form utilized by the University of Southwestern Louisiana to notify recipients of awards made to them and describe such awards did not meet NCAA requirements.

THE FACTS

A regular committee on scholarship and grants-in-aid was not operating at the University of Southwestern at that time. When the University joined the NCAA they did not realize that it was necessary to have such a committee approve all scholarships and so, technically, Southwestern again violated a rule of the NCAA.

[The state board had refused to fund the three black athletes, so this talk about a committee is superfluous. Committee or no committee, the scholarships could not have been approved, because the state board would allow no money to fund the three black athletes.]

As it was pointed out in the above facts—all monies contributed by the Lafayette Business League were run through the University's Administration Office, and neither the Athletic Staff nor any outside persons had any actual control over these monies.

The form used to sign Leslie Scott, Marvin Winkler and Elvin Ivory was the regular form used by the Gulf States Conference and provided to the school by GSC Commissioner Stanley Galloway.

This should not be held against USL. The NCAA apparently recognized the form [used] was drafted by the

GSC [since] they pointed out in a December 28th memorandum—"the Gulf States Conference has modified the form [to incorporate] the amount, duration, terms and conditions of awards made to student-athletes to bring it into conformity with the NCAA requirements."

[No such form existed at the time the black athletes were signed. There was no December 28 memorandum in the university archive files, but the statement, as presented by the paper, is a direct quote from the resolution, dated January 6, 1968. This is another instance in which the NCAA is clearly carrying water for the State Board of Education.]

NCAA CHARGE

WHEREAS, the Council has found the University of Southwestern Louisiana to have violated the provisions governing recruiting (NCAA Bylaw 6.1) in that:

1. Members of the University of Southwestern Louisiana's athletic staff recruited prospective student-athletes with the offers of institutional financial assistance and provided the prospects with written statements to the effect that such assistance would be available to them.

THE FACTS

This refers back to the scholarship forms that the GSC was using, and also to the fact that Southwestern had to rely on outside funds to give the athletes scholarships.

NCAA CHARGE

2. During the late summer of 1967, a representative of the University's athletic interests provided a prospective student-athlete with an unsecured loan in order to pay his air transportation to the University's campus for the purposes of reporting for 1967 preseason football practice and eventual enrollment at the University.

THE FACTS

Larry Highbaugh, a highly sought after Negro athlete from Indiana, decided that he would attend the University of Southwestern Louisiana but because his parents wanted the youth to attend Indiana University he did not have the money to report to USL for pre-season football practice.

Woodrow Crum, head basketball coach at Central High School in Lawrence, Indiana, gave Highbaugh $75 to fly to Lafayette. Crum got no security for the loan and since he was a friend of Beryl Shipley and his assistant Tom Cox, Crum was labeled [by Stanley Galloway, state board commissioner of athletics] a "representative of the University of Southwestern Louisiana's athletic interests."

[The word *gave* is improperly used by the paper; *loaned* is correct.]

This is a rule violation. But Art Bergstrom, NCAA assistant executive director, said in an interview with Will Grimsley of the Associated Press after the announcement of the NCAA action in New York that USL was not penalized for this infraction because, although it was a rule violation, it was not deemed serious enough to warrant a probation, since Highbaugh did not remain at USL and did not participate in pre-season football workouts.

[This was no rule violation; Crum had no official connection with USL and said so in a written statement. This is an example of how far the NCAA went in cooperating with Galloway and the state board.]

NCAA CHARGE

WHEREAS, the Council has found the University of Southwestern Louisiana to have violated the provisions governing recruiting NCAA Bylaw 6-2-(b), and Bylaw 6-7-(a) in that:

1. The University permitted an outside organization to pay the educational expenses of a prospective student athlete to attend the institution's 1966 summer session.

THE FACTS

Elvin Ivory attended summer school prior to the start of the 1966–67 school year and his educational expenses were covered by the Lafayette Business League. This again goes back to the fact that the University could not put Ivory on a regular scholarship.

[His being financed by an outside organization was a forced action caused by the board's illegal act of refusing to fund the scholarships for the three black athletes.]

NCAA CHARGE

WHEREAS, the council has found the University of Southwestern Louisiana to have violated the provisions governing recruiting (NCAA Bylaw 6-8) in that:

1. During the late summer and early fall of 1966, football coaches of the University recruited a student-athlete enrolled in another four-year institution without first contacting the director of athletics of that institution and obtaining his permission.

THE FACTS

Billy Mistric wished to leave Louisiana State University after playing his freshman year there. When he told his mother of this decision, she asked Billy to contact Daniel Roy, an assistant at USL who had coached Billy at Glen Oaks in Baton Rouge and had become very close to the boy. Billy asked Roy only what he thought about the move and Roy told him that he could not get involved since it would be a violation of the NCAA rules.

Billy later thought it over and came to the USL campus. LSU Athletic Director James J. Corbett then charged that USL had come on the campus and attempted to persuade the youth to leave LSU during the summer. The late LSU athletic director insisted that USL recruited Mistric away from the LSU campus, but this was proven not to be fact.

[Corbett's accusation was created from whole cloth and was proven to be entirely untrue.]

The rule violation was that Roy did not contact Corbett when the youth contacted him. The NCAA committee concluded that while the incident was a violation, it was

70

technical in nature and resulted from the prospective student-athlete actually, but unknowingly, maneuvering USL into the act of violation.

[No rules were broken, and the NCAA knew it. This was the second time during these proceedings that it had saved face.]

NCAA CHARGE

WHEREAS, the Council has found the University of Southwestern Louisiana to have violated the provisions governing playing and practice seasons (NCAA Bylaw 8-1 (b), in that:

1. Beginning on or about October 10, 1966, the head basketball coach of the University, with the knowledge and consent of the institution's director of athletics, conducted several practice sessions in basketball in order to evaluate the skills of certain candidates and determine the personnel of the University's 1966–67 basketball squads.

THE FACTS

Shipley, athletic director A.G. Urban and University President Clyde Rougeau were called on the carpet several times by the State Board of Education's athletic committee and Galloway when it was learned that the Negroes were going to attend the University. Shipley and Urban did not reveal to the athletic committee that the youths were contacted by USL. They, in fact, led the state board to believe that the Negroes had been sent by an outside organization to "test" USL.

It is obvious why Shipley and Urban left this impression. To admit the recruiting of the Negroes would have opened the door for the State Board's athletic committee to take punitive action against not only Rougeau but the entire university.

When the athletic committee finally found out the whole story during the NCAA investigation (one member of the state board confided that the athletic committee knew what was going on the entire time) they came out in the open with their attempts to hurt the basketball program and in particular Shipley.

Through the pressure from members of the state board, the executive committee of the Gulf States Conference was persuaded to adopt a resolution declaring Southwestern ineligible for the GSC title for two years. One member of the executive committee, composed of each school's athletic committee chairman, said he was not in favor of the resolution, feeling that USL had been punished enough, but that he had been instructed to vote for the resolution.

Then came the wave of criticism out of Lafayette and that is when the Lafayette Legislative team of state Senator Edgar Mouton, state Representative Luke LeBlanc and state Representatives-Elect Dan Guilliot and Fred Hayes requested a meeting with the State Board of Education and Education Supt. William Dodd.

The local legislators did not go to Baton Rouge with threats of race riots or to be used as "tools" by Negro racists [as reported by some news agencies]. They went to protest that their University was being punished too severely for violations brought on by the State Board's unwritten rule. At no time was there any threat of riots on the part of an outside organization.

It was during one of the early investigations on the part of the State Board's athletic committee and Galloway that the early practice was ordered. In a Lafayette motel room with President Rougeau, Urban, Shipley, Galloway and Smith present; Galloway said to Rougeau, "If I were president (of USL) I would find a way to keep them from playing. I would flunk them on the test (the test administered by each member of the NCAA to see if a student can project a scholastic average of 1.6).

Rougeau then informed Galloway that the Negroes had already passed the test. Galloway then instructed Shipley to hold an early practice and see how many Negroes were going to make the team.

[Actually, as Beryl pointed out in his January 4 letter, the purpose of the early practice was for Beryl to declare that all of the black athletes were incapable of making the team.]

Shipley told Galloway that [early practice] would be a violation of NCAA rules but Galloway responded by saying he would take full responsibility. Shipley held the early workouts and had Urban inform Galloway and the athletic committee that the three Negroes would be on the traveling squad.

Galloway appeared before the infractions committee of the NCAA and denied taking the responsibility for the early workouts. The NCAA [says it] doesn't deal in why a violation occurred, just if it did. The early practices were held under the instruction of Galloway, and USL is being penalized [for it].

[If "the NCAA doesn't deal in why a violation occurred, just if it did," then what was the underlying reason the football problems were forgiven?]

NCAA CONCLUSION

WHEREAS, the Council has noted that once the executive administration of the University of Southwestern Louisiana became aware of the existence of the arrangement whereby student-athletes received financial assistance from an outside organization, it terminated this arrangement;

[USL put them on regular scholarships after the board and USL were forced to do so by the equal rights investigator. The board's actions had violated the civil rights of the athletes months before this investigation even began.]

WHEREAS, the Council has recorded the fact that the Gulf States Conference has revised and placed into conformity with NCAA requirements the form utilized to notify recipients and describe amount, duration, terms and conditions of awards made to them;

[The form is really no longer needed. Black players would now receive the same scholarships as white players, no thanks to the NCAA.]

WHEREAS, the Council is concerned that during the period the Committee on Infractions was investigating alleged violations of the Association's legislation on the part of the University of Southwestern Louisiana members of the institution's coaching staff participated in an improper recruiting procedure which they should have known to be a violation of NCAA rules and regulations;

WHEREAS, the Council considers these activities to reflect a laxity in the administration of the University's program of intercollegiate athletics and an apparent lack of attention to NCAA rules and regulations on the part of certain members of its athletic coaching staff;

NOW, THEREFORE, BE IT RESOLVED, that the University of Southwestern Louisiana be placed on probation for a period of two years from this date (January 6, 1968), it being understood that prior to the expiration of this probationary period the NCAA Committee on Infractions shall review the athletic policies and practices of the institution;

BE IT FURTHER RESOLVED, that during the period of this probation the basketball team of the University shall end its season with the final, regularly scheduled in-season game and it shall not be permitted to participate in any post-season competition;

BE IT FINALLY RESOLVED, that record be made of the assistance and cooperation extended to the NCAA and its Committee on infractions by the University of Southwestern Louisiana and the office of the Commissioner of College Athletics, State of Louisiana.

[The first two *whereas* statements were designed to inform the public that the activities of USL and the board did not cause the punishment—that Shipley and his scofflaws did it all. The goal of the entire process was to punish Beryl and the basketball program, and the NCAA cooperated to the fullest.]

The ADVERTISER'S Conclusion

When you consider the entire USL case it is easy to see that only the Mistric and Highbaugh cases [football] would have been considered by the NCAA if it had not been for the State Board of Education's unwritten rule on giving Negro athletes scholarships. The Mistric and Highbaugh cases would have seemed minor and probably would have drawn no more than a reprimand.

Galloway, the commissioner of athletics for the State Board of Education, carried on most of the investigation for the NCAA and supplied them with the majority of information used to initiate the probe. Why didn't Galloway initiate an investigation of his own or on the part of the GSC, instead of taking the action to the NCAA?

Why didn't Galloway tell the Associated Press about the resolution adopted by [GSC's] executive committee? Why did he inform the AP that the matter was only casually discussed? Why did the GS Conference wait six weeks before deciding to take action on the NCAA resolution when it should have been the one to take action in the first place instead of referring it to the NCAA?

It seems that the State Board of Education's athletic committee has given full rein to Galloway's policing action against USL instead of having him attend to the duties of commissioner of athletics. It seems that his duties even involve calling parents of prospective athletes and informing them that they should not send their sons to USL.

Unfavorable publicity continues to haunt Shipley and USL. A report in Lake Charles said that Shipley would not return to USL next season because he had fallen into disfavor with higher-ups at Southwestern. In a Sunday edition of the Alexandria paper the entire resolution from the NCAA on USL was printed. This resolution was not released by the NCAA or USL [at that time] to be printed publicly and could have come only from Galloway or Tannehill. [And USL didn't get an official copy of the January 6 resolution until February 9.]

Just how much damage is going to be done to Southwest Louisiana's great University? Are narrow-minded, bigoted individuals going to continue to draw out the Southwestern case and penalize the University, Shipley and his fine team?

There have been veiled threats of more charges against USL from Galloway and Tannehill, but they have not come forward with the facts. If there are more charges let's bring them forward, and if not, then let's let the entire incident die and allow Southwestern to proceed on its path to academic and athletic greatness.

It is quite obvious that the violations are all technical in nature while the penalty imposed by the NCAA is very severe. The NCAA leaves the door open to review the situation at any time during the two-year period, but the NCAA will do so only at the request of the University administration.

Southwestern has an excellent chance of winning a national championship next season if the probation is lifted after one year. But the NCAA must review the case soon if they are to lift the ban by next Jan. 6. It is up to University officials to start the wheels turning in an attempt to give Southwestern a rehearing and it must be started immediately.

The university made no effort to shorten the two-year suspension of postseason play; no appeals were filed. But Beryl stripped some of the pleasure from his conference competitors. His team continued its winning ways and won the Gulf States Conference Championship during the next two regular seasons.

After the probationary period had passed in 1969, Beryl was told of another charge—and he was told it was the one that was decisive for the NCAA, and one of which he had been completely unaware. Dr. Ray Authement, USL vice president at the time and ultimately successor to USL President Clyde Rougeau, said to Beryl that none of the violations presented above were sufficiently serious for probationary action, as most observers had surmised. According to Dr. Authement, an additional charge, introduced to the NCAA after December 20, 1967, had caused the action. Dr. Authement said that if Beryl had not given Marvin Winkler a credit card in Indianapolis, Indiana, the NCAA would not have administered the two-year probation period to the school. This was an alleged violation, Authement said, that had been added to the charges. Yet none of the administration participants had deemed it necessary to inform Coach Shipley of it. Beryl had no knowledge of the charge and vehemently denied that he had given anyone a credit card.

Amazingly there has never been any other mention of such an incident, verbally or in writing. Shipley told Dr. Authement that if he had known of this accusation at the time, he could have easily proven that it was unfounded, and the school could have avoided the penalty.

But Dr. Authement's story about the credit card and its importance is highly questionable. The allegation has never been mentioned in any NCAA document that anyone has seen. It never reached newspaper, TV, and radio reporters who were actively involved at the time and reported on the events, and the administration never informed the coach of this allegation at any time prior to 1969.

Dr. Authement was a participant in all of these NCAA affairs during the entire period, yet the alleged violation was not mentioned until 1969. If Dr. Authement's story is true, and the credit card was the decisive factor, a simple question or two could have saved the university, its basketball program, and the Lafayette community from the unfavorable publicity that resulted.

Dr. Authement's story about the credit card, whether true or not, affected personal relationships. Based on his story, Shipley surmised that his supposed friend, Raymond Blanco, an assistant football coach at the time, was the person who had made the credit card charge. Blanco is now the university's vice president of student affairs, and the husband of Louisiana Governor Kathleen Blanco.

The whole incident is now in serious doubt. Close scrutiny of university records of that period, recently made available, has revealed nothing to confirm the credit card story or who reported it.

These questions concerning the veracity of the story didn't come to the fore until 2006, when university records for that period were finally obtained. There is absolutely nothing in them to indicate that any mention of a credit card for Marvin Winkler ever surfaced.

Even to this day stories are written that insinuate that the university fired everyone involved with the 1973 penalties. The intimation is that strong, decisive action was taken by the administration in dealing with the situation. In fact, the only athletic department employee fired during 1973 was Head Football Coach Russ Faulkinberry, and that was after nine games into a miserable winless season. Athletic Director "Whitey" Urban retired before the NCAA penalties were promulgated and was replaced by Toby Warren. Warren took responsibility for firing Faulkinberry and appointing Dan "Sonny" Roy as interim head football coach to serve for the last game of the season; another humiliating loss. Ironically Warren, a very good high school punter, had quit the USL football team, coached by Russ Faulkinberry, after only one year. Faulkinberry had criticized him for a "lack of desire."

Beryl Shipley resigned in May of 1973, three months before the NCAA "death penalty" ruling. Shipley maintains that his resignation was the result of the failure of the administration to live up to promises of salary increases and the frustration of being cut out of the loop regarding the university's defense against NCAA allegations.

Assistant Coach Tom Cox also resigned before the NCAA rulings. Cox had been asked by influential parties to stay on for consideration as Shipley's replacement but realized he would suffer the same treatment as Shipley should he choose to do so.

The truly unfortunate fallout of the entire 1967 episode is that it set up USL's ultimate punishment in 1973. One of the reasons for the severity of that punishment was the university's record of violations in the mid-60s—violations that were the direct result of racist retribution. Had the NCAA treated those alleged violations as pure segregationist's taunting of a coach and his program, it is unlikely the second set of violations would have grown to such a consequence.

Chapter Six

Recruiting 101

As in most endeavors in life, the more competitive you become, the tougher and more talented opposition you will face. Your goal is to escalate the quality of talent on your side so as to meet those challenges. Also, in most cases, the more successful you become, the more talent and quality will be attracted to your endeavor.

Nowhere is that more true than in the sports world. There is no doubt that John Wooden deserves his position in the Basketball Hall of Fame and as the icon of coaching success. However, winning ten NCAA championships, seven in a row from 1967 to 1973, certainly attracted even more talented high school players to his program. Wooden, in the smaller universe that college basketball was then (the NCAA tournament included only twenty-four teams), could pick the cream of the crop from throughout the nation. And, with most universities in the Deep South still segregated, he and a handful of other major university coaches also had their choice of the best black high school players below the Mason-Dixon line.

Landing seven-foot Lew Alcindor as a recruit in 1966 certainly ensured Wooden's success for the next four years. A seven-foot-tall basketball player was a unique prize at that time. Since then almost every team has one or several players nearly that tall or even taller. Alcindor later changed his name to the muslim Kareem Abdul-Jabar, and he and a bevy of other talented Bruins dominated the college game from 1967 through 1969. Wooden kept pulling in the talent and kept winning, topping off his sensational run with 6'10" Bill Walton leading the team to championships in 1973 and '74.

All told, Wooden accomplished records no other coach will probably ever come near: the ten championships included four 30–0 perfect seasons and 88 consecutive winning games.

It is a tribute to Shipley and his team that *Sports Illustrated's* Curry Kirkpatrick observed in a story near the end of the 1973 season that USL could be the only team in the tournament that could match up with UCLA. Kirkpatrick noted the outside shooting of Lamar and favorably rated Roy Ebron as one of the few in the nation who could go head-to-head with Walton.

As Shipley took on the SLI job and started whipping Gulf States Conference rivals on a regular basis, he was constantly looking for new talent. Basketball was decidedly a second-rate sport in the football-crazy state of Louisiana. Beryl knew if the program was to grow into his vision, he would have to attract more than the state had to offer in basketball talent. He had some pretty fair Louisiana players in the early years but was roaming far and wide in his recruitment efforts. Tim Thompson came in from Lexington, Kentucky from 1957 to '61 and averaged over fifteen points per game in the slow, low-scoring game that was college basketball at the time. Thompson received All-American Honorable Mention honors. Larry Simon hit almost fifteen per game during his 1958-62 tenure.

In 1960 Shipley scored his first, first-team All-American, Dean Church, a linguini-thin, cool shooting guard from Ashland, Kentucky. Church quickly became one of the leading scorers on the team, but he and Shipley clashed early and often. In Beryl's system it was his way or the highway.

Church remembered, "At the start of my junior year, I was rooming with a freshman named Henderson Payne from Kentucky and we both decided that we would be better off back in Kentucky than staying in Louisiana so we quit school and went home. When I got there, I went to work at a department store selling toys. It didn't take me long to understand how stupid I was to leave school. That year, USL was playing two games in Kentucky. I made up my mind that I would go see the games and ask Coach Shipley if I could come back."

Shipley recalls, "I had put Church in as this kid Payne's roommate because I thought Dean could give him some maturity and guidance. Next thing I know they're packing up to leave school and go home. I was so damn mad I told Church we'd escort him out of town and make sure he never came back."

In 1962 radio play-by-play announcer Ron Gomez was on his first road trip with the team. Gomez recalls, "Former head basketball coach J. C. 'Dutch' Reinhardt was now the trainer/manager for the team and did all travel arrangements. I had broadcast one year of LSU football as a color announcer and was familiar with how the Tigers traveled and a little taken aback by our arrangements. This was like joining a Gypsy caravan. First, no flying. We were on a chartered Greyhound bus for the seven-day trip. Second, Reinhardt had a belief that the only good hotels were the ones with transoms over the doors. So, that's where we stayed. They all must have been at least fifty years old. That's the first time I'd ever seen a radiator (heater). It was December so it really didn't matter that most didn't have air-conditioning. Third, meals; lunch consisted of a paper bag with a white bread sandwich, bologna, ham, cheese, it varied. The sandwich was accompanied by a cola and an apple or an orange or any other fruit we could buy from roadside vendors. It was served laptop on the bus while traveling. Dinner consisted of the nearest, least expensive cafeteria.

"As we traveled through the two-lane roads of the South, I was trying to learn the 'shuffle' offense from Shipley and get to know the team as best I could since the only game I had broadcast was the opener at Blackham Coliseum. Truth be known, I hadn't broadcast a basketball game in four years. In my first game, an 89–54 win over Nicholls State, Beryl had roared off the bench after a questionable call by an official. Since SID Bob Henderson had placed me at the very end of the scorer's table nearest the USL bench, my crowd microphone caught the full verbal fury of Beryl's anger. Then, as he stripped off his sport coat and flung it behind him, I caught the coat over my face and head. Needless to say, the rest of my home games for eighteen years were spent on the other end of the scorer's table.

"Having seen few basketball games in recent years and never having seen the 'shuffle,' I described the Nicholls defense at one point as 'shifting to a zone.' Several weeks later a young high school basketball coach, Bob Adamson, took me aside to let me know that the zone could not be played against the 'shuffle.' Adamson became a good friend, retired after moving up the ladder of the school system to become a high school principal. He also served as my basketball color announcer for high school and USL games for several years and, with his encyclopedic knowledge of basketball, did an exceptional job in that position.

"After losing to Alabama in Tuscaloosa by only six points, we headed for Tennessee Tech in Cookeville. After a ten-point loss there the next night, I started hearing some of the members of the team saying they had seen Church. I had heard about Dean Church so I knew they weren't having a religious experience. I asked Shipley about the circumstances of his leaving, but he wouldn't discuss the player or the reason for his dismissal from the squad.

"We continued our bus tour of murderer's row, four games in four different cities in four nights. When we lost to Kentucky Wesleyan in Owensboro by nineteen, Shipley wasn't worth talking to. I normally did a post-game interview with the coach, but after this loss, he sent Assistant Coach Tom Colwell out for the chat. Coincidentally this was future assistant coach Tom Cox's hometown and alma mater. Cox was a junior high school coach at the time and did some scouting for Shipley. Again, the chatter on the team was that Dean Church had followed the bus to Owensboro in a beat-up old rattletrap car and was desperately trying to talk with Shipley. Colwell acknowledged my question off the air regarding Dean's presence. He said this wasn't the time to talk to Shipley.

"We moved on down to Bowling Green, Kentucky to take on the legendary Coach Ed Diddle and his famous red towel. The Hilltoppers prevailed by thirteen and Shipley's mood grew darker. It wasn't looking good for Church. Finally during an overnight stay in Memphis on the way home, Beryl granted him an audience."

Church takes up the story: "It took me a long time waiting outside his room to get up enough nerve to knock on his door. The last time I had seen the coach, he was being held by two guys to keep him from beating me to a pulp and then having a car follow me to the city limits to make sure I left town.

"I finally saw the coach and asked if I could come back. He said that if I really wanted to finish school, I could, but only on his conditions and with no exceptions. I won't go in to all the conditions that I agreed to, but in the years 1964 and 1965, did anyone ever see me in a dirty car or shoes that were not shined?"

It turned into a mutually satisfying decision. Church went on to produce scoring and leadership for the Bulldogs and was honored in 1964 and '65 as GSC Player of the Year, NAIA first team All-American; AP first team Small College All-American and Louisiana Athlete of the Year in 1965; and was later inducted into both the USL and Louisiana Basketball Hall of Fame.

The story doesn't end there. Dean Church ultimately became a top-flight executive with Avondale Shipyards in South Louisiana, receiving many awards and recognition for his business achievements.

Shipley's strong stance in this situation was typical of his coaching and recruiting style and philosophy. He was the *head* basketball coach. He set the rules. He called the plays on the court and off.

Fred Saunders, one of Shipley's recruits from Columbus, Ohio, commented in 2001 on Beryl's direct attitude during his recruitment in 1969. "As one may be aware … the late '60s early '70s was a very interesting era. Up north you had what was called the Black Revolution or Age of Black Awareness. So, when Coach Shipley came to Columbus he said, 'We're going to put the school on the map, and don't you come here with that Black Power *stuff*.' Now, if you know and love Coach Shipley, you know that the word he used was not *stuff*. I told Coach, 'You've got a deal.'"

It's hard to believe a coach would speak that bluntly to a prospect if he thought he would have to coddle him or pay to keep him. At the same time, Beryl knew kids would need help at times, and he couldn't desert a kid once he signed on. Fred continued, "Coach Shipley was a man that what you see is what you get: shoot from the hip. His words were his bond. Shipley's words, 'How in hell are you going to bring a kid two thousand miles from his home and not take care of him.' Strong man."

Beryl was always known for his hard-nosed, no-nonsense brand of coaching and his superbly conditioned athletes.

During a Shipley Era reunion in Lafayette in 2001, one of the old friends who returned for the event was Red Hoggatt. Beryl had elevated Hoggatt to head football coach at SLI during his brief term as interim athletic director. Not coincidentally, Hoggatt had been football coach at Dobyns-Bennett High School in Kingsport, Tennessee, Shipley's alma mater.

Red reminisced about his days at SLI and said he used to sit in the Earl K. Long Gymnasium stands during some basketball practices. He said he had never seen a coach work boys so hard. He said he had always been demanding in the training of his football team members, but he never approached the demands of Coach Shipley. And he was positive, as he watched the workout, that all of the basketball boys would quit. Some did, but most didn't. He said that Beryl's training for his players emphasized physical fitness; his objective was a team of players who could participate in a full game at full speed without tiring to the point of losing their edge.

One of Shipley's more violent drills was known by the players as the "take a lick." One of the worst things Beryl could say about a player is that "he couldn't take a lick" or "he wouldn't take a lick." That, of course, was referring to standing one's ground while an opponent came charging through your position. Shipley's players were expected to take that lick whether the opposing player was 145-pound Jerry Flake or 280-pound Garland Williams. Remember this is basketball: a T-shirt, shorts, and sneakers, no pads or helmets. A non-contact sport. Right.

Sam Thomas, a team member during the years of 1960–64, posed the question during a discussion at the 2001 reunion, "I wonder if many of Coach Shipley's players remember his famous 'take the lick' drills, which usually followed an occasional loss, when he thought we had been too passive in our play. These drills were administered without pads and consisted of one player dribbling at full speed and running over a defensive player who was supposed to learn how to draw a charging foul."

Randy Price, a player (1955–59), remembered the drill well. Among the top six things he says he learned from Coach Shipley, his number-four was "Take that lick, [but] if you don't, stand without flinching and let [the] big redhead [Beryl] run over you." Shipley's basketball was definitely not a non-contact sport.

Once the team had moved most of its operations to Blackham Coliseum, Shipley utilized the tiered seating and steps in his training agenda. The big oval building was built primarily to house rodeos and had a dirt floor and chutes to hold the broncos and bulls on the west end of the arena. Green dyed sawdust covered the dirt during basketball season, when the portable wooden floor was laid out.

It was said that Garland Williams had more miles up and down the steps and around the top of the seats in Blackham than an orbiting astronaut. Williams, a burly 6'9" center who came to USL in 1968, was constantly fighting a weight problem. Williams didn't think it was a problem, Shipley did. Shipley had a weight set for Garland to check in at, say, 250 pounds. Williams would come in at 280. Shipley would say, "Hit the steps, pal." The few observers allowed into Shipley practices during the four years Williams was on the squad remember seeing the huge, lone figure going up and down the steps and around the Coliseum more than they saw him on the practice court. Yet Williams contributed in a large way to USL's successes.

In spite of the severe training and the dominance of Beryl's coaching style, there were seldom any incidents of animosity between players on his teams. Maybe they realized that such actions would never be tolerated.

Beryl remembered one event of trouble between team members occurred in 1958, before the team was integrated. "We were having a scrimmage one afternoon and I had a new recruit, a junior-college kid from Kentucky. I don't know why, but as they went down the floor, the kid tripped Bill McHorris [another graduate of Kingsport, Tennessee's Dobyns-Bennett High]. As they came down the floor again, the guy tripped him again. But when it happened for the third time, Bill asked him, 'Did you do that on purpose?' and the guy said, 'You figure it out.' McHorris went after him, and as things like that generally go, the other players almost immediately separated them.

"And that usually marked the end of the brawl. But I wanted to put an end to all that stuff. So, I just said to the bunch, we'll have to see who the best man is. Then I ran everybody out of the gym—the players, managers, janitors—everybody. That just left those two, and I told them to hit the center circle out there and let's see who the best man is. McHorris sprinted out there, ready to go, but the other kid came back toward me. He didn't want any part of McHorris.

"That was the only problem of that kind that I ever had in sixteen years at USL. I guess the word got around that I didn't tolerate bickering. Anyhow, there wasn't any that I noticed from that time on."

Tom Cox joined USL as assistant coach in the summer of 1965. Cox was a personable, natural athlete with a quick smile and easygoing demeanor, especially in contrast to Shipley's volatility. They formed a sort of "good cop, bad cop" kind of approach to the players. In '65–66 USL went 17–8, won the Gulf States Conference championship again, and went to the NAIA playoffs.

Once Shipley and Cox enrolled the three black players and endured the wrath of the State Board of Education, their own administration, their coaching colleagues, their basketball conference, and the NCAA, the feeling was "What the hell, let's go for it."

They started recruiting top-flight players from around the nation, but in particular in the Ohio, Indiana, Kentucky breeding ground of basketball. Shipley had been recruiting in the area since his early days at Southwestern, and Cox, being from Owensboro and having played there, had a relationship with many of the coaches and principals. As the years went by, the Southwestern coaches developed a solid group of fans and supporters among that group. The black coaches and principals, in particular, were close-knit, and as a whole, were sincerely looking out for the future of their young athletes. They saw the personal and friendly treatment the first black athletes were afforded in Lafayette, they knew of the history of Southwestern's early admission of black students, and they trusted and respected Shipley and Cox.

Shipley has fond memories of his relationships with several principals and coaches in the Midwest basketball hotbed. "Dr. Jack Gibbs, principal of Columbus East High School and Lee Williams, football and track coach, were guiding lights on the recruitment of Lamar and Ratleff. They advised us to sign Lamar so that we would have a much better chance with Ratleff. Amazingly our recruiter, Harry Garverick, who had visited the school several times, never met with either Gibbs or Williams. He was visiting the basketball coach who would have nothing to do with the decision these players would make.

"Gibbs and Williams treated us like royalty. On my second trip they handled my hotel reservations. I was picked up at the airport by Coach Williams who had me in a suite in a local hotel. After two days of visitation, on checking out, I was amazed to learn that my suite had been comped. You'd have thought that I was being recruited. These two guys, who were so influential and so respected in Columbus, believed in Tom and me and our school. They were proud of the fact that this relatively small southern university was the first in the South to integrate academically and athletically. Their hospitality was repeated on several other occasions.

"On Gibbs' and Williams' advice, we signed Bo Lamar to a scholarship. This put us in good position for signing Ratleff. At an all-star football game, in which Ratleff was playing end, his father told me he thought his son would sign with us. That was about three in the afternoon. By 5:00 p.m. we learned we had lost him to Jerry 'Tark the Shark' Tarkanian with a phone call. When you lose a talent like Ratleff to a phone call when you are right there in person, it's a humbling experience for a basketball coach.

"Dr. Gibbs and Coach Williams were also close friends with Coach Tom Simpson, Fred Saunders's basketball coach. With their help we were able to sign Fred. Dr. Gibbs and coach Williams are deceased now but we stayed in touch as friends through all these years through phone calls and Christmas cards. Dr. Simpson and I still stay in touch, even to this day."

When USL went to Evansville, Indiana for the final-four college division championship tournament in 1971, Gibbs, Williams, and many of the Columbus East parents were on hand. They mixed with and bonded with the hundreds of USL fans who had made the trip, black and white. These were class people, understandably proud and righteous. Evansville had never seen a party like the one the Cajun fans put on that weekend.

At the USL headquarters hotel, bartenders, waiters and waitresses, and musical combos were paid extra from collections taken up among Cajun fans to stay open, keep serving, and keep playing until the wee hours of the mornings.

The story has been told many times that Bo Lamar was not the prime recruiting target at his high school. Columbus East High School was the hottest basketball school in the Midwest in the late '60s and maybe the best Ohio high school team in history. They lost one game in a three-year run. There were three main reasons for their success: Nick Conner, 6'6" center who played much taller with his phenomenal leaping ability; Ed Ratleff, a 6'6" hot-shooting, smooth-ball-handling forward/guard; and a skinny six-foot guard with a huge afro hairdo known as Dwight "Bo-pete" Lamar. Lamar was the ball handler and assist specialist since Conner and Ratleff were such prolific scorers. Naturally the two big men were the most highly recruited players in the Midwest.

Shipley and Cox spent a lot of time with the coaches, principals, teachers, friends, and families of all three players. They were trying to find out everything they could about them, anything that would give them an edge.

Up to the last week before the signing date, they still thought they had a decent chance of signing Conner and Ratleff. Lamar had only attracted the attention of one other minor university and would be a bonus pick.

It didn't come off. One big phone call from Tark the Shark turned the tide and Ratleff ended up at Long Beach State, signing with Coach Jerry Tarkanian's 49ers.

Meanwhile, Conner decided to stay close to home by signing with Illinois.

Both went on to outstanding careers. Ratleff averaged 22.6 points per game and made All-American twice while playing for Tarkanian and both had NBA careers. Conner died at age fifty-five in 2005 of lung cancer.

USL had taken its best shot but didn't come up empty-handed. Lamar was offered a scholarship and ended up as the only player to ever lead the nation in scoring in both the college division and Division I of the NCAA.

Not surprisingly, some of USL's most distasteful recruiting battles took place right in their own backyard, where the enemies were closer and more bitter.

In 1972 Beryl went to W.O. Boston High School, Lake Charles, Louisiana, to sign Edmond Lawrence, an athletic, seven-foot center. Seven-foot high school seniors in south Louisiana were as rare as dinosaurs. With Shipley and school staff looking on, Lawrence signed the national letter of intent to attend USL. The event was immediately announced to the W.O. Boston High students over the school's public address system: "Edmond has signed with USL."

The next step was mandatory. Beryl had to get official permission for the agreement from Edmond's parents. Edmond's mother greeted him at the family home. Beryl told her Edmond had agreed to attend USL and he needed her signature. She said she wanted her husband to do the signing but he was out working in a rice field about a mile away. She and Beryl drove to the rice field, blew the car horn to summon Mr. Lawrence, and the wife waved to him. He came to the car and his wife told him of their son's decision and asked him to sign the papers. When he had finished signing, Beryl asked if anyone from McNeese State had been to see him. (Beryl knew that McNeese, in Lake Charles, had been heavily recruiting Edmond.) The father said no one but Beryl had been around. Beryl returned to Lafayette with the prized documents in hand.

Twenty-four hours later, Beryl received a telegram from the Southland Conference commissioner, Dick Oliver—no phone call or any other communication, a telegram—informing him that Edmond Lawrence had been *assigned* to McNeese State. It said that Edmond had signed with McNeese before he had signed with Beryl. Beryl knew the telegrammed information was untrue, but the Conference had ruled, and there was nothing he could do about it. His administration, as usual, had no comment and offered no assistance in correcting the situation.

Sportswriter J.C. Hatcher, in his *Advertiser* column "Sports Lowdown" on April 27, 1972, held nothing back when he wrote:

"If you play in a sewer ditch, you are going to get a little stink on you." Those simple, but truthful, words came from the mouth of my old grandfather and were uttered when I was but a small boy. My grandfather was admonishing me to hang around in good company. He was telling me "you are what your friends are."

My grandfather has since died but his words still linger in the back of my mind. Every now and then they will come out of nowhere. Sort of like the Durango Kid or the Lone Ranger or State Farm Insurance—when you need a trusted friend, the words are there.

Such was the case last week. It was a dreary Friday and a press conference was in process. Beryl Shipley, the imminent basketball coach at the University of Southwestern Louisiana, had the floor. He was trying to explain what had happened on the signing of Edmond Lawrence. Shipley was actually at a loss of words. For the first time in my memory, the red haired country boy could not explain the situation. I have seen this guy handle some tough situations, and with ease. But, as he spoke about the "double-signing" of Edmond Lawrence, tears almost emerged from his eyes; on several occasions his voice cracked; he was upset, mad and fired up.

The Edmond Lawrence Case, or the "Who signed what first" ordeal, has sparked controversy between USL and McNeese State. Southwestern legitimately signed the young basketball player to a Louisiana State Board of Education Letter of Intent, a Southland Conference Letter of Intent and a "national" letter of intent.

USL signed the lad to the first two letters on Tuesday (April 18) and he inked the "national" document on Wednesday (April 19). All of this was announced by USL officials on Thursday (April 20). Some 24 hours later McNeese announced that it had signed Lawrence first, and on all three letters-of-intent at that.

McNeese State says it signed Lawrence first on all three contracts. The Cowboy officials have not proved this, they just say it is the truth. Jesse James said he never robbed a bank and Al Capone was innocent of everything, according to Al Capone.

Stanley Galloway, a former coach and now the Commissioner of State College Athletics, a job he will not have very much longer, and Dick Oliver, the czar of the Southland Conference, both supposedly investigated the double-signing by USL and McNeese. Neither Galloway nor Oliver investigated. They both looked over the documents and came to the conclusion that the form that McNeese submitted was dated prior to the documents that USL had submitted, in all instances. Now, for Oliver and Galloway to come up with such judgments must rank with Sherlock Holmes' escapades around Scotland Yard. Boy, they really had to get out and dig to secure the necessary information to make that decision. My five-year-old son could have read the forms and stated, with authority, that McNeese's forms carried an earlier date (or time) than those presented by USL.

We expected Galloway to rule in McNeese's favor. He has consistently opposed Southwestern in everything. Galloway was turned down as USL's head football coach in 1961 (when Russ Faulkinberry was hired) and Galloway has been getting even ever since.

Last Friday he admitted he did not have any of the documents, but he thought that Lawrence belonged to McNeese. Now that makes a lot of sense. The papers could have been signed by "The Three Stooges," and Galloway would have ruled in McNeese's favor.

Galloway takes his orders from the State Board of Education members Fred Tannehill and Boyd Woodard, and those two have also opposed Southwestern in the progress made in the field of athletics.

But Oliver making his ruling without holding any kind of hearing is a puzzle. I have known Oliver for many years and respect him as a "hard-nosed" individual.

I had thoroughly expected him to investigate the whole ordeal, leaving no stone unturned in an effort to find out what really happened in the signing of Edmond Lawrence.

Oliver may still accomplish this necessary inquiry. He is not likely to let the rumblings of his decision cause harm to the Southland Conference.

Southwestern officials have to be shaking their heads. USL forced the breakup of the old Gulf States Conference last May to get out of the "sewer ditch" and to get away from politics, and to get away from Stanley Galloway.

USL and Louisiana Tech joined the Southland Conference. McNeese was left in the cold with no conference affiliation. Politicians in the state of Louisiana forced USL to co-sponsor McNeese's application to enter the Southland conference.

Just recently McNeese was caught by Oliver with an ineligible football player. Several schools in Louisiana had attempted to recruit the footballer, but his grades were too low to allow him to compete, except at McNeese.

McNeese had him in school and out for grid drills, which is a violation of every rule in the book. Mr. Galloway did not publicly rule on this matter.

What can be done in the Lawrence matter?

1—Oliver should have a complete investigation.

2—He should give all parties involved in the case (Reigel, Shipley, Lawrence, the automobile dealer and the rest) a polygraph test.

3—He should get a hand writing expert to authenticate the signatures on every contract.

4—He should explain how he ruled in McNeese's favor, even though McNeese signed the kid to the wrong contract (McNeese signed him to a grant-in-aid, which is against the rules. He should have been signed to a pre-enrollment pact).

If Oliver cannot handle the investigation, he should seek the help of the NCAA.

And if Oliver does not accomplish these deeds, the University of Southwestern Louisiana should withdraw from the Southland Conference immediately.

And with that withdrawal, break all relations with McNeese State—football, basketball, track, baseball, tennis, golf, archery, swimming, ice hockey.

Let's make another attempt to get out of the "sewer ditch." It's beginning to smell again.

Again, strong words, hard facts, falling on deaf ears.

That was it. No investigation was held by Oliver, Galloway, the NCAA, or anyone involved with USL or McNeese.

It was probably just as well. The other big shoe was about to drop.

Chapter Seven

NCAA versus USL, Round two

Fall 1972. Practice for the new basketball season was in full swing, expectations were skyrocketing, and USL fans were in high anxiety. The new season would open in Las Vegas, Nevada against the Runnin' Rebels. Two 727 jets had already been chartered and seats were filling up fast.

Most of last season's 25-and-4 team were back. They had reached the second round of the NCAA tournament the previous year, ended the season ranked in the top ten, and would probably start the season with a similar ranking. Bo Lamar had led the nation in scoring in Division I, Ebron was one of the top rebounders in the country, and Saunders, Bisbano, and Robert Wilson made the one-three-one trap zone defense work. Newcomers Larry Fogle and Andre Brown were ready to prove their worth. History was waiting.

Shipley's ambitious scheduling included, in addition to the Southland Conference home-and-home, a Bayou Classic featuring Marshall and St. Joseph's of Pennsylvania. The Cajuns would entertain Mercer at Blackham Coliseum and take on perennial powers Cincinnati, Houston, and Jacksonville on the road and close out the season with two games in Hawaii. That trip was also already filling up airline seats. Season tickets were almost sold out.

Yet, with all these delirious preparations, disaster was lurking. For more than a year, Shipley had been trying to verify a rumor he had heard in the summer of 1971. Attending a College Sports Information Directors Association (CoSIDA) convention in Chicago, a friend of his said, "I hear they're after you again, Ship." Reed Greene, athletic director at the University of Southern Mississippi, said he had heard the USL administration had notified the NCAA that it was investigating Shipley's recruiting practices. Later a private investigator friend informed Beryl that a private firm had been engaged by his old nemesis, the State Board of Education, to do personal surveillance on Shipley.

Shipley, to this day, is amazed that neither his president, Dr. Clyde Rougeau, nor anyone from the university administration ever advised him of the impending disaster. "At one time Dr. Rougeau and I would talk on the phone almost daily. He would call me four or five times a week. I felt we were good friends. I can't say for sure, but coincidentally, shortly after Raymond Blanco became dean of men, my relationship with the president cooled considerably. I never heard from him and my calls to him went unanswered. I don't know, could it have been jealousy over the success of our basketball program? I guess I'll never know," Shipley said.

On November 2, 1972, the USL administration received a letter from the NCAA notifying it of the culmination of an investigation and containing an official inquiry. There were thirty-two pages of alleged violations. Shipley and Cox received a copy of the letter and the official inquiry. That would be the last, the only, documents concerning this investigation that the coaches saw until August 2006, thirty-three years later. All the correspondence exchanged between the university and the NCAA concerning the investigation, the allegations, and the ultimate penalties were never submitted for review or comment to the principal individuals involved in the case.

An official inquiry is the first public notice of an NCAA investigation, and it presents the allegations of violations received up to that point. The school is required to review these allegations, question and obtain information from the athletic department and others directly involved, and respond to each allegation.

The next year was one of confusion, frustration, and despair for the faithful USL basketball fans, the players, and coaches. Most fans who watched the drama unfold could not understand how this was happening. Most truly believed, and still do, that the university administration vigorously defended their beloved basketball program and went down only after exhausting all remedies.

However, Shipley still believes the administration itself was a source of much of the misleading and fraudulent information and some persons in it were guilty of aiding and abetting the investigation and supporting the excessive punishment.

The NCAA, as standard practice, demands that the official inquiry be copied and a response be inserted below each allegation. The NCAA is supposed to review the responses and revise, eliminate, or maintain allegations in accordance with the responses presented, and then advance to the second step, a numbered case file. This file presents the NCAA's case, and it, for the first time, reveals the sources of the allegations. It also presents the final allegations, revised to reflect the university's responses.

The third step occurs fifteen days later when the case is presented to the NCAA Council, which evaluates the case file presentation and renders decisions based on its merits.

Coach Shipley had been tilting windmills for years. Although he had successfully reconstructed his life after the 1973 debacle and was comfortably retired, the old competitive spirit still burned. He wanted to get to the bottom of the NCAA destruction of his program. He and his wife, Dolores, had collected reams of newspaper clippings, personal memos, USL documents, and personal notes. He had enlisted writers, locally and out of state, to take on his redemption project, without success.

In 2006 Beryl's older brother, Tom, was enlisted to help Beryl sort out all the details and uncover the mysteries still surrounding the whole convoluted affair.

Through solid research work and with the help of Beryl's many friends still at the university, files of the period were recovered from the ULL library archives. One of the documents was the July 20, 1973 Case 390 file, which was developed from the official inquiry and university responses.

Neither Beryl nor Tom Cox had ever seen this document before. As they read it for the first time on August 4, 2006, it was, coincidentally, the thirty-third anniversary of the NCAA Council's decision, the so-called death penalty given USL on August 4, 1973.

The July case file document was revealing. For the first time, the coaches saw the names of the individuals who had initiated the allegations of violations. The case, with the accusers' names, had been prepared twenty-two days after the June 28 date of the university's response to the NCAA's official inquiry.

From that material the Shipleys learned that the NCAA's committee on infractions had received information on possible USL violations of regulations in the spring of 1971. During its inquiry into this matter, the committee "developed other information alleging numerous additional violations of the Association's legislation." During the "late summer and early fall 1972, the University [informed the NCAA that it had] initiated an investigation of its athletic department with particular emphasis on the recruitment and retention of student-athletes in the basketball program."

But when all archive files had been reviewed, it was discovered that there was extensive information for the '60s, but almost all of the correspondence for the 1970s was missing. Beryl went back to his archive sources but was told no other files existed.

Beryl and Tom Cox had originally seen only the November 2, 1972 initial inquiry. They hadn't even seen the final document that completed the episode and dictated the punishment. Without that and other NCAA/university correspondence of the 1970–73 period, there was a huge gap of information unavailable. One document from the archives, issued to form the NCAA case, included a historical review of NCAA/university communications that led to the initial inquiries, the basis for USL's Case 390. Its contents detailed specific information, dates, and documents on NCAA/university/board communications during the 1970–74 period. It turned out to be an inventory of the missing documentation.

Requests were made to the NCAA for copies of the missing files with no success. Requests were then made directly to USL President Ray Authement. The request for specific documents was made to the president in a letter dated September 2006. When there was no response, phone calls were placed to the president's office without success. The president was unavailable.

In the meantime, Tom was pursuing every possible avenue. He had even drafted a newspaper ad that he intended to run throughout the state, requesting help in locating the missing information. Finally, in mid-October, Dr. Authement responded. After detailed discussions, the president acknowledged that there were eight more folders of papers available. The president agreed to have the documents copied, at Shipley's expense, and send him the requested material.

With that information in hand, the whole pattern became obvious. As in the 1967 case, the NCAA had no intention of taking into account testimony other than that of those who had reported the alleged violations. The missing documents included testimony by those accused and other witnesses, documentation, and evidence that was obviously ignored. The NCAA was not to be bothered by facts. Their mind was made up.

Chapter Eight

Gotcha!

According to NCAA records, the new investigation of allegations began on July 8, 1970 and continued until September 22, 1972. The records show that it conducted ninety-six different interviews with people located in many different states in the nation. To build its case, the association spent more than two years of effort. The official inquiry, which required response from the university, was dated November 2, 1972.

Compounding the university's problems was the stipulation that such response "must be on file with [four committee members in four different states] by December 13, 1972."

Six weeks to compile an answer to two years of investigations was an impossible demand. A delay was requested, and the NCAA agreed to a delay of the response until March 1 but requested university representatives attend a meeting of the NCAA council on December 19, at which the findings of the association's investigation would be presented.

In other words, the NCAA intended to go forward with the case without the benefit of an official, written response. The university sent three representatives to the meeting, but they were not allowed to present a defense. They tried to explain that, in the time allowed, no defense was possible and requested the NCAA allow USL to respond on the previously agreed upon date of March 1, 1973.

The NCAA disregarded that request and presented its case to the committee. The committee subsequently filed Confidential Report No. 74, dated December 22, 1972, with Case 390 (ten pages) attached. The report and case file were sent with a cover letter dated December 28, 1972 and received by

USL on January 3, 1973. At that time the case was based only on university-reported allegations of improprieties, derived from USL's initial response to the official inquiry presented with Dr. Rougeau's October 9, 1972 report. The case was to be presented to the council on January 9, 1973, and "[represented] the Committee on Infractions' findings of violations of NCAA legislation based upon specific information reported by the University (for which this Committee also had developed supportive evidence)."

A copy of Dr. Rougeau's October 9 letter was included in the documents supplied in the fall of 2006 by Dr. Authement. Dr. Rougeau's letter did not present one single "finding of violations of NCAA allegation" on which the case could have been justified. The closest the letter comes to that is this one sentence: "Our investigation has uncovered certain irregularities surrounding the procedures employed by certain members of the athletic staff in recruiting, determining eligibility, and in providing aid to student athletes."

But a very important element was missing. At the end of the letter was the word *enclosure*. There was no copy of such included with the document. Further research disclosed what is believed to be that enclosure attached to a later Rougeau letter to the Athletic Committee, Louisiana State Board of Education, dated October 24. It read:

> It is the purpose of this report to provide specific infor-mation concerning irregularities in each of the areas afore-mentioned: Recruiting, Determining Eligibility, Providing Financial Aid to Student Athletes. Except in the area of responsibility for the administration of the athletic program in general and the basketball program in particular, the Uni-versity does not wish to assess, for any of the irregularities uncovered in its investigation, a degree of culpability of any particular member of our athletic staff, past or present, or of individuals not directly associated with the athletic program of the University.
>
> I. Recruiting
>
> a. Money in amounts ranging from $15-$20 was pro-vided to prospective student athletes on visits to the campus. This was in lieu of having a second party paying entertainment expenses for the visiting ath-lete.
>
> b. University records indicate payments made (from outside funds) for two plane trips to the campus for

each of two student athletes. Though credits have been issued to the University to cover these costs, the University regards this as irregular.

c. Automobile transportation to and from a job site was provided a prospective student athlete.

II. Determining Eligibility

a. Incorrect grade-point averages were used to predict a 1.6 g.p.a. on two student athletes. These averages were submitted to the Testing Center on a special form used by the Athletic Department.

b. An altered high school transcript was used in calculating the grade-point average of a student athlete.

c. Grants-in-aid were awarded two student athletes who had not completed the necessary procedures employed by the University in predicting the 1.6 and in awarding the grant-in-aid.

III. Providing Aid to Student Athletes

a. The loan of private automobiles was made to student athletes for dating purposes.

b. Gasoline was made available to student athletes for use in their private automobiles. This practice, in part, was initiated to allow students to drive to and from practice sessions held away from the main campus.

c. Payment of grants-in-aid for student-athletes who had not predicted the 1.6 GPA (same as II-c) were approved and made.

d. Loans were made to/or endorsed for certain student athletes.

e. Automobile transportation was provided student athletes returning to the campus after a school break.

That's a pretty damning litany of findings apparently admitted to by the university. They are, in fact, a repetition of the same allegations, though fewer in number, as were listed in the November 2, 1972 official inquiry. Obviously the university was admitting to all the charges.

The sad truth is the university had not done a comprehensive investigation. Only a few of the accusers were interviewed, making the university's findings no better than, and, actually endorsing, the NCAA's contentions. The university had carried out its investigation, reported in Dr. Rougeau's October 9, 1972 letter, without interrogating a single one of the accused individuals. This cavalier, almost dismissive action made the outcome of the case a foregone conclusion, a slam dunk.

Later individuals within the community but not associated officially with the university volunteered their help. These were people who truly cared about the future of the athletic program and the university's reputation. Bob Wright, John Allen Bernard and Senator Edgar "Sonny" Mouton, all attorneys, took charge of the case. Because of them a thorough investigation took place. Accusations were vehemently denied. Almost all of the allegations, large and small, were countered. Unfortunately this mountain of evidence was not produced until USL's June 28, 1973 response, at which time it was promptly ignored.

The December 22 case file, received by USL on January 3, 1973, was slated to be presented to the council on January 9—six days later—at the Palmer House in Chicago. This meant that the university was not to be allowed an official response to any of the allegations. This sounds arbitrary, but it is probable that the NCAA assumed that Dr. Rougeau's investigation results, supplied in his October 9 letter, was sufficient proof to NCAA members that their findings had been correct and no further response from the university was necessary.

By this time the public reaction to the ongoing events had forced the university hierarchy to deny its acquiescence and apparent acceptance of the impending NCAA action. They finally accepted the outside help. Several prominent attorneys and state legislators were actively seeking ways to block the NCAA's steamroller. It should be mentioned that attorneys John Allen Bernard and Bob Wright and members of their firms as well as state Senator Edgar "Sonny" Mouton, also an attorney, worked countless hours and produced reams of documents at no charge to the university or state.

By January 5 the basketball team was ripping through opponents, undefeated in their first seven games and averaging more than ninety-seven points per game. But Shipley and his closest friends and supporters were not happy. Beryl had sought the advice of attorneys Wright and Bernard. The two were staunch fans and had traveled with the team on most road trips ever since its first appearance in the NAIA tournament in Kansas City.

Faced with the NCAA's recalcitrance and the January 9 meeting in Chicago looming, the team flew back to Lafayette in a chartered plane after beating Texas-Pan-American in Edinburgh. They made no more than a pit stop in Lafayette on Friday then headed out again that afternoon by commercial airline for a noon Saturday TV game with Jacksonville in Florida. The team and its followers would fly to New York City after the game in Jacksonville late Saturday afternoon for another big game on Long Island.

Wright, Allen, and several other key supporters were on the Florida trip. Emotions were running high concerning the impending NCAA action. Friday night, after dinner in Jacksonville, the entourage gathered in Coach Shipley's suite. After hours of discussion of alternative plans, some of it loud and rancorous, the decision was made to file an injunction against the NCAA to restrain it from taking immediate action against the university in Case 390.

Ron Gomez was in the suite during the discussion and relates the following: "Anger, hurt, frustration, all the emotions had built up to a crescendo over the past couple of months. Wright and Bernard argued the case for an injunction. When it was decided to go forward, Senator Edgar 'Sonny' Mouton, also an attorney, was called at his home in Lafayette. Using three phones in the suite, Wright, Bernard, and Shipley discussed the arguments and the language of the plea."

Mouton agreed to draft the injunction with the help of one of Wright's colleagues, Mark Bienvenu. Being a well-connected politician, Mouton called and got Louisiana Attorney General William Guste's permission to sign the suit in the A.G.'s name and file it on behalf of the state board and the university. They would then get Dr. Rougeau to sign it and Mouton would drive to Abbeville in the morning to the home of federal judge Richard Putnam for his signature. Mouton also grudgingly reminded the group that one of his daughters was getting married the next day as well.

Wright called Judge Putnam at his home. He had known the judge for many years and had tried cases before him. In the course of the conversation, Bob, a master trial lawyer, pleaded the case for the better part of an hour. When the judge had all his questions answered and agreed to sign the injunction, Bob told him, in all sincerity, "You're going to be really proud that you helped these young men and the university, Judge. They're going to be on national TV at noon tomorrow. Be sure to watch them. You'll be proud of what you did."

On Saturday morning, January 6, 1973, Senator Mouton pulled enough strings to get the Lafayette Parish Court House opened and for a clerk to accept and file a civil action suit instituted by the "Attorney General of the State of Louisiana for the Board of Education for the State of Louisiana, individually and on behalf of the University of Southwestern Louisiana versus the National Collegiate Athletic Association." It was a "Petition for Preliminary Injunction and Temporary Restraining Order."

The petition described the efforts the university had made to comply and explained why the time to conduct a comprehensive investigation was too short, the efforts made by the attorney general to obtain sufficient time, and the NCAA's subsequent denial.

It related that three university representatives who had attended the December 19, 1972 meeting with the committee had not been able to present a defense. They had merely tried to explain that, in the time allowed, no defense was possible, and request the NCAA allow USL to respond on the previously agreed upon date of March 1, 1973. By signature of Judge Putnam, a preliminary injunction was granted, enjoining the NCAA from proceeding further until August 15. Eventually the association had the suit nullified in federal court only to see it get new life in a Louisiana state court.

But for now the NCAA was restrained, Mouton made it back in time for his daughter's wedding, and presumably Judge Putnam settled into his easy chair to watch USL versus Jacksonville on national TV.

The Cajuns played the worst game of their collective careers, maybe the worst in USL history, losing by 42 points 120–78. It was unbelievably embarrassing. Years later Fred Saunders and Bo Lamar admitted to Gomez the factors leading to the wipeout. "They said, with all the NCAA problems and the legal discussions, the coaches had failed to tell them this was a noon tip-off. They expected the game to be the usual 7:30 starting time. In addition, they had scouted out the coaches' suite and surmised that, with all the shouting, drinking, and debating going on, there would be no bed check, so the majority of the team spent the night cavorting on the beach until sunup. When the breakfast call came, most of them hadn't slept more than an hour."

Shipley's problems were compounded. The NCAA was now restrained from dropping the hammer on Tuesday, as expected, but he now had a team in disarray while heading for a huge showdown against nationally ranked Cincinnati at the Nassau Coliseum in Uniondale, New York on Long Island.

In the meantime, the NCAA "confidential case file" was leaked to the media. A New York newspaper reporter tracked Shipley and the team down in the concourse of the New York airport as they arrived from Jacksonville. Beryl was outraged. He told the reporter he and his university had not even been able to answer the charges and here they were released to the press. He said, in so many words, that the NCAA were racists and were politically motivated by Louisiana segregationists.

After checking in to a motel and changing, the team headed for a workout at the Nassau Coliseum. During the practice another reporter showed up. This one was from the *New York Times*.

The Monday edition of the *Times* carried the headline: "S.W. Louisiana Coach Calls NCAA Charges Political" and began "The basketball coach of

100

the University of Southwestern Louisiana said today that charges of mass recruiting violations against his school were either 'political' or 'picayune' and had grown partly from his success in enrolling black players in the Deep South."

In the third paragraph, the article continued: But Shipley insisted that "95 percent of our trouble" with the NCAA stemmed from charges made by a graduate assistant the coach dismissed two years ago. The trouble, he said, thrived in a climate fed by two things: resentment by established teams that his school was now a basketball power and resentment by some state officials over his use of black stars.

Later in the article, Shipley reiterated, "95 percent of our trouble started after we had to fire a guy in the spring of 1971, a graduate assistant who did scouting and recruiting for me." Shipley declined to identify the former graduate assistant, but he said, "Any time you have anybody who leaves a place bitter, he's going to do anything to hurt you. I could write a book about why I fired him."

Shipley was asked to comment on reports in Louisiana newspapers that more than 120 violations would be charged at the meeting of the NCAA on Tuesday in Chicago. The violations reportedly included the use of substitutes to take entrance examinations for basketball prospects. "I don't know what the NCAA is criticizing us for, but the main thing in the past was that some of our procedures were not set up properly. We'd still like more time to answer the charges, and we can't understand why the NCAA wouldn't act in good faith after the school acted in good faith. We need time to go out and get our side of the story. I deny that we had subs take exams for players. A lot of the other charges are picayune. Some we admitted, some we don't feel are wrong, even if the NCAA says they are. We didn't try to fool anybody or sneak a kid into school. If they want us to change anything, we will. I'm not trying to fight the Establishment."

Beryl was flying blind. He was answering questions concerning a list of charges he had never seen and would not see in its entirety until 2006. He had heard from good sources who his accusers were but, at that time, had no proof.

This was a bad time to get cross-wise with the coach. Larry Fogle, always on the brink of trouble, did. Fogle was a superb freshman guard from Brooklyn, New York. Tom Cox had recruited out of the housing projects of the ghetto. He was tough and street-smart. He also was a phenomenal athlete with all the talent needed for All-American status. After a couple of months of playing number six and seven, he had worked his way up to the first five and was to start in the Cincinnati game.

He and Beryl had words about Fogle's desire to visit his old neighborhood while they were on Long Island. Shipley wouldn't allow it and Fogle pitched a fit. When the smoke had cleared, Shipley had kicked Fogle off the team and told him if he wanted to come back he'd have to find his way back to Lafayette, Louisiana on his own.

The Cajuns, still smarting from all the adversity and the humiliating loss to Jacksonville, couldn't shake the monkey off their backs. They trailed Cincinnati by nineteen points at halftime.

There is no transcript of what transpired in the locker room during intermission, but Shipley must have blistered the paint. The team came back playing like the champions they could be to beat the Bearcats by six.

Fogle found his way back to Louisiana a few days later, was sufficiently contrite, and returned to the team. That breakout second half against Cincinnati seemed to lift the Cajuns above their frustration and the confusion of the NCAA debacle. They proceeded to reel off ten straight wins and won fourteen of the next fifteen games.

USL had bought some time, but the NCAA was relentless. On January 11, Warren Brown wired Dr. Rougeau that if he would see to it that the court's restraining order was vacated, the NCAA Council would meet in private dining room nine at 9:30 a.m., Sunday, January 14, at the Palmer House.

Brown stated that the council would not act upon the report until USL representatives, if any, had an opportunity to be heard.

Dr. Rougeau did not respond to Brown's request until the seventeenth, explaining that his office had been closed due to inclement weather and that the telegram had been mailed rather than phoned or hand-delivered by Western Union. The meeting was presumably held but not attended by USL representatives.

The NCAA naturally appealed the temporary injunction. On February 15, while the appeal was pending, another proposal was made to the NCAA. USL agreed to join the NCAA in a mutual agreement of dismissal of the injunction suit. USL would agree to voluntarily withdraw from consideration of any post-season tournament bid, and the NCAA would voluntarily agree to grant USL an extension until August 15, 1973, to allow USL to properly respond to the charges.

On the same day, the proposal was discussed further with NCAA officials and their attorneys, and USL attorneys asked that a decision be rendered by the afternoon of the sixteenth. The NCAA responded that it could not respond by that time but could by the nineteenth. On the nineteenth they rejected the proposal. The association had never been in a court battle such as this and they were determined not to set any precedents. They had to win or face more future challenges that could destroy the NCAA.

On February 20, John Allen Bernard, named by William Guste Jr., Attorney General for the State of Louisiana, as special counsel, wrote a letter to J. Winston Fontenot, the Lafayette attorney hired by the NCAA to represent them in Louisiana. He summarized the exchange of the previous five days and concluded it by saying:

> Frankly, it is difficult to understand what reason the NCAA can have for not agreeing to the proposal. In view of the NCAA's attitude we wish at this time to advise the NCAA, through you as its attorney, that the aforesaid proposal is withdrawn. Regardless of the outcome of the present litigation, the State Board of Education, acting on its own behalf and on behalf of USL, intends to exercise, by every available means, all remedies that may be available either within the NCAA itself or by further court action or both.

The NCAA obviously had no interest in considering USL's defensive response. After the release of the allegations to the press, they had to have a conviction or face harsh criticism from their members as well as the media.

The Cajuns held on long enough to get a bid and play in the NCAA tournament. On March 10 they romped to a satisfying 102–89 victory over the University of Houston at Ames, Iowa. This was the same Cougar team that had taken a questionably officiated 82–80 win in Houston on February 10 at the height of the NCAA frenzy. During that game the Houston band played "Hey, Big Spender" repeatedly. They were, of course, alluding to the allegations of USL players being paid. After the game, Houston players were seen leaving their dressing room in classy, *Superfly* street clothes and getting into their late-model cars.

With the circumstances surrounding the end of their season, it is not surprising that tension was seething on the team. Roy Ebron, relishing his role as the recognized challenger to Bill Walton, had scored twenty-four points and pulled down eleven rebounds in a superb effort against the Cougars. Now he decided to assert himself by not shaving and, by the second round of play, held in Houston, was sporting a week-old beard. Shipley's rules strictly forbade facial hair. It was hard enough for the disciplinarian coach to allow Afro hairdos, much less beards. Ebron was told to shave or not show up for the game against Kansas State, one of the top seeded teams in the tournament.

Several of Ebron's personal entourage, who felt they had a stake in the big center's NBA future, pleaded, cajoled, and threatened him. He reluctantly shaved at the last minute but was not allowed to start the game. When he did get into the game, he played as though he was sleepwalking, hitting only five of fifteen field goals, most from point-blank range and committed several crucial turnovers. K-State won 66–63, eliminating the Cajuns and ending speculation of a match-up with UCLA in the Final Four to be held in New Orleans.

The season was over but the gloom lingered on. Who were the accusers? Who were these people that the NCAA put the full faith and reputation of their association behind? Who were the individuals Shipley had referred to in the *New York Times* interview as bitter people, a graduate assistant whom he had to fire, whom he described as a person "who leaves a place bitter, he's going to do anything to hurt you. I could write a book about why I fired him."

In those days at USL, the coaching staff consisted of a head coach and one assistant. There wasn't much budget to spread around, much less buy players. The head coach was making less than fifteen thousand dollars a year and the assistant, eleven thousand. The basketball program needed help in contacting potential recruits on the road and doing a vast number of other things the coaches couldn't handle for lack of time. Some students were interested in athletics and chose to help. Some of the student coaches were interested because they had a desire to pursue coaching as a career. For instance, Don Landry in 1960, Rocke Roy in 1965–66, and Jimmy Dykes and Allen Van Winkle in 1969–73 were considered part of the staff but were unpaid. Others, like Jerry Meaux, just loved the game and admired Shipley. He volunteered to do whatever was needed—scouting other teams, assessing possible recruits, driving the car, whatever—just for his own personal satisfaction.

One assistant was neither a student nor a volunteer. Harry Garverick was hired at five hundred dollars per month in 1969 as a recruiter. His job was to screen high school and junior college students who were reputed to be good athletes. The information on these would come to the head or assistant coach, generally, from almost any source: high school coaches, USL fans, friends of one coach or the other. Garverick would be assigned to investigate the prospect and would travel when necessary to assess the talent and possibly approach the potential recruit on behalf of USL. He carried the title of assistant coach but had little experience as a coach and did no floor coaching at all at USL.

Harry, married with kids, soon gained a reputation of having an eye for the girls. Shipley and Cox began to get rumors and complaints that Garverick was using his position for pursuits other than recruiting. He attended high school games and tournaments as a part of his job, but he reportedly used the events and his position as an assistant coach with a potential path to a college scholarship to further other objectives. USL's coaches received complaints that one of Garverick's favorite enticements was filling a bathtub with ice, beer, and soft drinks before a game, then inviting recruits, their girlfriends, and cheerleaders to a post-game party in his hotel room.

In one instance Garverick was scouting a tournament in which Pensacola Jr. College was playing. One of the female cheerleaders reported improper behavior on Garverick's part to the Pensacola coach. The coach called Tom Cox and told him that USL was never to recruit at his school again.

As reports of Garverick's extracurricular activities began to surface, the final straw occurred during the NCAA College Division Tournament in Evansville, Indiana, in March 1971. Coach Shipley was called by a tearful wife of one of the players. She told him Garverick had made sexual advances toward her and become physically abusive when she rebuffed him. After listening to her story and doing some checking with others to verify her story, Beryl called Garverick in and terminated him immediately.

Shipley later learned that Lafayette law enforcement officers were very familiar with his assistant. According to both the Lafayette City Police and Lafayette Parish sheriff's office, Harry Garverick, the guy in whom the university, the state board, and the NCAA were to put their trust as their prime witness against Beryl Shipley and his program, definitely had a behavioral problem, and a penchant for younger girls.

It seems that Garverick, married with children, was using a nineteen-year-old girl for sexual purposes and suggesting a possible blackmail scheme.

Coach Shipley was apprised of his assistant's law enforcement problems by a member of the Lafayette City Police. He still has transcripts of the 1969 official records.

The city police report relates the arrest of a nineteen-year-old woman on a charge of dispensing LSD. While being questioned, the woman told officers she had been given money by Harry Garverick and said she had been shacking up with him for some time at various motels in the area and at the apartment that she identified as her residence. The woman told officers she had become a regular mistress of Garverick, who had enticed her on several occasions to "entertain" visiting coaches and players who were visiting Lafayette.

She also said she had smoked pot and taken some pills with Garverick on several occasions. According to the report, he had also asked her to call the wife of a prominent local businessman with whom she had a relationship. He told her to tell the man she would call his wife if he didn't come up with money. She said she had called the wife on one occasion but refused to do it again because the man had been good to her and had paid three thousand dollars to an attorney who was representing her on previous charges.

The same woman was also interrogated by the Lafayette Parish sheriff's office concerning a narcotics violation.

Without a doubt, the worst decision Beryl Shipley ever made was hiring Harry Garverick as a recruiting assistant.

The NCAA had prematurely released its allegations to the public, and interested parties were beginning to realize who the prime accusers were.

Garverick became the NCAA's—and because they originally accepted the veracity of the charges, the university's—principal informant of violation allegations. Another less-than-credible source was a former player that Shipley ran off, Frank Kluz.

Garverick and Kluz were both from Ohio. He brought Kluz to USL's attention in 1969. He was a borderline recruit, but Shipley and Cox accepted Garverick's recommendation and signed him to a scholarship. Frank played for only one season (1970–71) and didn't get much game time. According to Shipley, Kluz wouldn't or couldn't follow the coaches' game instructions, and he lacked a basic characteristic that Coach Shipley considered fundamental: he wouldn't "take the lick."

Beryl's players had to be aggressive, and Frank Kluz, Beryl decided early on, didn't have the heart for it. In addition he was having academic problems.

Frank had gotten no playing time in the two games of the College Division Tournament in Evansville, and he complained bitterly to anyone and everyone who would listen. In the following days, he didn't attend a single class. Beryl had a standing request with all university professors: "Please, give our guys who need it all the scholastic help that you can (because of their limited opportunities in previous years and the time demands of major college basketball practices and travel), but let me know when any player cuts classes." When the team was in town, it was mandatory that they attend classes. If a player's class attendance did not satisfy Beryl, the player's status on the team was in jeopardy, and so was his scholarship agreement. Frank Kluz was terminated as a player for poor class attendance.

Harry Garverick and Frank Kluz, both carrying grievances against Coach Shipley, subsequently joined forces, with Kluz playing a minor role, to do what they could to help bring the basketball program down.

On September 29, 1971, the two good friends were both interviewed by an NCAA investigator, Kluz at Lancaster, Ohio and Garverick at Chillicothe, Ohio.

These were the two main characters on which the NCAA based its case for most of the violations against the USL basketball program.

After Dr. Clyde Rougeau's sudden decision to retire in early 1973, the university's response was finalized by acting president Dr. Ray Authement and mailed to the NCAA June 28, 1973. This document is the one Shipley finally uncovered in late 2006. It was a very comprehensive three-volume report. Volume I consisted of 118 typewritten pages that responded to each specific allegation. As instructed by the NCAA, it repeated each allegation as presented in the official inquiry, followed by the university's response to it. Volume II, Supporting Exhibits, provided details requested by the NCAA: details on scholarships, grade transcripts, SAT material, and other academic records. This was 122 typewritten pages. Volume III, Appendix of Statements, provided the signed statements of the individual respondents and quotes from interviewees and witnesses. It consisted of seventy-two typewritten pages.

Allowing normal mail delivery time, the NCAA should have received the material just prior to the July 4 holiday. It is assumed the staff would begin the process of reading and analyzing the complex details of this 312-page document shortly after the holiday. Presumably they would then discuss the contents with their investigators and the accusers. They would have to weigh the evidence presented against the proof that the accusers had given the association. Trained, legitimate investigators would want to make follow-up interviews with many of the university's witnesses who refuted the NCAA's witnesses. And, of course, the accusers were not all located at NCAA headquarters.

It is almost inconceivable and unbelievable that the NCAA, which took two years developing Case 390, could present a final report from the NCAA Committee on Infractions just more than two weeks after receiving the USL response. The final report, forty-five pages long, was virtually unchanged and just as damning as the allegations presented the previous fall. Thus, the final step, the resolution from the NCAA Council, was dated August 4, 1973—fifteen days after delivery of Case File 390. It strains logic to believe that the NCAA read or took any follow-up action on the evidence presented in the university's 312-page response.

The resolution basically terminated USL's membership in the NCAA, banned for four years all USL sports teams from post-season play, suspended the basketball program from competition for two years (the death penalty), and banned all USL athletics from any national television appearances.

Case File 390 essentially was a carbon copy of the same allegations contained in the official inquiry of November 1972. Not one notarized statement of denial, not one statement from USL witnesses was acknowledged, much less rebutted. It is obvious to any rational person that the NCAA, in league with the Louisiana State Board of Education, some members of the USL administration staff, and others, had its mind set when it issued the official inquiry on November 2, 1972, and nothing the university could have produced would have made one iota of difference.

If any member of the NCAA had tabulated the individual gifts and totaled the amount of money that the two coaches were allegedly doling out, he would have realized that the accusations were ridiculous. The kind of money the NCAA was talking about—cars, monthly stipends, houses, travel allowances—would have been impossible to find, much less justify in the Lafayette economy at that time.

The NCAA had investigated the Century Club and other outside organizations during the 1967 investigation and had ascertained that they were in no position to contribute funds to aid the coaches and the university. Yet the association accepted the words of a couple of bitter rejects.

State Senator Mouton, in response to the NCAA action, called it almost criminal. In a release published in the *Lafayette Advertiser,* he also castigated some members of the media:

> The NCAA, in a totally autocratic manner, refused to disclose its sources or to validate its findings and merely points the finger of fault in a shotgun manner at individuals, at athletes, at administrators and at the entire community. You who survive under a theory of constitutional law should grant that same right of survival to others, the principle of due process, the principle of innocent until proven guilty and the principle of the accused having the right to examine the accuser.
>
> USL has been prejudged by you and other individuals and yet you [members of the media] have not read the charges, you do not know the source of the charges and you cannot prove the validity of those sources. Were I to tell you that a key witness for the NCAA was an ex-coach, investigated by the local law enforcement agencies for extortion, for narcotics and for NSF checks, would you think him to be a creditable [sic] witness?

The NCAA was the accuser, the judge, and the jury. Any accused university had no recourse when attacked except to take its case to the civil courts. The situation was stacked against them by NCAA procedures. Only large institutions or well-endowed individuals had the deep financial pockets required to fight them in court. USL officials decided they either couldn't afford this procedure or they didn't have the heart to proceed.

Shipley still shakes his head and wonders, "Why Warren Brown and David Berst, those two investigators sent down here by Walter Byers, never once contacted coach Tom Cox or me. I gotta believe they were sent down here to come up with any conviction they could come up with. I had the unfortunate experience of catching these two guys on their first investigation, their maiden voyage. The worst part of it was that they used info from any reprobate they could find."

In 2004 in a hearing before the House of Representatives, Committee on the Judiciary, Subcommittee on the Constitution, One Hundred Eighth Congress, a hearing was held on the fairness of the NCAA. The following was the introductory statement:

> This hearing is about fairness, particularly the fairness the NCAA displays in enforcing its rules. Merited or not, the NCAA has at least the perception of a fairness problem. Evidence of this is found in newspapers, such as stories regarding the NCAA's decision not to restore eligibility to Jeremy Bloom, who is with us today, and Mike Williams. It is found in courtrooms, where two former Alabama assistant coaches have sued the NCAA for alleged violations of procedural due process. It is also found in State legislatures, such as the State of Nevada, which passed statutes providing particular due process rights for NCAA investigations conducted within their States. And it is found in the NCAA's own 1991 study conducted by former Solicitor General Rex Lee, that proposed 11 recommendations the NCAA should undertake to improve fairness in its procedures.
>
> It has been 13 years since Congress last examined the procedures that the NCAA uses to investigate and enforce its rules. In that time, the NCAA has made several changes. However, the NCAA has failed to take action on several recommendations of its own 1991 study, most notably, those relating to the hiring of independent judges to hear infractions cases and the opening of these proceedings to all. This hearing will examine those recommendations and the NCAA's decisions not to implement them.

It is interesting to note that USL, and its NCAA record, was never mentioned in Walter Byers' book *Unsportsmanlike Conduct*.

The sports media almost unanimously reported in January 1973 that USL's record of violations was the worst in NCAA history. Incredibly Byers never mentions USL in his book. As executive director of the NCAA from 1951 to 1987, he was directly involved in the USL proceedings, so he had firsthand knowledge of all that went on. The penalties heaped on USL were far worse than the two—University of Kentucky (1952) and Southern Methodist University (1987)—that he defined as the only "death penalty" cases in his book.

Quoting from the August 5, 1973 resolution of the USL case concerning its penalties: "For a period of two years from this date, the University of Southwestern Louisiana shall not permit its intercollegiate basketball teams to participate against outside competition." For two years, no ballgames.

Yet the worst penalty ever, according to Byers in his book, involved the University of Kentucky in 1952—twenty years before USL's. The Kentucky violations were for illegal payments to players and point shaving in collusion with gambling interests. Note that the violations were not for early practices or raising outside funds for black athletes.

Byers related, "The conference and NCAA combined to eliminate Kentucky from competition for an *entire basketball season*. For 33 years afterward, faintness of heart prevented imposition of such a heavy punishment on any big-name Division I-A university. The penalty was reinvented in 1985 at the NCAA Integrity Convention, labeled by the media the 'death penalty,' and used in 1987 after a series of hand-in-glove violations involving top management, coaches, and players engulfed in a respected school, Southern Methodist University of Dallas." Notice the designation "big-name Division I-A university." Obviously Byers considered the destruction of the USL program as a small-name, insignificant case.

Byers listed the University of Nevada, Las Vegas (and Coach Jerry "Tark the Shark" Tarkanian) as the poster child for "greased admissions, suspect grades, under-the-table payments." But, he says, "In fairness, however, it was not strikingly different [from] the Kentucky case of the 1950s, UCLA in the 1960s, Michigan State in the 1970s, Southern Methodist in the 1980s, and Florida State or any other cases yet to surface in the 1990s."

It might come as a surprise to Mr. Byers, but in 1972 and 1973 USL was a big-name, Division 1-A university, ranked both years in the nation's top ten basketball polls. This was a case the NCAA promoted, in 1972–73 as "the worst in NCAA history." Yet the president of the association, at the time the instigator of both USL investigations, makes no mention of it in his book.

In 1998 Jerry Tarkanian exacted his pound of flesh from the NCAA when the association agreed to pay him two and a half million dollars to settle a long-disputed lawsuit. The settlement put an end to twenty-six years of NCAA investigations, charges, penalties, and litigation. Tarkanian was one coach who did not roll over for the almighty NCAA. He and his university brought all the way to the U.S. Supreme Court their argument that the NCAA had no right to order the coach's firing. When the high court ruled against the NCAA in 1988, Tarkanian and his wife filed a tort suit in civil court in Nevada. After another six years of litigation, the NCAA decided not to pursue defense of the case and made the settlement. The date of the settlement was April 1, April Fools' Day.

Could it be that Walter Byers, in retrospect, was actually ashamed of the NCAA's part in the whole USL situation and left it out of his book because of a troubled conscience? Perhaps he eventually realized that the entire procedure was unfair and obviously driven by racial prejudice, and that he and his association had been accomplices to the continuation of racism and segregationist practices.

He had to know that he could have focused the same investigative procedures on practically any university in the nation, particularly those with black student athletes, with comparable unfair charges. It would have been a little more difficult with them, because he probably would not have had the help from education governing authorities in other states or the investigated university's administration.

In his book Byers refers to the UNLV case as historic: "The ambitious have-nots of yesteryear enjoy the moneyed good times of today. They are clustered together with other rich schools in major athletic conferences and look with scorn at the new breed of opportunist colleges that use shenanigans similar to those that made today's nouveau riche well-to-do in the first place." Wow, Walter Byers explained the entire university athletic scene in that one paragraph. Yet he condoned his investigators' humiliating and enthusiastic destruction of one of the wannabe middle-level programs whose crimes were primarily impatient, ambitious dreams.

With his credentials and experience, Byers knew—and his writing proved he knew—that characters like Garverick, Kluz, and other discontents are universal and that the same allegations of violations could have been found in comparable numbers at practically every member school of the NCAA.

To this day Shipley is baffled that neither Warren Brown nor David Berst, the chief investigators for the NCAA, ever contacted him or his assistant, Tom Cox, during the months of investigation during 1972 and 1973. The only time he saw either of them was during and following the mid-1960s episode. He spent about an hour with Brown at that time and about a half-hour with Berst sometime in 1969. He was never asked about the firing of Harry Garverick.

Beryl resigned in May 1973, before the NCAA's procedures were finalized, even before a comprehensive response to the allegations was formulated. In mid-summer USL hired a new coach, Rolland Todd. He had coached the Portland Trailblazers of the National Basketball Association (NBA) and at the University of Nevada, Las Vegas. When USL was banned from intercollegiate basketball for two years, there was no job, so by mutual agreement with USL President Dr. Ray Authement, his relationship with the university was terminated.

Todd was quoted in an *Advertiser* news report, "The NCAA made an example of them (USL). There were a lot of charges but I would say that out of the 140 to 150 violations you could walk onto any major college basketball campus and gather 135 similar charges on one day ... [The NCAA] has made it impossible for enthusiastic schools to do a job demanded by the public. I don't know what the answer is, but I know what they're doing is not the answer."

Chapter Nine

Point – Counterpoint

An initial examination of the NCAA's list of allegations is overwhelming and daunting. Someone leafing through it with only a cursory perusal will first notice a bad taste in the mouth, then an involuntary shaking of the head, and next wondering how such a dynamic program could go so wrong.

Obviously most sportswriters did just such a cursory read-through. Bill Carter of the Alexandria (Louisiana) *Town Talk*, Joe Planas of the Baton Rouge *Advocate*, Roger Brandt of the Opelousas *Daily World*, and Marty Mulé of the New Orleans *Times Picayune* were particularly scathing in their reporting of the alleged violations. Unfortunately few reporters did detailed research and instead just fed off the initial stories.

Planas (now deceased), noted for his sarcasm, wrote a column while substituting for the regular *Advocate* columnist, Bernell Ballard. He titled it "Tail-Wagging Once More," and in it noted:

> This fair state's attorney general, Mr. William Guste sought a restraining order against the National Collegiate Athletic Association from taking further action against basketball powerful University of Southwestern Louisiana in Lafayette.
>
> And Mr. Guste's yearning for such a restraining order was rewarded by a signature of U. S. District Court Judge Richard Putnam.
>
> And now, in the words of Mr. Guste, that gives poor little USL time to defend itself against a reported 125 re-

cruiting violations. One of the alleged recruiting violations involves just a minor little basic dishonesty whereby a brainier fellow than the prospective basketball signee sits and takes the ACT or college entrance examination for the shooting star. This practice might not be exclusively done at only two La. colleges.

The other college to which he refers is not named. After seven or eight more paragraphs of more of the same, Planas closed with:

Anyway, good luck USL when that oppressive monster comes knocking on your Cajun door.

And may the state's top legal representative spare no time—or expense—in aiding your cause.

After all, what's 125 alleged violations between basketball and the taxpayers.

Planas and the other *Advocate* sportswriters had long been recognized as LSU's non-gymnastic cheerleaders who for years never missed a chance to take a shot at USL. Only in recent years, since the paper's circulation has increased significantly in Acadiana, have they given Cajun teams relatively unbiased coverage.

Unfortunately that bias against USL, and especially against Beryl Shipley, has continued through the years in the state's sports pages. Several attempts have been made to have Beryl recognized and inducted into the Louisiana Sports Writers Hall of Fame. He is, after all, one of the winningest coaches in the history of the state. Most recently Gerald Hebert, former manager of the local Coca-Cola plant and now internal fundraiser for the USL athletic department, gathered together several people to work on that project again.

At the initial meeting were former assistant coach Tom Cox, former USL sports information director and current sportswriter with the Lafayette *Advertiser* Dan Mcdonald, former broadcaster Ron Gomez, and several others. Cox volunteered to talk with a couple of New Orleans members of the writers' group to see if they would help. He said if he got any encouragement, he'd be glad to travel around the state talking with other members.

Cox met with an Associated Press writer and one from the New Orleans *Times Picayune*. Before he started his pitch, he told them if there was any doubt in their minds that he would be telling the truth about USL's case with the NCAA, he would submit to a lie detector test and pay for it himself. They said that would not be necessary.

Cox related, "I told them the story—about the whole history. I went through all that stuff and I got two responses. The AP guy said the problems happened on Beryl's watch. I said, 'Let me ask you something. Whose watch was it on at Louisiana Tech when it went on probation and Scotty Robertson was there?' (Robertson was inducted into the Hall of Fame some years ago.) The other writer said Beryl ought to tell the story to the sportswriters, and I said, 'You can forget that. Beryl wouldn't cross the street to talk to one of you guys. You ought to know that. As much havoc as you've created in his life, there's no way in hell he will allow you another chance to spit in his face.'"

Shipley still has not been voted into the LSW Hall of Fame. Perhaps some of the younger writers, untainted by the prejudice of the '60s and '70s, will read this and correct this gross inequity.

Whereas the NCAA obviously accepted all accusations, including those from the disreputable former assistant, Harry Garverick, and his failed recruit, Frank Kluz, it obviously ignored testimony submitted by the university that had been gathered by volunteer investigators at their own expense. Some of the testimony was from some of Lafayette's most prominent businessmen.

The Case 390 document foretells the stance taken by the NCAA concerning the university's formal response:

> The Committee has noted that in the development of its response to the official inquiry, the University relied primarily upon information reported by individuals associated with the athletic interests of the University (i.e., University coaches, enrolled student-athletes, representatives of the institution's athletic interests and institutional employees). **[Who else were they expected to interview? Uninvolved citizens? Nursing home inhabitants? Since the university did not have the names of the accusers and others interviewed by the NCAA, who else could they interview?]** The information provided by these individuals often is in direct conflict with the information reported to the Committee by the sources identified at the conclusion of each finding ... Further, it has been the Committee's experience that oftentimes individuals closely associated with an institution might be motivated to provide information which would protect the institution's athletic interests; finally, that those individuals who are directly involved in alleged violations may be motivated to provide information which would protect their own personal interests.

In other words, the NCAA had predetermined that any evidence, sworn statements, or other defense presented by the university were all lies, but accusations by people like Garverick and Kluz were beyond reproach. They had interviewed ninety-six people all over the United States over a two-year period, but the vast majority of the accusations initiated with Garverick. The university, with no funds for such a search, and working with volunteer investigators, was notified in the November 2, 1972 document that responses to the allegations "must be on file by December 13, 1972."

Rather than reprint the entire 128-page response document, the following are excerpts of the most important allegations with the university's response. In the original document, the responses are sprinkled with references to sworn affidavits and statements as well as other evidence that was attached. In practically each response, reference is made to a signed or sworn statement. Those references have been deleted for the sake of brevity. Some statements are underlined due to their pertinence and importance. Remember that these responses were backed with more than seventy pages of signed testimony from the witnesses.

The university's response leads with this eloquent recap and plea:

> In view of the somewhat complicated history of these allegations and the resulting nationwide publicity concerning them **[much of it in error]**, the University feels that it should begin its response to the N.C.A.A. Official Inquiry with a brief review of those events which have had a direct relationship to this case. Consequently, a chronological record of these events is presented below.
>
> On October 18, 1971, the NCAA Committee on Infractions, by letter advised the USL Athletic Director that it was conducting a preliminary inquiry into the athletic policies and practices of USL. No charges were specified at that time. Nothing further was heard from the NCAA until November 1, 1972. In the meantime, on October 9, 1972, by letter addressed to Warren S. Brown, Assistant Executive Director of the NCAA, President Rougeau advised that USL itself had conducted an investigation on and in the immediate vicinity of the campus, and had taken certain action, as outlined in the letter based on the investigation. It was expressly stated in a letter of October 24th, to the Athletic Committee of the Louisiana State Board of Education that the University did not assess, for any of the irregularities, any degree of culpability of any particular member of the athletic

staff. No specific findings or violations were made as to any particular coach, other USL employee, USL student athlete, or any other person. <u>The University took the action that it did in an effort to show good faith and comply with the basic objectives of the NCAA, did so without completing a full investigation and without interrogating any of the essential witnesses or persons involved in the allegations</u>, and did so because it was determined that it was best to take certain precautionary action by setting forth guidelines and prohibitions for members of the Athletic Department.

On November 2, 1972, Warren S. Brown, Secretary, NCAA Committee on Infractions, addressed a letter to President Rougeau advising him that an "official inquiry" was being undertaken and that the letter and the attachment thereto constituted an Official Inquiry. The Committee directed that the University file its response to the charges by December 13, 1972, and further advised that the Committee would meet on December 19, 1972, in Fort Lauderdale, Florida, at which time USL's response would be considered, and an appearance by a USL representative was invited. On November 9, 1972, the day following receipt of the official inquiry letter, the University initiated an investigation into the charges specified in an effort to be able to respond to them. However, it was impossible for the University to make an adequate investigation and file suitable responses to the charges within the time allowed. Accordingly, an extension of time was requested and by letter dated December 6, 1972, Mr. Brown notified President Rougeau that the Committee had approved USL's request for a delay to respond to the official inquiry, granting USL until March 1, 1973, but nevertheless requesting that representatives of USL appear before the Committee, on December 19, 1972, at Fort Lauderdale, Florida, to explain in detail the action previously taken by the University itself.

President Rougeau and the Executive Vice President of USL **[There was no "executive VP" at the time. The writer probably meant the academic VP, who was Ray Authement]** were engaged in critical out of town activities on behalf of USL at the time, which greatly impaired the ability of USL to comply with the request in the letter of December 6, 1972. Accordingly, President Rougeau phoned the NCAA requesting that USL not be compelled to appear on such short notice, and advising that because of the incompleteness of the University's own investigation, a great deal of additional information would necessarily be required in order to explain the action taken by the University and the action taken was of a precautionary nature only. Nevertheless, the NCAA insisted that the University send representatives to the December 19, 1972, meeting, and USL, in a further effort to show good faith and to cooperate as fully as possible with the NCAA, sent three USL employees to said meeting.

Then, by letter dated December 28, 1972, but not received by USL until January 3, 1973, the Committee on Infractions forwarded to President Rougeau what it referred to as "NCAA Committee on Infractions Report of Case Number 390", stating that the document set forth the results of the Committee's inquiry into certain athletic policies and practices of the University of Southwestern Louisiana and that the report was being forwarded in accordance with Section 4 of the Official Procedures. The letter further advised that the report would be submitted to the NCAA Council at the Palmer House, Chicago, Illinois, beginning at 9:15 a.m. on January 9, 1973, only six days after receipt of the letter by USL. Immediately upon receipt of the letter of December 28, on January 3, 1973, the officials of USL again met to determine whether or not there would be an opportunity to fairly and adequately make a presentation on behalf of USL before the Council on January 9, 1973, and understandably, concluded that this would be impossible, and, accordingly, notified the governing authority of the University, the State Board of Education. The matter was referred by the State Board of Education to the Attorney General for the State of Louisiana, who, on January 4, 1973, telephoned and wired representatives of the NCAA, requesting a delay of the proposed hearing on January 9, 1973, and requesting that any and all allegations or charges against USL not be heard until USL had a reasonable opportunity to investigate same and develop its evidence, certainly no earlier than March 1, 1973, as the NCAA had previously agreed. The NCAA responded negatively. It was at this time that a petition was filed seeking to enjoin the hearing before the Council on January 9,

1973. Subsequently, the trial court granted a preliminary injunction, enjoining the NCAA from proceeding further with reference to the allegations against USL until August 15, 1973. Following appeal, the ruling of the trial court was reversed.

It was widely rumored and speculated that USL sought to enjoin the NCAA for the purpose of insuring USL's eligibility for post-season basketball tournaments. Such speculation was completely unfounded. The charges leveled against USL were voluminous and involved numerous witnesses who resided all over the United States. It was earnestly felt by the officials of USL that the charges could not be adequately investigated and responded to within the time allotted by the NCAA. The injunction was sought for one purpose and one purpose only, and that was to afford the University an opportunity to properly investigate and respond to the charges.

That the injunction was not sought for the purpose of assuring USL's eligibility for post-season play is amply demonstrated by the fact that on February 15, 1973, while the appeal was still pending in the Court of Appeals, Third Circuit, State of Louisiana, and before said Court of Appeals had issued its ruling reversing the trial court, a proposal to settle the issues presented in the injunction suit was made on behalf of the State Board of Education and USL to the NCAA. Under this proposal, the State Board of Education offered to agree to a dismissal of the injunction suit and to dissolution of the injunction against the NCAA, together with voluntary withdrawal by USL from consideration for any post-season basketball tournament bid, if the NCAA would voluntarily grant to USL an extension within which to reply to the charges. This proposal was conveyed to the NCAA through J. Winston Fontenot, the attorney representing the NCAA in the injunction proceedings, and through attorneys for the NCAA in Kansas City. This proposal was rejected by representatives of the NCAA.

The foregoing statement has been made not because we feel the Committee on Infractions is uninformed on the proceedings leading to the hearing on July 13, 1973, but rather, for the sincere purpose of showing to the Committee that the University has never acted in an arbitrary manner or with any intent to defy the NCAA, but rather for the sole purpose of attempting, in good faith, to make a complete and sincere response for the numerous allegations against the Institution and persons directly or indirectly associated therewith.

The next nine pages of the response were the university's answer to procedural practices. USL admitted to administrative faults in scholarship, eligibility, and financial aid procedures, outlined the changes that had been made, and assured the NCAA that all procedural problems had been corrected.

Then the document turned to the personnel and player accusations.

Accusation 3: It is alleged that during the summer 1971, then student-athlete Frank Kluz attended summer school at the University on a work-aid scholarship without working the required number of hours to legitimately receive money from the program; further, assistant coach Tom Cox informed Kluz that he would receive an $86.40 check each month from the University during the summer from the work-aid program without having to work; finally, that Kluz actually received two checks, each amounting to $86.40, for which he rendered no services.

Response: The University must deny that Mr. Frank Kluz attended Summer School during the 1971 Summer Session on a work-aid scholarship without working the required number of hours to legitimately receive money from the program. University "Payroll Voucher-Time Record" sheets for the periods June 1–July 2, 1971, and July 5–August 6, 1971, show that Mr. Kluz worked the required 54 hours in each time period for his $86.40 in pay. That these records are correct is <u>certified</u> by Ms. Bonnie Mallet, the person responsible for supervising the work performed by Mr. Kluz. In addition, Mr. A.G. Urban, Athletic Director of the University, approved these time sheets.

As to that portion of this allegation which indicates that Coach Tom Cox informed Mr. Kluz that he would receive an $86.40 check each month from the University during the 1971 summer without having to work, Coach Cox has submitted a statement denying this allegation.

Accusation 4: It is alleged that while the University's intercollegiate basketball team was in Las Vegas, Nevada, on or about January 23, 1971, the majority of the team members were provided spending money in amounts ranging from $5 to $20 by J.Y. Foreman and Robert F. Wright, representatives of the athletic interests of the University of Southwestern Louisiana, to be used for their own entertainment in Las Vegas; further, then student-athlete Bill Roniger received $10 from Foreman at the Houston airport on the way to Las Vegas; further, that Wright provided money to purchase poker chips in a Las Vegas casino for then student-athlete Frank Kluz and student-athlete Denny Wright; finally, that Tom Cox cashed Foreman's personal check and then gave the money to then assistant coach Harry Garverick for distribution to other team members. Please indicate whether this information is substantially correct and submit evidence to support your response.

Response: In accordance with statements by Mr. J.Y. Foreman and Mr. Robert F. Wright, the University must deny that these two gentlemen provided spending money for the majority of the basketball team members in amounts ranging from $5 to $20 while in Las Vegas, Nevada, on or about January 23, 1971.

The University must also deny that student-athlete Bill Roniger received $10 from Mr. J.Y. Foreman at the Houston airport on the way to Las Vegas since both Mr. J.Y. Foreman and Mr. Bill Roniger have issued statements to this effect.

Mr. Robert F. Wright's version of the alleged poker chip-casino incident is given in his statement which is summarized as follows: **[Corroborated by Denny Wright's statement as well.]**

"One evening while in Las Vegas, I was playing "21" and my nephew, Denny Wright, and a couple of other student-athletes were standing nearby. When my party was ready to leave, I had a few (5 to 10) $1.00 chips left. I left these with my nephew, Denny Wright, with the comment 'Don't lose them all at one time.' I have been providing financial assistance to my nephew, Denny Wright, for several years. This assistance has been provided before Denny entered USL and while he has been enrolled at USL, but has nothing to do with his being on the University basketball squad."

In view of this statement, the University must contend that Mr. Wright was not "giving financial aid" to his nephew when he gave him the poker chips and that this incident had nothing to do with the fact that his nephew was also a member of the basketball team.

In reply to the allegation that Coach Tom Cox cashed Mr. J.Y. Foreman's personal check and then gave the money to Harry Garverick for distribution to other team members, the University calls the Committee's attention to the statements of Coach Tom Cox and Mr. J.Y. Foreman. Coach Cox denies any knowledge of such an incident, as does Mr. Foreman. In fact, <u>Mr. Foreman has offered to make his personal checking account records available to substantiate his denial.</u>

Accusation 5: J.Y. Foreman paid for the cost of expenses incurred by student-athlete Dwight Lamar in traveling via commercial airline from his home, Columbus, Ohio, to Lafayette, Louisiana, following the 1971 NCAA College Division Basketball Championship in Evansville, Indiana. Lamar had returned to his home for a visit with family and friends following completion of the tournament before returning to the University's campus.

Response: In reply to this allegation, the University submits portions of the statements of Mr. J.Y. Foreman and Mr. Dwight Lamar. Mr. Foreman denies that he paid for the expenses incurred by Mr. Lamar in traveling via commercial airline from his home, Columbus, Ohio, to Lafayette, Louisiana, following the 1971 NCAA College Division Basketball Championship in Evansville, Indiana. Additionally, Mr. Lamar admits having made such a trip, but emphatically denies that Mr. Foreman paid his expenses for this trip. He says that he paid his own expenses.

In light of these statements, the University must deny this allegation.

Accusation 6: Information available to the Committee on Infractions indicates that several University student-athletes have been provided transportation between the institution's campus and their hometowns either at the expense of the University, its athletic staff members or other representatives of its athletic interests. Specifically, it is alleged that:

> a. Student-athlete Dwight Lamar was provided free commercial airline transportation between Lafayette and Columbus, Ohio, during the 1970 and 1971 Christmas vacations as well as the 1972 Easter vacation. Arrangements for these flights were made with the Acadiana Travel Agency, Lafayette, Louisiana, and expenses paid either by the University or a representative of its athletic interests with full knowledge of the University's basketball coaching staff.

Response: A check of the records at Acadiana Travel Agency reveals that then student-athlete Dwight Lamar purchased tickets for flights between Lafayette and Columbus, Ohio during the 1970 and 1971 Christmas vacations. There is no record of him purchasing an airline ticket during the 1972 Easter vacation. According to Mr. Dwight Lamar's statement, he "paid for every trip he made between these cities."

Head Coach Beryl Shipley and Assistant Coach Tom Cox have both given statements which contain a denial of any knowledge of the events described in this allegation.

In consideration of the statements referred to above, the University must deny this allegation.

> b. Then student-athlete Marvin Winkler was provided free commercial airline transportation between Lafayette and Indianapolis, Indiana, during the 1967 and 1968 Christmas vacations. This transportation and payment of the resultant expenses was arranged by head basketball coach Beryl Shipley and Tom Cox.

Response: In reference to this allegation, Mr. Marvin Winkler, Coach Beryl Shipley and Coach Tom Cox have given written testimony. As can be seen by reading these statements, all three of these people deny that Mr. Winkler was provided free commercial airline transportation between

Lafayette and Indianapolis, Indiana during the 1967 and 1968 Christmas vacations.

Because of the content of these three statements, the University must deny this allegation.

> c. Student-athlete Fred Saunders was provided free commercial airline transportation during the 1971 Easter vacation and on one other occasion subsequent to his enrollment between Lafayette and Columbus, Ohio. On both occasions, Beryl Shipley made arrangements for the transportation with the Acadiana Travel Agency and authorized Saunders to contact travel agent Tony Medina, [sic] who had Saunders sign receipts in return for round-trip tickets. The cost of the tickets was then billed to the University.

Response: In reply to this allegation, the University presents statements from Mr. Fred Saunders, Coach Beryl Shipley, and Mr. Anthony Mannina.

Mr. Saunders states that as far as he can remember, he has paid for all airline tickets he received with the exception of the trip taken when he visited USL on his official visit.

Coach Shipley denies any knowledge of the incidents as described in this allegation. He points out that Fred Saunders could not have signed a receipt and had anything billed to the University since he does not have that authority.

Acadiana Travel Agent Mr. Anthony Mannina states, "Beryl Shipley never made arrangements with Acadiana Travel Service for commercial airlines transportation for Fred Saunders. As far as I know he never authorized Saunders to contact me for such arrangements, and I never had Saunders sign receipts in return for round trip tickets, and the cost of no such tickets was ever billed to the University. Whenever Saunders arranged through Acadiana Travel Service for transportation, he did so on his own and it was a cash basis."

In view of these three statements, the University feels it must deny this allegation.

> d. Then student-athlete Garland Williams was provided free commercial airline transportation between Lafayette and Washington, D.C., approximately two

times each year during his four years of attendance at the University. This transportation and payment of the resultant expenses was arranged by Tom Cox and Beryl Shipley, and occurred during the Christmas, Easter and summer vacation periods beginning with the 1967 fall semester and ending with the 1971 spring semester.

Response: In response to the charges contained in this allegation, the University submits statements from Coach Beryl Shipley and Coach Tom Cox. The University would like to point out at this time that it has not had the opportunity to obtain a statement from Mr. Garland Williams since all efforts to locate the young man have met with defeat.

Coach Beryl Shipley states, "I did not arrange for any such transportation for Garland Williams as alleged and did not arrange for payment of any such resultant expenses. As far as I know, no free commercial air transportation was provided to Garland Williams as alleged."

Coach Cox comments, "… It is quite possible that he (Coach Shipley) made arrangements for Mr. Williams by calling the airlines or travel agency for reservations, but I did not pay or arrange for the payment of expenses in connection with any such reservations."

A search of the University Business Office records show no receipts for trips taken by Mr. Garland Williams. Further, the only record of a trip for Mr. Williams which could be located at Acadiana Travel Agency was during the Christmas, 1970, vacation. Mr. Williams paid for this ticket himself.

In view of this evidence, the University is obliged to deny the charges contained in this allegation.

    e. Then student-athlete Frank Kluz was provided $50 cash by Beryl Shipley and $20 cash by an unidentified representative of the University's athletic interests to pay for transportation expenses incurred by Kluz and his wife to travel between Lafayette and Lancaster, Ohio, shortly after the 1970 Bayou Classic. Kluz received the money directly from Shipley and the representative during a party at Shipley's home on or about December 20, 1970.

Response: In reply to this allegation the University submits a statement from Coach Beryl Shipley in which he denies that he ever provided cash to Mr. Frank Kluz at any time except for amounts authorized to be provided for meal money on basketball road trips.

In view of Coach Shipley's statement, the University must deny this allegation.

> f. Then student-athlete Wilbert Loftin was provided free automobile transportation by then assistant coach Harry Garverick to Tyler, Texas, during the 1970 Thanksgiving vacation.

Response: As a reply to this allegation, the University calls the Committee's attention to the statement by Mr. Wilbert Loftin in which he states, "Harry Garverick did not provide me with free automobile transportation from Lafayette to my home in Tyler, Texas, during the 1970 Thanksgiving vacation."

Taking due cognizance of this statement by Mr. Loftin, the University must deny this allegation.

> g. During the 1971 Easter vacation, then student-athlete Wilbert Loftin was provided free commercial airline transportation between Lafayette and a location in New Mexico in order for the young man to visit his girlfriend. The arrangements for this transportation was made with the Acadiana Travel Agency and paid by the University as a recruiting expense incurred by assistant coach Al Van Winkle. This arrangement was authorized by the basketball coaching staff.

Response: Mr. Loftin states that the trip to New Mexico which he took in the Spring of 1971 was paid for by himself. In addition, Mr. Van Winkle denied that he paid for or arranged a trip to New Mexico for Mr. Loftin. In fact, he denied any knowledge of the incident.

In support of these statements, we have been unable to locate any record of such a trip at Acadiana Travel Agency and a check into University travel records from April 1, 1971, through June 30, 1971, disclosed no record of a trip to New Mexico by Mr. Van Winkle during that time.

Mr. Anthony Mannina, Travel Agent at Acadiana Travel Agency notes that, "Any such transportation arranged through Acadiana Travel Service was arranged by Loftin himself and paid for on a cash basis. The cost of such transportation was not paid by the University nor was it paid as a recruiting expense incurred by Assistant Coach Al Van Winkle or anyone else."

Considering the foregoing evidence, the University must deny this allegation.

> h. Then student-athlete Payton Townsend was provided free commercial airline transportation to travel between Lafayette and Cincinnati, Ohio, during at least two Christmas holidays with the expense of the transportation being paid either by the University or a representative of its athletic interests with full knowledge of the basketball coaching staff.

Response: As evidence concerning this allegation, the University transmits to the Committee statements from Mr. Payton Townsend, Coach Beryl Shipley and Coach Tom Cox.

Mr. Townsend admits that he did travel to Cincinnati, Ohio, on at least two Christmas holidays, but states that his parents paid for the expenses of the trips. He further states that at no time did the University or a representative of its athletic interests contribute to the trips to Cincinnati.

Both Coach Shipley and Coach Cox fervently deny any knowledge of or involvement in providing expenses for Mr. Townsend on the trips mentioned above.

Taking into account these statements, the University must deny this allegation.

> i. Student-athlete Roy Ebron was provided free commercial airline transportation to travel between Lafayette and Norfolk, Virginia, on at least four occasions during the 1970 and 1971 Christmas vacations, and at the conclusion of the 1971 and 1972 academic years. Arrangements for this transportation were made by Tom Cox and paid for by the University or a representative of its athletic interests.

Response: In reply to this allegation the University presents statements from Mr. Roy Ebron and Coach Tom Cox. Mr. Ebron contends that on these four occasions when he traveled between Lafayette and Norfolk, Virginia that his expenses were paid for by his family. Coach Cox states that he has made arrangements for Mr. Ebron's airline reservations several times during the past three years, but that he has never paid for those tickets or arranged for payment of those tickets.

With due consideration for these statements, the University must deny this allegation.

Accusation: Student-athlete Wayne Herbert traveled from Cleveland, Ohio, to Lafayette during the summer 1971 on a commercial airline. Sometime after Herbert's arrival in Lafayette, Tom Cox reimbursed the young man's mother in the amount of $50 as a partial payment of the expenses she incurred to pay for the cost of the airline ticket.

Response: In its response to the charges as set forth in this allegation, the University will draw upon the statements of Mrs. Charles Herbert, Mr. Wayne Herbert, and Coach Tom Cox.

Mrs. Herbert, in her statement, declares that the expense involved in her son, Wayne Herbert, traveling from Cleveland, Ohio, to Lafayette during the summer of 1971 was borne by her alone. No one helped with these expenses by giving her $50.00.

Mr. Wayne Herbert likewise indicates that he believes that his mother paid the expenses involved in his trip to Lafayette, Louisiana during that summer.

Coach Cox denies that he has ever reimbursed Mrs. Herbert for any kind of expenses including travel expenses.

In consideration of these statements, the University feels it must conclude that these charges are unfounded.

The committee then asked basically the same questions, concerning transportation, as above, with the same names: Lamar, Winkler, Williams, Saunders, et al. The university response continued to direct the committee's attention to the attached statements by all the players mentioned as well as the coaches and travel agents.

The questioning then shifted from the players' travel to other people who supposedly traveled with them.

Question 7: A review of the University's records related to its payment of transportation expenses for individuals through the Acadiana Travel Agency includes several individuals unidentifiable to the Committee. Because of the apparent numerous alleged violations related to improper transportation for enrolled and prospective student-athletes and their friends or relatives, the Committee is concerned at the possibility of additional violations in this area. Accordingly, please identify the following individuals who traveled to the University from the location and on the date indicated, provide a statement of the purpose of their visit and relationship at that time to the University, identify the athletic department staff members arranging for the transportation, and provide the address and telephone number of each individual:

> a. J. Milbourne who accompanied student-athlete Roy Ebron on his official campus visit from Newport News, Virginia, May 15, 1970.

Response: J. Milbourne was the high school coach of Roy Ebron who accompanied Mr. Ebron on his visit to the University. The University paid Mr. Milbourne's expenses during this trip since after all arrangements had been made for Mr. Ebron to visit the University, the University was notified that Mr. Ebron would not feel comfortable visiting USL unless he was accompanied by his coach. To the best of the University's knowledge, Mr. Milbourne currently resides in Newport News, Virginia.

> b. Doug Cook and Dean Rougas who traveled to the University on May 11, 1971, from Denver, Colorado.

Response: Both Mr. Doug Cook and Mr. Dean Rougas were prospective student-athletes who were on an official visit to the University from Pueblo Central High School in Pueblo, Colorado. Both of these young men were contacted by former Coach Harry Garverick who arranged for their campus visit. The University is presently unaware of the current addresses and telephone numbers of these young men, but believes that both are attending Colorado State University.

 c. Lynn Bartimore and Byran Ambrozech who traveled to the University from Los Angeles on May 14, 1971.

Response: Mr. Byran Ambrozech was a prospective junior college transfer student-athlete from near Los Angeles. Miss Lynn Bartimore was Mr. Ambrozech's fiancée at the time of this visit (it is believed they married shortly after visiting USL). Arrangements for Mr. Ambrozech's campus visit were made by Assistant Coach Allen Van Winkle. The University does not know the current address and telephone number of Mr. Ambrozech, but believes he completed his studies at Brigham Young University last spring.

The University admits that it paid for the expenses of Miss Bartimore while on this trip in violation of NCAA regulations.

 d. Tom Clark who traveled to the University from Los Angeles on August 18, 1971.

Response: The University does not recognize the name "Tom Clark," and feels sure that the person in question was Mr. James Henry Clark who enrolled in this University for the 1971 Fall Semester. Mr. Clark is mentioned in Allegation 34, and information concerning him is presented there.

 e. Gerald Wilson and Kenneth Dunham who traveled to the University from Houston, Texas, on January 27, 1972.

Response: Mr. Gerald Wilson and Mr. Kenneth Dunham were prospective student-athletes (football) from Jeff Davis High School in Houston, Texas, who were invited to visit the campus last year. Airline tickets were mailed to these young men, but inclement weather prohibited their visiting on January 27, 1972. Neither young man ever actually visited the campus, one returning his ticket and the other having his ticket canceled by the University (see statement by Head Football Coach Russ Faulkinberry). These trips were originally arranged by Coach Donald Lockwood. The University does not know the current addresses and/or telephone numbers of either of these young men.

> f. The person who accompanied prospective student-athlete Charles Jordan on April 7, 1972, between Indianapolis, Indiana, and Lafayette.

Response: A statement from Mr. Charles Jordan verifies the fact that no one accompanied him on his visit from Indianapolis, Indiana to Lafayette, Louisiana.

> g. Steve Fielder, D. Harris, Jack Wolf and C. Williams who traveled to the University from Columbus, Ohio, on August 5, 1970, March 28, 1972, June 30, 1970, and April 14, 1972, respectively.

Response: Mr. Steve Fields (Fielder) was a prospective student-athlete from De Sales High School in Columbus, Ohio, who visited the University on August 5, 1970.

Mr. D. Harris was a prospective student-athlete from Lutheran East High School in Cleveland, Ohio, who visited the University on March 28, 1972.

Mr. Jack Wolf was a prospective student-athlete from Whetston High School in Columbus, Ohio, who visited the University on June 30, 1970.

Mr. C. (Chuky) Williams was a prospective student-athlete from Columbus, Ohio, who attended Kansas State University during the last academic year.

The University is not aware of the current addresses and/or telephone numbers of these young men. Their travel arrangements were made by Coaches Beryl Shipley and Tom Cox.

> h. Mike Franklin who traveled to the University from Newport News, Virginia, on June 7, 1971.

Response: Mr. Mike Franklin was a prospective student-athlete from Booker T. Washington High School in Newport News, Virginia. Coach Tom Cox arranged for Mr. Franklin to visit our campus in June of 1971, but Mr. Franklin did not show up. The University is not aware of the current address and/or telephone number of Mr. Franklin.

The committee's questions then turned from air travel to the purchase of gasoline for automobiles; obviously a serious threat to the integrity of college athletics.

Question 8: Information available to the Committee on Infractions indicates that during the last several years numerous University student-athletes have been provided gasoline for the personal operation of their automobiles at the expense of the University and/or members of its athletic department staff; further, that arrangements for this gasoline were made by or with full knowledge of these staff members; finally, that the cost of the gasoline was normally charged to oil company (Esso, Texaco or Gulf) credit cards issued to members of the basketball coaching staff and in turn paid for by the University.

Response: Sometime around 1965, the University began holding its basketball practice sessions and its home games in Blackham Coliseum which is located a considerable distance off campus. A problem immediately arose as to how to transport the basketball team members from their on-campus residence to the off-campus practice sessions and games. The basketball coaches, Beryl Shipley and Tom Cox, consulted with the then Business Manager of the University, Mr. Richard C. Delcambre. According to Mr. Delcambre's statement, he gave the coaches permission to reimburse those student-athletes who had automobiles for transporting their fellow student-athletes between the campus and Blackham Coliseum for practice sessions and home games.

Instead of paying these student-athletes a mileage allowance, it was agreed that those students who used their private automobiles for transporting their fellow student-athletes should be allowed to obtain gasoline for their cars every now and then at the University's expense.

This practice was instituted (as best anyone can recall) in the fall of the 1965–66 academic year, and continued until last fall when it was questioned by an NCAA investigator. It was the impression of the University that the reimbursement of "actual and necessary expenses on intercollegiate athletic trips (including reasonable trips to practice sites other than those of the institution)" were allowable under the NCAA constitution, Article Three, Section (g)-(1), and that this repayment of gasoline which had been used in such trips was allowable.

Gasoline accusation a: During the 1970–71 academic year, student-athlete Wayne Herbert obtained free gasoline at a Gulf service station in Lafayette, Louisiana, on approximately five to ten occasions by charging the cost to the University credit card issued to Harry Garverick. On at least five occasions during the 1970–71 and 1971–72 academic years, Herbert also obtained gasoline from an Esso service station in Lafayette which was charged to the University credit card issued to Tom Cox.

Response: In responding to this allegation the University will use statements from Mr. Wayne Herbert and Coach Tom Cox.

Mr. Herbert states that indeed on a few occasions he was furnished free gasoline, but only under the guidelines as stated above. Coach Cox's statement verifies that of Mr. Herbert, and specifically states that Mr. Herbert received the gasoline only because he was transporting student-athletes.

In view of these statements, the University must deny that it was providing free gasoline to Mr. Herbert because he was a student-athlete.

Gasoline accusation b: Former student-athlete Frank Kluz obtained free gasoline on numerous occasions for his automobile during the 1970–71 academic year at the Esso service station located on South College Street, Lafayette. When his automobile needed gasoline, Kluz would contact Tom Cox to obtain permission, and then proceed to the station and report to the attendant that the purchase was approved by Cox. Thereafter, Cox would arrange for the payment of these charges usually through the use of the University credit card issued to him.

Response: A statement from Coach Tom Cox indicates that Mr. Frank Kluz was permitted to charge gasoline for his personal automobile on a University credit card only to replace the gasoline he had used in transporting basketball players from campus to an off-campus practice site (Blackham Coliseum).

Since the University was aware that this practice was being followed, and further, thought it was within NCAA guidelines, the University, although admitting that Mr. Kluz was given gasoline, must deny the implication of this allegation that this gasoline was provided because Mr. Kluz was a student-athlete.

Gasoline accusation c: Former student-athlete Tom Turner obtained one free tank of gasoline for his automobile from the Gulf service station, Lafayette, each week during the months of September and October 1970 until he withdrew from the institution on or about October 12, 1970. The arrangements for Turner's free gasoline were made and authorized by Harry Garverick and charged to the University credit card issued to Garverick.

Response: According to the statement of Mr. Tom Turner, he received gasoline for his car on one or two occasions. This gasoline was to replace gasoline which Mr. Turner had used while assisting with the University business of registering students.

In view of this statement, the University must deny that Mr. Turner received one free tank of gasoline each week during September and early October, 1970.

Gasoline accusation d: Former student-athlete Jeff Rhodes obtained free gasoline for his automobile from a Texaco service station, Lafayette, on approximately six to eight occasions while enrolled at the University during the 1968–69 and 1969–70 academic years. Usually, Tom Cox provided Rhodes with a University credit card issued to Cox in order to charge the cost of the gasoline. On two occasions without possession of the credit card, Rhodes was permitted to charge the cost of the gasoline only after the service station attendant telephoned Cox for specific authorization.

Response: In support of its reply to this allegation, the University submits statements from Mr. Jeff Rhodes and Coach Tom Cox.

According to Mr. Rhodes, he was provided gasoline only in accordance with the arrangement that had been worked out between the basketball coaches and the Business Office of the University; i.e. as reimbursement for using his private automobile to transport fellow student-athletes to and from basketball practice and home games at Blackham Coliseum which is located off campus.

Coach Cox's statement verifies the account given by Mr. Rhodes.

With due consideration for these two statements, the University admits that Mr. Jeff Rhodes received gasoline paid for by the University, but denies any violation of either University or NCAA rules in so doing.

Gasoline accusation e: On numerous occasions subsequent to his enrollment, student-athlete Fred Saunders has obtained free gasoline for his automobile at an Esso service station in Lafayette. Arrangements for the purchase of the gasoline were made by Tom Cox and the costs charged to Cox or the University.

Response: The University submits statements by Mr. Fred Saunders and Coach Tom Cox.

Mr. Saunders admits that on 4 or 5 occasions he received gasoline for his automobile as repayment for gasoline used in transporting student-athletes from campus to Blackham Coliseum. Coach Cox verifies Mr. Saunders' statement concerning this allegation.

Taking note of these statements, the University admits that Mr. Saunders received gasoline paid for by the University, but denies any wrongdoing or infraction of NCAA rules.

Gasoline accusation f: It is the policy of Beryl Shipley to permit student-athletes on the University's intercollegiate basketball team to obtain free gasoline during the basketball season from several oil company service stations in Lafayette. Shipley and Cox contact the service stations and inform the attendants that a player will report to obtain gasoline. The cost of the gasoline is charged to a University credit card and paid by the University.

Response: The University policy under which student-athletes were permitted to obtain gasoline paid for by USL for their private automobiles has been described above. As to this allegation, Coaches Beryl Shipley and Tom Cox have given statements setting forth their positions and policies concerning this practice. The University finds that Coach Shipley and Coach Cox were acting under proper University authority in providing gasoline to student-athletes as outlined above.

The questioning continued into the alleged gasoline violations, taking a somewhat different tact but basically repeating the previous questions; asking that all student-athletes receiving gasoline be named, who paid, what years this occurred, and whether this practice was still continuing. The university's responses were the same as to previous questions: referring to sworn statements.

The next line of questions involved allegations of free long-distance calls afforded to players; another dangerous practice obviously not found in any other NCAA member school.

Question 9: Information available to the Committee on Infractions indicates that several student-athletes at the University have been permitted by the University's basketball coaches to place long distance telephone calls at the expense of the University. Specifically, it is alleged that:

a. Student-athlete Fred Saunders was permitted to make free long distance telephone calls on approximately ten occasions during the 1970–71 academic year. These calls originated from the offices of the basketball coaches when the telephone was made available to Saunders by Cox or Shipley to contact his parents or other individuals. The calls were charged to the University or its department of athletics.

Response: In response to this allegation, the University wishes to call the Committee's attention to portions of the statements of Mr. Fred Saunders, Coach Beryl Shipley, and Coach Tom Cox which are contained in the accompanying volume marked "Appendix of Statements."

According to Mr. Saunders, "on a few occasions since I have been at Southwestern the coaches would have occasion to call my home for one reason or another, and sometimes I would be permitted to talk briefly with my parents."

Coach Cox replies that he does "not recall ever placing a call for Fred Saunders or making the phone available for his use."

Coach Shipley recalls that there may have been some occasions when a minor emergency which required him to call a student-athlete's parents existed and that while he was talking to the parents the student-athlete might simply have gotten on the phone to speak briefly with his parents. He does note, however, that "on no occasion were student-athletes permitted to make free long distance calls such as alleged in this allegation.

In view of the contents of this statement, the University must deny that "Fred Saunders was permitted to make free long distance telephone calls on approximately ten occasions during the 1970–71 academic year."

   a. Student-athlete Wayne Herbert was permitted by the basketball coaches (Cox and Shipley) to make free long distance telephone calls on numerous occasions during the 1970–71 and 1971–72 academic years in order to contact his mother in Cleveland, Ohio. The calls originated in the offices of the basketball coaches and were charged to the University or its department of athletics.

Response: In reply to the charges contained in this allegation, the University submits statements by Mr. Wayne Herbert, Coach Beryl Shipley and Coach Tom Cox.

Mr. Herbert states that only on one or two occasions when he happened to be around while one of the coaches was talking to his mother did he ever talk long-distance without charge. Coaches Shipley and Cox verify this observation.

In view of these statements, the University must deny that Mr. Wayne Herbert was permitted to make numerous free long-distance telephone calls.

    c. Former student-athlete Payton Townsend was per-
       mitted to make free long distance telephone calls
       on numerous occasions during his enrollment at the
       University beginning with the 1968 fall semester
       and ending with the 1972 spring semester in order
       to contact his parents in Hamilton, Ohio. These calls
       originated in the offices of the basketball coaches and
       in turn charged to the University or its department
       of athletics.

Response: The University presents statements by Mr.
Payton Townsend, Coach Beryl Shipley and Coach Tom
Cox in response to this allegation.

Mr. Townsend notes that "On occasions, when the
coaches at USL were contacting my parents, I was permitted to speak to my parents."

Coach Cox states that he has never authorized Payton
Townsend to make long distance phone calls from the University. He further notes that "I have personally had occasion
to make calls to Payton Townsend's parents on many occasions when we were attempting to recruit Payton's younger
brothers—Willie and Mike."

Coach Shipley also denies that student-athletes were
allowed to make free long distance phone calls from the
University.

In consideration of these statements, the University
must deny that Mr. Payton Townsend was allowed to make
free long distance telephone calls on numerous occasions
during his enrollment at the University.

    d. Former student-athlete Tom Turner was permitted to
       make a long distance telephone call at the Universi-
       ty's expense during the 1970 fall semester. On this
       occasion, Beryl Shipley actually dialed the number
       for Turner from his office (Shipley's) and then al-
       lowed Turner to complete the call to his mother in
       Vincennes, Indiana.

Response: In a statement presented in the Appendix
of Statements, Mr. Tom Turner says of this allegation, "On
one occasion I walked into Coach Shipley's office while he
was talking to my parents by telephone. During this call he

permitted me to talk briefly to my parents. This is the only conversation I had on the telephone while in Lafayette that was not paid for by me."

Coach Shipley vigorously denies that student-athletes were permitted to make free long distance phone calls.

Taking into account these statements, the University feels that it must deny this allegation as stated.

> e. Former student-athlete Frank Kluz was permitted to make long distance telephone calls at the expense of the University or its department of athletics on several occasions during the 1970–71 academic year. When Kluz wished to place these calls (usually to his parents in Lancaster, Ohio), he would contact Tom Cox, who in turn would request the operator to place the call before transferring it to Kluz. When Cox could not be located, Kluz would identify himself to the operator as Cox and then place the call.

Response: Coach Tom Cox offers the following statement in reply to this allegation: "I have never placed, nor permitted Frank Kluz to place, long-distance calls from the coaches' office."

In view of this statement from Coach Cox, if Mr. Frank Kluz was placing long distance telephone calls himself from University telephones as you indicate in this allegation, then he is guilty of fraud and misrepresentation at the least and perhaps more.

With due cognizance of the contents of both the allegation and Coach Cox's statement, the University must deny the first part of this allegation and claim no knowledge of the second part. However, if the Infractions Committee has information which would substantiate the second part of this allegation, then it should turn such evidence over to the University for possible action against Mr. Kluz.

In summary, the University must admit that there were some occasions when a student-athlete was permitted to speak to his parents when one of the coaches had reason to contact them by telephone and the student-athlete was nearby. However, the University has found no evidence to support the contention that the "wholesale free long distance

telephone service" which is pictured in these allegations is
to any extent true.

Question 10: Information available to the Committee
on Infractions indicates that several University student-athletes have received clothing at the expense of and/or through
the arrangements of members of the University's basketball
coaching staff. Specifically, it is alleged that student-athletes Roy Ebron, Dwight Lamar and Fred Saunders, and
former student-athletes Garland Williams, Wilbert Loftin
and Payton Townsend received free clothing from Abdalla's
Clothing Store, Lafayette, by charging their purchases to the
accounts of Beryl Shipley and Tom Cox.

Further, on one occasion during his attendance at the
University, Williams received clothing from the King Size
Company (Washington, D.C.) C.O.D. in the amount of approximately $100—the cash for the payment of this charge
being provided to Williams by Tom Cox.

The Committee would appreciate receiving the University's explanation and comments concerning the alleged
provision of free clothing for student-athletes. In responding, please indicate whether the information regarding
each allegation involving the individual student-athletes is
substantially correct and submit evidence to support your
response. In this regard, please submit all records of the accounts held by Shipley and Cox at Abdalla's Clothing Store
including records available from Shipley and Cox as well as
the Store.

Response: In responding to the charges contained in
this allegation, the University will utilize portions of the
statements of Mr. Roy Ebron, Mr. Dwight Lamar, Mr. Fred
Saunders, Mr. Payton Townsend, Coach Beryl Shipley, and
Coach Tom Cox

The four student-athletes all contend that they have not
received any free clothing from Abdalla's Department Store
as stated in this allegation. Specifically Mr. Ebron states, "I
was not offered … , nor free clothing.…" Mr. Lamar denies
that he "ever made a purchase or charged any clothing at
Abdalla's to either the account of Coach Shipley or Coach
Cox." Mr. Townsend states, "At no time did I receive cloth-

ing from Abdalla's Department Store," and Mr. Saunders also denies that he ever charged anything at Abdalla's to the accounts of either Coach Shipley or Coach Cox.

Coach Shipley responds to this allegation as follows, "I did not ever authorize or permit any of the named student-athletes to obtain clothing from Abdalla's Clothing Store or any other clothing store by charging their purchases to my account. No such clothing was ever provided at my expense nor through any arrangement made by me. I naturally have not kept my charge slips at Abdalla's or other clothing stores for a long period of time and dispose of some when I pay my bills. However, <u>I signed an authorization for an investigator from the NCAA, whose name I do not recall, authorizing him to check the records of my accounts at Abdalla's as well as any other clothing store</u>."

Coach Cox comments, "At no time have any athletes been permitted to charge clothes to my account at Abdalla's Clothing Store. Also, I do not have any knowledge of any king-size C.O.D. clothing bills for Garland Williams, and I certainly did not pay for such a bill. <u>I gave permission to the N.C.A.A. to check my account at Abdalla's</u>."

<u>In addition to these statements, the University has included copies of both Coach Shipley's and Coach Cox's Abdalla's account sheets from 1969 to present</u>. Neither Coach had kept their copies of the monthly statements from Abdalla's. The University can find nothing irregular concerning these accounts.

In consideration of the above evidence, the University must deny the charge that student-athletes are being provided free clothing as stated in this allegation.

Questioning then shifted to allegations regarding legal assistance. It is obvious that any USL fan, anyone who attended the games, or especially people who followed the team on road trips were identified by the NCAA as "representatives of the university's athletic interest."

Question 11: It is alleged that Robert F. Wright, a representative of the University's athletic interests, provided cost-free legal assistance during 1969 to then student-athlete Garland Williams. Williams had accumulated a large telephone bill of approximately $350 to $500 while using the telephone of a student living in the University dormitory.

This student was a nephew of a district attorney living in Jefferson Davis Parish, Louisiana, and his (the student's) mother threatened legal action against Williams unless the bill was paid. Williams requested Wright's assistance, and Wright then convinced the student's family to accept a personal note that Williams would repay the telephone charges in the near future. The matter was dropped and Williams was not charged by Wright for his services and has never paid Wright.

Please indicate whether this information is substantially correct and submit evidence to support your response.

In view of the previous line of questions, why did Williams not just use the university's phones in the coaches' offices?

Response: Mr. Robert F. Wright has submitted a statement concerning this allegation. It is reproduced here:

"Following the termination of a basketball career, Garland Williams was residing in a dormitory at the University of Southwestern Louisiana next to the young man who was the nephew of the District Attorney of Jefferson Davis Parish which is near Lafayette, Louisiana. Apparently, Garland Williams had run up a substantial telephone bill and the young man turned the bill over to his uncle, the District Attorney, for collection.

Since I am a lawyer and have known Bernard Marcantel, the District Attorney, on a personal basis for many years, Garland asked me to contact the District Attorney to see if something could be worked out. I did call Bernard Marcantel and advised him that Garland Williams would be graduating from school in a couple of months and would thereafter either sign a professional contract or go to work and would be able to pay the telephone bill. Mr. Marcantel agreed that if Garland would sign a promissory note for the amount involved that suit would not be filed. Garland did sign the note and I have had no contact with the situation since. I did not charge Garland Williams any fee for these "services." I have performed innumerable courtesies for many friends and acquaintances and would not have

142

thought of charging anyone for such an insignificant favor or "service"."

In view of this statement of Mr. Wright's, the University must deny that cost-free legal assistance was provided to Garland Williams during 1969.

Having thoroughly covered accusations of violations concerning players' travel expenses (all refuted), the NCAA then dug into travel by family members and friends.

Question 12: Information available to the Committee on Infractions indicates that members of the University's basketball coaching staff or representatives of its athletic interests arranged for payment of the transportation costs incurred by relatives of student-athletes to travel between their homes and the campus to attend intercollegiate basketball contests in which the University's basketball team competed. Specifically, it is charged that:

a. Mrs. Lulu Burton, mother of student-athlete Roy Ebron, her son (Samuel) and daughter (Lucy) were provided round-trip commercial airline transportation between Norfolk, Virginia, and Lafayette, Louisiana, in December 1970 to attend the Bayou Classic Basketball tournament; further, Mrs. Burton, her daughter and son were also provided free lodging at the Sheraton Townhouse Motel and received free meals. The cost of the transportation, room and board was paid by Robert F. Wright, a representative of the University's athletic interests with full knowledge of the basketball coaching staff.

Response: As its response to the charges contained in this allegation, the University submits statements from Mrs. Lulu Burton, Mr. Roy Ebron, Mr. Robert F. Wright and Coach Beryl Shipley.

In her statement Mrs. Burton emphatically denies that Mr. Robert F. Wright paid for either transportation or other expenses of herself, her daughter, Lucy, or her son, Samuel, in their December 1970, trip to Lafayette, Louisiana. She states that she was personally responsible for all expenses in connection with this travel.

Mr. Wright's statement reads, "I categorically deny that I paid or contributed to the cost of transportation, room and board or any other expense incurred by Mrs. Lulu Burton or her daughter or her son in connection with their alleged visit to Lafayette, Louisiana in December, 1970."

Mr. Ebron states that, "As far as I know, when my mother, brother and sister visited Lafayette for the Bayou Classic Basketball Tournament, they paid their own expenses."

Coach Shipley says that he has no knowledge of and certainly did not help arrange for the payment of the transportation, room, and board of Mrs. Burton and her two children.

In consideration of these four statements, the University must conclude that the charges as contained in this allegation are false.

b. Mrs. Lamar, mother of student-athlete Dwight Lamar, was provided commercial airline transportation between Columbus, Ohio, and Lafayette, Louisiana, in December 1970 to attend the Bayou Classic basketball tournament; further, she was provided free lodging at the Sheraton Townhouse Motel. The cost of the transportation and lodging was paid by the University or a representative of its athletic interests with full knowledge of the University's basketball coaching staff.

Response: In reply to the charges contained in this allegation, the University submits statements from Mr. Dwight Lamar and Coach Beryl Shipley.

Mr. Lamar's statement reads, "It is alleged that my mother was provided free airline transportation to Lafayette in December of 1970, together with cost of lodging, etc. I again deny these allegations. I wish to further state that <u>my mother has never been in the state of Louisiana, nor the City of Lafayette</u>."

Coach Shipley denies that any such transportation and lodging was paid for by the University and disclaims any knowledge of the events mentioned in these charges. He further states that he understands <u>Mrs. Lamar has never been on an airplane in her life and never been in the state of Louisiana</u>.

Considering these two statements, the University must deny the truth of the charges contained in this allegation.

The NCAA also wanted to know if the university allowed players to keep year-old, used warm-ups and/or uniform parts.

Question 13: Information available to the Committee on Infractions indicates that it is the policy of the University's basketball coaches to permit members of the University's intercollegiate basketball team to retain travel uniforms issued by the department of athletics after one year of use.

Specifically, it is alleged that at least one former student-athlete, Bill Roniger, was allowed to keep the travel jackets issued to him during his freshman and sophomore years (1969–70 and 1970–71 academic years) at the University.

Please indicate whether this information is substantially correct and submit evidence to support your response. In responding, please describe the policy concerning the retention of travel uniforms by student-athletes participating in each intercollegiate sport at the University. Also, identify all members of the University's intercollegiate basketball team who have been permitted to retain their travel jackets during the last four academic years and indicate the years in question.

It is interesting to note that even the phrasing of the questions tends to assume that the accusations are correct. "Whether it is substantially correct," not "Is this correct?" describes the policy, not "Was there such a policy?" and "Identify team members who have been permitted ... and what years." This is similar to the infamous question, "When did you stop beating your wife?"

Response: In response to this allegation, the University submits statements from Mr. William Roniger, Coach Beryl Shipley, and Coach Tom Cox.

Mr. Roniger, in his statement, says: "I have no recollection of having kept any travel jackets."

Additionally, both Coach Shipley and Coach Cox deny that Mr. Roniger was allowed to keep his travel jacket after only one year of use.

As to the University's policy concerning travel uniforms, Coach Shipley states, "it is not and was not a policy of the University basketball coaches to permit members of the basketball team to retain travel uniforms as alleged. No member of the University's basketball team has been permitted to retain his travel jacket, not even senior members of the basketball team."

In accordance with this policy, no member of the University's basketball team during the past four years has been allowed to retain his travel jacket.

Taking cognizance of these statements, the University must deny this allegation.

Unlike Kansas' deal with Wilt Chamberlain and other substantiated cases, USL is accused of "loaning" cars to athletes.

Question 14: Information available to the Committee on Infractions indicates that several student-athletes at the University have been provided the regular or periodic use of automobiles without charge. Specifically, it is alleged that:

a. J.Y. Foreman, a representative of the University's athletic interests, has loaned his personal automobile cost-free to student-athletes Fred Saunders and Roy Ebron, and to former student-athlete Payton Townsend on approximately ten to fifteen total occasions during their attendance at the University. This automobile was operated on these occasions at no expense to the young men.

Response: In answer to this allegation, the University presents statements from Mr. J.Y. Foreman and Mr. Fred Saunders.

Mr. Foreman states, "I did on a few occasions loan my personal automobile to Fred Saunders, Roy Ebron, and Payton Townsend, inasmuch as they did not have automobiles. However, if they needed gas, etc., they paid for some.

I would like to mention, however, that I have also loaned my automobile on various occasions to non-athletes, including students of U.S.L., for their personal use."

Mr. Saunders' statement indicates that Mr. Foreman did loan him his car on occasion. However, he states that this was never pre-arranged and that there were times when he requested to borrow the automobile and was refused by Mr. Foreman. He further states that his borrowing Mr. Foreman's automobile had nothing to do with the fact that he was a student-athlete.

In view of these replies to this allegation, the University must admit that Mr. Foreman did loan his private automobile to the three young men in question. However, according to Mr. Foreman's statement, the automobile was not necessarily operated at no expense to these young men.

> b. Student-athletes Dwight Lamar, Fred Saunders, and Bill Roniger were provided the use of Harry Garverick's personal automobile on several occasions during their attendance at the University.

Response: In reply to this allegation, the University submits statements from Mr. Dwight Lamar, Mr. Fred Saunders, and Mr. William Roniger.

Unfortunately Mr. Garverick had been fired by the university and, being the principal supplier of allegations, was not available for questioning.

Both Mr. Lamar and Mr. Saunders indicate in their statements that they were allowed the use of Mr. Harry Garverick's personal automobile two or three and one or two times, respectively. However, Mr. Roniger claims that he does not recall ever having borrowed or been given the use of Coach Garverick's automobile.

With due consideration for the allegation and the responses of these three young men, the University admits that Mr. Lamar and Mr. Saunders were provided the use of Mr. Harry Garverick's private automobile on a few occasions during their attendance at the University.

    c. Robert F. Wright, a representative of the University's athletic interests, has loaned his personal automobile to student-athlete Roy Ebron and former student-athlete Marvin Winkler on several occasions during their attendance at the University.

Response: In support of their reply to this allegation, the University submits statements from Mr. Robert F. Wright and Mr. Marvin Winkler.

Mr. Wright's statement indicates that he did loan his automobile to Mr. Roy Ebron on two or three occasions prior to Mr. Ebron obtaining a car of his own. This was done on isolated occasions without any prearrangement, and in no way was connected to the fact that Mr. Ebron was a student-athlete.

Mr. Wright implies that the same circumstances surround the fact that he loaned his automobile to Mr. Marvin Winkler.

On the other hand, Mr. Winkler's statement states that he did borrow Mr. Wright's automobile on two or three occasions.

In consideration of the content of the above statements, the University must admit that Mr. Robert F. Wright loaned his personal automobile to student-athletes Ebron and Winkler a few times.

    c. For several days after his enrollment for the 1970 Fall semester, then student-athlete Tom Turner was permitted the use of a rent-a-car arranged by the University's department of athletics. The rental cost was paid by the University.

Response: As a response to this allegation, the University offers a statement from Mr. Tom Turner.

Mr. Turner states: "Shortly after my enrollment in Fall, 1970, I obtained a rental car for a few weeks from a company that I had made a promise to buy a Volkswagen from. This was all at my own expense."

Further, <u>a check of the University's financial records</u> <u>showed that there was no record of any car rented by the</u> <u>University during August or September, 1970.</u>

In view of these statements, the University must deny this allegation.

Question 15: Information available to the Committee on Infractions indicates that student-athletes at the University have received financial assistance other than that administered by the University. Specifically, it is alleged that:

> a. Student-athlete Dwight Lamar has on several occasions received cash for his performance in intercollegiate basketball games. These cash rewards were received from representatives of the University's athletic interests usually after the completion of the basketball games when Lamar was approached before leaving the site of the contest. On one such occasion during the 1970–71 basketball season, Lamar received approximately $100 from Robert Wright, a representative of the University's athletic interests, following the University's basketball game with Oral Roberts University.

Response: The University's response to this allegation is based on statements by Mr. Dwight Lamar and Mr. Robert F. Wright.

Mr. Wright answers: "I specifically deny that I gave Dwight Lamar approximately $100 or any other amount following a game with Oral Roberts University or after any other game."

Mr. Lamar states: "With regard to the allegation that I received cash on several occasions following basketball games and that I received $100 from Robert Wright, representative of USL, following a game with Oral Roberts: These allegations are denied."

With due regard for these statements, the University must deny this allegation.

    b. On several occasions, Harry Garverick provided cash from his own resources to student-athlete Dwight Lamar in amounts ranging from $5 to $10. This cash was used by Lamar for personal reasons and was never repaid to Garverick.

Response: In his statement, Mr. Dwight Lamar responds, "It is absolutely untrue that Harry Garverick ever gave me cash. As far as I know, Mr. Garverick was always wanting to borrow money himself, and I would certainly never have attempted to borrow money from him."

In light of Mr. Lamar's statement, the University must deny this allegation.

    c. On at least two occasions, Robert Wright, a representative of the University's athletic interests, gave money to student-athlete Dwight Lamar in amounts ranging from $15 to $20. These benefits were supposedly in the form of loans for which Lamar did not sign a promissory note and was not charged interest. One time, the money was given to Lamar in Evansville, Indiana, during the 1971 NCAA College Division Basketball Championship. Another time, money was given to Lamar after a basketball game during the 1971–72 basketball season.

Response: In support of its reply to this allegation, the University presents statements from Mr. Robert F. Wright and Mr. Dwight Lamar.

Mr. Wright's statement says in part, "I specifically deny having given any money to Dwight Lamar except, as I have advised NCAA investigators, when I did lend Dwight Lamar $20 or $25 in Evansville, Indiana, following the NCAA College Division Basketball Championship. It is true that I charged him no interest and did not make him sign a promissory note."

Mr. Lamar's statement verifies that of Mr. Wright, setting the amount borrowed at $20. Mr. Lamar also points out that this loan was repaid a few days later.

With due consideration for the information contained in these statements, the University must deny this allegation.

    d. Former student-athlete Garland Williams received cash on numerous occasions during his enrollment at the University, as follows:

    (1) During his freshman year, he was provided approximately $15 by Robert Wright, a representative of the University's athletic interests, for his performance in an intercollegiate basketball game:

Response: According to a statement by Mr. Robert Wright, "this allegation is specifically denied."

Since the University has been unable to locate Mr. Williams even though it has repeatedly attempted to do so, it has not been able to obtain a statement from Mr. Williams concerning this allegation.

In the absence of a statement by Mr. Williams and with due consideration for the statement of Mr. Wright, the University must deny the charges as contained in this allegation.

    (2) During Williams' first three years of attendance at the University, he received approximately $5 to $10 cash a week in addition to his full athletic grant-in-aid. This money usually was delivered to Williams each week by former student-athlete Marvin Winkler, who obtained the money from Tom Cox or other representatives of the University's athletic interests, although on several occasions Williams obtained the money directly from Cox.

Response: Coach Tom Cox states, "The only time I gave Mr. Winkler and G. Williams $5 and $10 was for meal money for the days when the basketball team was traveling."

Since the University has been unable to make contact with Mr. Williams, Coach Cox's statement is the sole piece of evidence which we can consider concerning the validity of these charges. With due consideration for this fact, the University must contend that the charges contained in this allegation are false.

e. Student-athlete Fred Saunders received cash on numerous occasions, as follows:

(1) Following the 1972 game between the University and Louisiana Polytechnic University, Saunders received $10 cash both from Robert Wright and J.Y. Foreman, representatives of the University's athletic interests.

Response: In response to this allegation, the University offers statements from Mr. Fred Saunders, Mr. Robert F. Wright and Mr. J.Y. Foreman.

Mr. Fred Saunders specifically denies, "that he ever received any cash" as referred to in these charges. In addition, Mr. Wright also states, "This allegation is specifically denied," while Mr. Foreman observes, "I did not give cash to Saunders as alleged."

In consideration of these three denials of this allegation, the University must join in labeling this allegation as false.

(2) Following the 1972 basketball game between the University and Eastern Kentucky University, Saunders received $10 cash from Foreman.

Response: Both Mr. Fred Saunders and Mr. J.Y. Foreman specifically deny that there was an exchange of cash as described in this allegation.

(3) On approximately eight occasions subsequent to his enrollment, Saunders received cash loans from Beryl Shipley and Tom Cox in amounts ranging from $10 to $20 although no interest was charged on these loans and the money was never repaid.

Response: As a reply to this allegation, the University offers statements from Mr. Fred Saunders, Coach Beryl Shipley and Coach Tom Cox.

All three of these gentlemen deny that there were any money transactions as described in this allegation. Further, Coach Shipley states that the only occasion on which he ever provided money for any student-athlete was to give them authorized meal money on road trips.

In consideration of these three statements, the University must insist that this allegation is false.

> (4) On numerous occasions subsequent to Saunders' enrollment, Harry Garverick provided from his own resources cash to Saunders in amounts ranging from $5 to $10—these amounts not being repaid by Saunders.

Response: According to a statement by Fred Saunders, this allegation, as with the last three allegations, is specifically denied. Mr. Saunders states that he never received any cash as referred to in these allegations.

In view of this statement by Mr. Saunders, the University must deny this allegation.

> f. Student-athlete Roy Ebron has on several occasions received cash for his performances in intercollegiate basketball games from Tom Cox, Beryl Shipley and Harry Garverick. He has also received cash from representatives of the University's athletic interests, Robert Wright and J.Y. Foreman. This cash ranged in amounts from $10 to $30 and was usually given to Ebron after the completion of the University basketball games although on several occasions cash was given to him by Cox and Shipley upon request.

Response: The University submits statements from Mr. Roy Ebron, Coach Beryl Shipley, Coach Tom Cox, Mr. J.Y. Foreman, and Mr. Robert Wright.

All five of these statements indicate a strong denial that there was an exchange of money between Mr. Ebron and the other gentlemen. Again, two coaches and the student-athlete mentioned in this allegation report that the only time there was an exchange of cash between anyone, it was to pay for the student-athlete's eating expenses on road trips.

With due regard for the content of these statements, the University must specifically deny this allegation.

Question 16: It is alleged that on several occasions during the 1970–71 academic year, maintenance (rotation of tires, changing of oil, etc.) was performed on the automobile owned by then student-athlete Frank Kluz at the Esso service station located on South College, Lafayette; further, that Kluz did not pay for the cost of this maintenance; rather, he signed a ticket for the charges, the payment of which was arranged by Tom Cox or Beryl Shipley. Please indicate whether this information is substantially correct and submit evidence to support your response.

Response: As a portion of its response to this allegation, the University submits statements from Coach Beryl Shipley and Coach Tom Cox.

Coach Shipley states, "I never did arrange for the payment of any such charges as alleged and have no knowledge that any such maintenance was provided." Coach Cox replies, "This is absolutely a false allegation."

In view of these two denials of the facts as set forth in this allegation, the University must deny that Mr. Frank Kluz was provided the automobile services mentioned in this allegation.

Question 17: It is alleged that during August and September 1970, student-athlete Tom Turner was provided approximately $185 in cash by Tom Cox to pay for the first month's rent for an apartment for Turner and his wife; further, Cox also paid for the cost of Turner's electric bill for this first month. Please indicate whether this information is substantially correct.

Response: In response to this allegation, the University submits statements from Mr. Tom Turner and Coach Tom Cox.

Mr. Turner states very specifically that he paid for his first month's rent himself from personal funds and an advancement on his first month's scholarship check. He categorically denies that he ever received $185 in cash from Coach Cox and states, "During my stay in Lafayette no one paid my utilities except myself."

Coach Cox avers that he "did not give Tom Turner $185 to pay for his rent and have never paid his electric bill."

With due consideration for the allegation and these two denials, the University must contend that the charges contained in this allegation are untrue.

Question 18: It is alleged that student-athletes Dwight Lamar and Payton Townsend, and then-prospective student-athletes Roy Ebron, Fred Saunders, Calvin Wade, Wayne Herbert and Rick Wasilewski were transported at no expense to the young men to the University for the purpose of enrolling for the 1970 fall semester. Specifically, it is alleged that Harry Garverick transported Herbert (Cleveland) and Wasilewski (Detroit) in an automobile from their homes to Springfield, Ohio, where they were provided cost-free overnight room and board at the home of Garverick's brother; further, that Tom Cox transported Ebron, Saunders, Lamar, and Wade via automobile from Columbus to Springfield where all individuals involved were provided breakfast in the home of Garverick's brother at no expense to the young men; further, that after departing Springfield for Lafayette, then student-athlete Payton Townsend was met in Cincinnati and transported to the University's campus.

Further, that approximately one week prior to this trip to the University's campus, Ebron was transported by Garverick via automobile at no cost to the young man from Lafayette to Columbus where Ebron traveled via commercial airlines to his home in Norfolk, Virginia, through the use of an airline ticket prepaid by the University; finally, that Ebron returned to Columbus from Norfolk by use of a commercial airline ticket paid for by Garverick from his recruiting expense money and was then transported to Springfield.

Please indicate whether this information is substantially correct and submit evidence to support your response.

Response: (a) In reply to the initial allegation concerning transportation of student-athletes and prospective student-athletes to the University for the purpose of enrolling for the 1970 Fall Semester, the University submits statements from Coach Tom Cox, Mr. Roy Ebron, Mr. Dwight Lamar, Mr. Fred Saunders, Mr. Wayne Herbert, and Mr. Rick Wasilewski.

As indicated in these statements, the information contained in this portion of the allegation is substantially correct. There does seem to be some question concerning the "free overnight room and board at the home of Garverick's brother," but this point is not critical to these charges.

(b) In its response to the latter portion of this allegation, the University will draw upon a statement by Mr. Roy Ebron. Mr. Ebron freely admits that he rode with Coach Harry Garverick from Lafayette, Louisiana, to Columbus, Ohio. However, he specifically denies that he used a ticket prepaid by the University on his airplane trip from Columbus, Ohio, to Norfolk, Virginia or that he used an airline ticket paid for by Mr. Garverick from his recruiting expense money to fly back from Norfolk, Virginia, to Columbus, Ohio. Mr. Ebron admits that he made this round-trip flight, but insists that he bought and paid for the ticket himself.

In view of Mr. Ebron's statement, the University admits that Coach Garverick transported Mr. Ebron from Lafayette to Columbus, Ohio, but must deny that portion of this allegation concerning airline tickets and transportation.

Question 19: Information available to the Committee on Infractions indicates that Scott Hudler, a prospective student-athlete from Houston Reagan High School, signed a grant-in-aid agreement with the University in June 1972. The University's head track coach, Robert Cole, acted in place of the institution's regular scholarship awards authority by informing Hudler that the terms of this grant-in-aid agreement provided for a "half scholarship" for four years with the understanding that if Hudler pole vaulted 15 feet while competing for the University, the aid would be increased to a full scholarship.

Upon learning of this scholarship arrangement, Dick Oliver, commissioner, Southland Conference, informed the prospective student-athlete that he would not be permitted to enroll at the University. Please indicate whether this information is substantially correct. Also, please submit a copy of all written statements signed by the young man and/or the University related to the institutional financial aid which was to be awarded to him.

Response: In response to this allegation, the University submits a statement of Coach Robert Cole. This statement tells a similar story with an important difference. The allegation states that Mr. Hudler was "informed" that his aid would be increased to a full scholarship if he vaulted 15 feet. Coach Cole reports that Mr. Hudler "asked" what he would have to do to get a full scholarship and that he (Coach Cole) told him he would have to jump 15 feet 6 inches or better.

In view of Coach Cole's statement, the University agrees that the information contained in the allegation is substantially correct except as noted above.

In reply to the Committee on Infraction's request for copies of all written statements signed by Mr. Hudler and/or the University related to the institutional financial aid which was to be awarded to him, the University has no record of any written statements as described herein.

Question 20: It is alleged that former University student-athlete Rick Wasilewski was contacted by telephone in April 1972 by Tom Cox; further, that Cox attempted to persuade Wasilewski to misinform the NCAA regarding violations of the Association's legislation by the University of which the young man was knowledgeable; further, that Cox informed Wasilewski that the University was being investigated by the NCAA, and that he (Cox) was trying to work out a story which all of the present and former student-athletes involved in the violations could relate when questioned by representatives of the NCAA; finally, that Cox indicated he would like for Wasilewski to return to the

University if he so desired and that he would be "well taken care of" if he did return.

Please indicate whether this information is substantially correct and submit evidence to support your response.

Response: In support of its response to this allegation, the University submits statements from Mr. Rick Wasilewski and Coach Tom Cox.

Mr. Wasilewski's statement concerning these charges reads, "It is true that Coach Cox contacted me by phone in April, 1972. During this conversation he discussed the manner in which I was transported to the campus to enroll for school in the fall of 1970 (see Allegation 18). Coach Cox could not remember which car I rode in, as there was more than one car and several athletes involved. We discussed this at length, but at no time has Coach Cox ever asked me to lie or misinform the NCAA."

Coach Cox's statement concerning this allegation states, "It is (a) completely false accusation that I tried to persuade Rick Wasilewski to misinform the N.C.A.A. It is a fact that the only violation involving Rick I admitted to when questioned the first time by Ralph McFillen was that mentioned in Allegation 18. I did not tell Rick that he would be 'well taken care of.' I understand that Rick's statement is attached."

Since both persons mentioned in the charges contained in this allegation deny that Coach Cox attempted to persuade Mr. Wasilewski to misinform the N.C.A.A. by telephone in April, 1972, the University must insist that these charges have no basis in fact and are completely untrue.

Question 21: It is alleged that the University paid for the costs incurred by then prospective student-athletes Fred McDonald (San Francisco) and Willie Williams (Atlanta) to travel to Lafayette to enroll for the fall semester, 1971–72 academic year; further, that arrangements for this transportation were made by Tom Cox with Tony Medina **[spelling?]** at the Acadiana Travel Agency; finally, that the cost of this transportation was charged to the University and paid by it. Please indicate whether this information is substantially correct and submit evidence to support your response.

Response: In reply to the charges contained in this allegation, the University offers statements from Coach Tom Cox, Mr. Anthony J. Mannina, Mr. Fred McDonald, and Mr. Willie Williams.

Both Mr. McDonald and Mr. Williams state that they paid for the airline tickets which were sent to them by Acadiana Travel Agency in the fall of 1971.

Coach Cox concedes that he may have made the reservations for both Mr. McDonald and Mr. Williams, but to his knowledge both student-athletes paid for their tickets when they arrived in Lafayette.

Mr. Anthony J. Mannina (Medina in the allegations), a travel agent at the Acadiana Travel Agency, states that the University was billed for the ticket in question in this allegation through an error on the part of Acadiana Travel Agency. This error was not discovered until an N.C.A.A. investigator questioned the University's payment of a second trip for both of these student-athletes. This error has now been corrected, and the University's payment for these tickets has been refunded. The Committee is referred to the statement of Mr. Anthony J. Mannina for a more complete discussion of the error which caused the double billing and the subsequent correction of the mistake.

Taking into consideration the statements of these four individuals, the University feels it must deny the charges contained in this allegation.

Question 22: It is alleged that during the summer 1970 then prospective student-athlete Wilbert Loftin visited student-athlete Dwight Lamar in Columbus, Ohio; further, that Loftin was then provided commercial airline transportation through the arrangements of Harry Garverick and at the expense of the University to travel from Columbus to Lafayette to begin a summer job; further, that Loftin was transported to his job as a construction laborer with the T.L. James Construction Company, Lafayette, by Garverick at approximately 5:50 each week-day morning during the summer until the beginning of the 1970 fall semester.

Please indicate whether this information is substantially correct and submit evidence to support your response.

Response: In response to this allegation, the University submits a statement from Mr. Wilbert Loftin.

Mr. Loftin states, "In answer to the allegation ... that the University of Southwestern Louisiana paid my traveling expenses from Columbus, Ohio, to Lafayette, Louisiana, in the summer of 1970, this is to state that I paid my own transportation."

A check of the University's travel records for June, 1970, do not show any flight from Columbus, Ohio, to Lafayette, Louisiana nor does Acadiana Travel Agency have a record of any such flight being charged to the University.

Further, Mr. Loftin continues, "While I was working for a construction company in Lafayette during that same summer, Mr. Harry Garverick worked for the same company. On occasion, Mr. Garverick gave me a ride to work. On other occasions, I was able to catch rides with other people who worked for that company."

In view of the contents of this statement by Mr. Wilbert Loftin, the University must deny that Mr. Loftin was furnished free commercial airline transportation as specified above. Because of Mr. Loftin's statement, the University must admit that Mr. Loftin rode to work on occasion that summer with Mr. Garverick. However, it must deny that this transportation was in any way connected with the fact that Mr. Loftin was a student-athlete and was instead an act of friendship on Mr. Garverick's part.

Question 23: Information available to the Committee on Infractions indicates that members of the University's athletic staff as well as other representatives of the University's athletic interests solicited the enrollment of prospective student-athletes by promise and/or provision of improper inducements. Specifically, it is charged that:

a. John Mills, then a prospective student-athlete from Laymon High School, Canton, Ohio, visited the University's campus in May 1971 and at that time was promised by Tom Cox that if he (Mills) enrolled at the University, he would receive extra money when needed, free gasoline for his car, and free transportation home subsequent to his enrollment.

Response: The University's response to this allegation is based upon a statement by Coach Tom Cox. Coach Cox states, "I did not offer John Mills extra money when needed, nor free transportation home. As to free gasoline for his car, he did not have a car, therefore, I could not have offered him free gasoline." Coach Cox continues, giving information concerning a request from Mr. Mills that the coaches buy him a motorcycle. When the request was refused, Coach Cox thinks that this angered Mr. Mills and caused him to not come to USL and to harbor some ill feelings for this University.

With due consideration for this allegation and Coach Cox's statement, the University must deny this allegation.

1) Later during the summer 1971, Cox and Harry Garverick visited Mills in Canton and persuaded him to sign a "national" letter-of-intent to enter the University. On this occasion, Mills was handed $20 in cash by Cox, who suggested that Mills use the money to entertain his parents.

Response: Coach Cox, in his statement, specifically denies giving Mr. Mills $20 as alleged above. Because of this, the University too must deny this allegation.

2) On or about June 7, 1971, Mills and two of his friends were apprehended by the police for a speeding violation in Virginia Beach, Virginia, for which Mills was fined $61. Mills telephoned Beryl Shipley, who in turn wired $61 to pay the fine.

Response: In replying to this allegation, Coach Beryl Shipley has given a statement which says: "One night I received a call from John Mills advising me that he had been apprehended for speeding in Virginia Beach, Virginia. He told me that he did not want to call his parents and asked me to wire $61 to pay the fine and that he would repay me when he got back home. I did wire the $61 to the proper official, because Mills was in trouble and I felt sorry for him and because he had promised to repay me. Mills never did repay me, despite his promise."

In consideration of the above statement of Coach Shipley, the University must assume that Coach Shipley made a bad loan of $61 to Mr. John Mills, for which he suffered the consequences—the loss of his $61.

> b. Frank Kendrick, then a prospective student-athlete from Indianapolis, Indiana, visited the University's campus in July 1970 and at that time was promised by Tom Cox that if he (Kendrick) enrolled at the University, he would receive in addition to a full scholarship, $100 per month, free clothing, free gasoline for his car, free air transportation to his home on holidays, free transportation for his parents to see him play and free laundry service.

Response: The University submits statements by Mr. Frank Kendrick and Coach Tom Cox in support of its position concerning this allegation.

Both Coach Cox and Mr. Kenrick deny that there was any offer of $100 per month, free clothing, free gasoline for Mr. Kendrick's car, free air transportation to Mr. Kendrick's home on holidays, and free transportation to Mr. Kendrick's parents. Coach Cox admits that he did offer Mr. Kendrick room, board, books, tuition, and laundry money.

In view of these two statements, the University must deny this allegation.

> c. Bill Roniger, then a prospective student-athlete from Brother Martin High School, New Orleans, Louisiana, visited the University's campus during the summer 1969 and at that time was promised by Tom Cox that if he (Roniger) would enroll at the University, he would be provided free transportation to travel between the campus and his home.

Response: The University submits statements by Mr. William Roniger and by Coach Tom Cox in support of its position on this allegation.

Mr. Roniger and Coach Cox both state that this allegation is untrue. Therefore the University must reject it also as being untrue.

    d. Frank Kluz, then a prospective student-athlete from Chipola Junior College, Marianna, Florida, visited the University during the spring 1970, and at that time was promised by Tom Cox that if he (Kluz) would enroll at the University, he would receive in addition to a full scholarship approximately $35 per month, free gasoline for his car, free transportation home during vacation periods and expense-free long distance telephone calls. In addition, Frank Kluz, Sr., father of the prospective student-athlete, was promised by Cox that he (Mr. Kluz) and his wife would be provided free motel accommodations in Dayton, Ohio, to watch their son participate in the University's game against the University of Dayton scheduled during the 1970–71 intercollegiate basketball season.

Response: As its response to this allegation, the University submits a statement from Coach Tom Cox. Coach Cox states, "I did not offer Frank Kluz $35 per month, free gas for his car, free transportation, nor long-distance calls. I did not offer his parents free motel accommodations, only that we would be playing close to his parent's home in Dayton and Cincinnati, and they would have the opportunity to see him play."

Due to this denial by Coach Cox, the University rejects the contention that Mr. Kluz and his parents were made offers as described above.

    e. During the recruitment of Roy Ebron, then a prospective student-athlete from Norfolk, Virginia, Tom Cox promised Ebron that if he (Ebron) enrolled at the University, he would receive in addition to a full scholarship, $450 per month, free clothing, free air transportation for his parents to travel to the campus to see him play, free air transportation to travel between the campus and his home during vacation periods, free laundry service, a substitute to take his ACT test in October 1970 to satisfy the prediction requirements of the NCAA 1.600 rule, and free transportation to the campus for his enrollment in the fall of 1970.

Response: In responding to this allegation the University will use the statements of Mr. Roy Ebron and Coach Tom Cox.

Mr. Ebron specifically denies this allegation, stating, "... the coaches offered me a basketball scholarship which they said would include tuition, room, board, books, and laundry. I was not offered $450 per month or any sum of money, nor free clothing, free air transportation for my parents, or for me, nor did anyone arrange for someone to take my ACT test in October 1970."

Coach Cox likewise denies that this allegation is true. He says that the accusations that he had offered Mr. Ebron these inducements is another allegation that is surely preposterous and completely false.

With due consideration of the content of these statements, the University must deny the truth of this allegation.

> f. Rick Wasilewski, then a prospective student-athlete from New Boston, Michigan, visited the University during the spring 1970 accompanied by his high school basketball coach, Dave Court, and was promised by Tom Cox that if he (Wasilewski) enrolled at the University, he would receive extra spending money and free clothes. In addition, Wasilewski and Court each were provided $20 cash by Cox during this campus visit to be spent as they desired.

Response: In support of its response to the charges contained in this allegation, the University will make reference to statements from Mr. Rick Wasilewski and Coach Tom Cox.

Mr. Rick Wasilewski's statement is quite specific concerning the facts surrounding these charges. He states, "I do not recall Coach Cox ever giving me money and he certainly never offered me clothes or anything other than room, board, tuition and laundry money." Mr. Rick Wasilewski obviously is denying the charges of this allegation.

Coach Tom Cox's statement concerning this incident reads "Rick Wasilewski was not promised by me free clothes and "extra" spending money. I did not give Rick $20, but did give the money to one of our own athletes to entertain

Rick during his visit. I did not give Coach Court $20 during his visit."

In reviewing the content of these two statements and contrasting them with the charges of this allegation, the University must come to the conclusion that the charges as set forth are completely false.

> g. Roland Grant, then a prospective student-athlete from South Philadelphia High School, Philadelphia, Pennsylvania, was visited by Beryl Shipley and offered an automobile and extra cash if he (Grant) would enroll at the University. Further, Shipley offered Grant a monthly cash living allowance for his mother who at that time was suffering from severe asthma and unable to work.

Response: The University has made persistent attempts to make contact with Mr. Roland Grant, but the mere mention of NCAA and he seems to just disappear. Consequently, we have not been able to secure a statement from him.

The response to this charge will be based on a statement of Coach Beryl Shipley in which he says, "I did meet Roland Grant while I was attending a post-season basketball tournament in Philadelphia in which Grant was participating. I did not offer him an automobile nor did I offer him cash if he would enroll at the University, and I did not offer a monthly living allowance for his mother, whom I never met or talked to. The purpose of my visit was to try to get him to visit the University, but he never did and I never talked to him again by phone or in person."

In consideration of this statement from Coach Shipley, the University must deny the charges which comprise this allegation.

> h. Mickey Heard, then a prospective student-athlete from Wilbur Cross High School, New Haven, Connecticut, visited the University in January 1972. During a telephone conversation prior to this visit, Beryl Shipley promised Heard that if he (Heard) enrolled at the University, he would receive in addition

to a full scholarship, $200 per month for his mother who had a heart condition and was unable to work, an automobile, a stereo, a television and a substitute to take his SAT test to establish eligibility under the NCAA 1.600 rule. After Heard's visit to the University, Heard was contacted by then graduate assistant coach Manny Goldstein who promised him that if he enrolled at the University he would receive an automobile, $200 per month for his mother, payment of his mother's telephone bill and a large undisclosed amount of money the day Heard signed a letter-of-intent to enter the University.

Response: In reply to the charges in this allegation, the University submits statements from Mr. Manny Goldstein, Coach Beryl Shipley, and Mr. Charles Cosper.

The University would first like to state that it has been denied access to Mr. Mickey Heard by athletic officials at the Louisiana State University. Mr. Charles Cosper, the University's representative who attempted to contact Mr. Heard, has given a statement which outlines the chronological order of his actions in attempting to interview Mr. Heard. Since the University has not been able to interview Mr. Heard, it feels that it has not had a proper opportunity to investigate the charges made in this allegation.

Mr. Goldstein states that he made no promises of inducements to Mr. Heard such as listed in this allegation. This charge, according to Mr. Goldstein, is specifically denied.

Coach Beryl Shipley states that he never talked to Mickey Heard by phone or otherwise prior to his visit to the University, and categorically denies that he offered him (Heard) such inducements as $200 per month for his mother, an automobile, a stereo, a television, and a substitute to take his SAT test. Coach Shipley further states, "all of the arrangements for Heard's visit were made with his high school coach, Bob Saulsbury, who did not permit Heard to visit any campus unless arrangements were made for Saulsbury and his wife to come with Heard. I can only assume that Saulsbury and his wife also accompanied Heard on his visits to other campuses."

166

In view of these two statements, and in the absence of information from Mr. Heard, the University must come to the conclusion that the charges contained in this allegation are false.

> i. During the recruitment of Tom Turner, then a prospective student-athlete from Vincennes Junior College, Vincennes, Indiana, Tom Cox promised that if he (Turner) would enroll at the University he would receive in addition to a full scholarship, an expense-free apartment, free gasoline for his car, free long distance telephone calls, free transportation home during school vacation periods and free transportation for his parents to travel to the University to watch him play.

Response: The University offers statements from Mr. Tom Turner and Coach Tom Cox as a portion of its response to this allegation.

Mr. Turner states that Tom Cox has "never promised me anything other than a full grant-in-aid." He continues, "He did not at any time offer me an expense-free apartment, free gasoline for my car, free long distance telephone calls, or free transportation home during vacations. And to my knowledge he never promised free trips to my parents to see me play."

Coach Cox likewise denies that he offered the inducements mentioned in this allegation to Mr. Turner.

In view of these two statements, the University must deny this allegation.

> 1) Further, Turner and his wife were provided with the cost-free use of an automobile and trailer rented by the University in order for them to travel to the campus for Turner to enroll for the 1970 fall semester and to transport their personal belongings. Specifically, the automobile was driven to Indianapolis from Lafayette by then student-athlete Marvin Winkler and delivered to Turner who was transported to Indianapolis from Vincennes, Indiana, by Harry Garver-

167

ick; further, Garverick then arranged for Turner to obtain a trailer at no expense to the young man.

Response: The statement of Mr. Tom Turner describes the same event in a somewhat different manner. According to Mr. Turner, "The automobile that I drove to Lafayette from Indianapolis was an automobile that Marvin Winkler had leased from Royal Rental Agency of Lafayette and did not wish to drive back home because he wanted to stay in Indianapolis. However, he needed to have the car returned before his lease expired, so I agreed to drive it back for him. Coach Garverick was with Winkler when they came through Vincennes. I leased, with my own money, a Hertz trailer to carry our belongings to Lafayette."

Mr. Marvin Winkler's statement completely verifies Mr. Turner's story.

Consequently, the University must insist that the true facts do not match those contained in the allegation and hence must also deny this allegation.

> i. During the recruitment of Garland Williams, then a prospective student-athlete from Mackin High School, Washington, D.C., Tom Cox promised Williams that if he (Williams) enrolled at the University, he would receive extra cash in the amount of $10 per week, free clothes and free transportation home during school holidays.

Response: The University submits a statement from Coach Tom Cox in support of its reply to this allegation. The Committee should also consider the fact that the University, despite all its efforts, has been unable to locate Mr. Garland Williams in order to secure a statement from him.

Coach Cox's statement reads, "I did not offer Garland Williams extra cash, free clothes, nor free transportation home during holidays."

In view of Coach Cox's denial of these charges, and in the absence of any other information concerning this charge, the University denies that Mr. Williams was offered the inducements mentioned in this allegation.

> 1) Further, during the summer 1967 Tom Cox accompanied Williams to Mackin High School when he

(Cox) gave the young man approximately $130 for payment of charges owed by Williams at the school. The payment of these charges was necessary in order for Williams' transcript to be released by the school.

Response: Again, Coach Cox's statement says, "I did not give him (Garland Williams) $130 to pay Mackin School fees...."

For the reasons stated above, the University also denies this allegation.

2) Further, Tom Cox provided a commercial airline ticket to Williams to travel from Washington, D.C., to Lafayette to enroll at the University for the 1967 fall semester. Williams did not pay for the cost of this ticket.

Response: Coach Cox's statement continues, "... and I did not provide him (Garland Williams) with an airline ticket to enroll at our University."

Again, following the reasoning given above, the University must deny that Coach Cox provided Mr. Williams with a commercial airline ticket as described in this allegation.

j. During the recruitment of Greg Procell, then prospective student-athlete from Ebarb High School, Ebarb, Louisiana, a representative of the University's athletic interests, Kenneth Hebert, gave the young man approximately $100 in cash in order to influence his enrollment at the University. This cash was provided to Hebert by Shipley and given to Procell during his senior year in high school. During the summer 1970, Beryl Shipley arranged a job for Greg Procell at Ocean Protein Company, Cameron, Louisiana; further, Shipley met Procell in Shreveport, Louisiana, and transported the young man to Lafayette where he (Procell) was housed in a University dormitory for approximately two days before being transported by Shipley from Lafayette to Cameron to begin the summer job; further, that after Procell worked only two days he was transported from Cameron to Lafayette by Harry Garverick where he remained in a University dormitory for one day before returning to Shreveport on a bus; further, prior to boarding the bus, Procell was given approximately $50 cash by Tom Cox. Procell did not pay for any of the expenses related to the transportation described herein and did not pay for the cost of staying in the University dormitory; further, Procell had already visited the University's campus on another occasion during the spring 1970 at the expense of the University. During the recruitment of Greg Procell, Beryl Shipley promised the young man a $500 wardrobe, an automobile and extra spending money when needed subsequent to the young man's enrollment.

Response: In response to this allegation, the University submits the statements of Coach Beryl Shipley and Coach Tom Cox.

With reference to the $100 supposedly paid to Mr. Procell, Coach Shipley states, "I never did provide to Kenneth Hebert $100 in cash or any other amount for him to give to Procell in order to influence his enrollment at the University." The University also made several attempts to reach Mr. Kenneth Hebert for verification of Coach Shipley's statement. However, Mr. Hebert is out of the country, working somewhere in Arabia. However, the University feels that Coach Shipley's statement is sufficient to allow us to deny this allegation.

As regards the second allegation concerning a job, Coach Shipley states, "I did get Procell a job with Ocean Protein in Cameron, Louisiana. At the request of Mr. William Lowery, Personnel Manager of said company, I transported Procell to Cameron, Louisiana, to meet with his boss on the job site. I was accompanied on this trip by Father Julius Robichaux, then pastor at Our Lady of Wisdom Church on the USL campus. I did not pick Procell up in Shreveport. He came to Lafayette and the day he arrived in Lafayette Father Robichaux and I drove him to Cameron as requested by Mr. Lowery. He did not reside in a school dormitory two days prior to my taking him to Cameron. By the time I got back to Lafayette after taking Procell to Cameron, Procell had called my wife and advised that he did not like the job at Cameron and that he wanted to leave and go to work at a Coca Cola plant in Shreveport. I did send Harry Garverick to get Procell and upon his return to Lafayette I told him that I did not think he would fit in at USL."

In view of this statement from Coach Shipley, the University admits to transporting Mr. Greg Procell from Lafayette to his place of employment at Cameron, Louisiana and back as described above. It denies that Mr. Procell was transported from Shreveport and that he spent time residing in a dormitory at USL.

As to that portion of this allegation that indicates Coach Tom Cox gave approximately $50 to Greg Procell, Coach Cox's statement specifically denies that he gave Mr. Procell money in any amount at any time. In addition, Coach Shipley denies that he ever offered Mr. Procell any of the alleged inducements or any other inducements in an attempt to persuade him to attend USL.

With due consideration for these statements, the University finds that it must deny the latter part of this allegation concerning promises made to Mr. Procell while he was being recruited.

l.   Fred Saunders, then a prospective student-athlete from Columbus, Ohio, was given $20 cash by Beryl Shipley in the spring 1970 when Shipley and Saunders were leaving the Top Floor Party House Restaurant, Columbus where they had eaten lunch.

Response: In reply to this allegation, the University has submitted statements from Mr. Fred Saunders and Coach Beryl Shipley.

Coach Shipley's statement concerning this alleged incident states, "I do not recall any restaurant named the Top Floor Party House Restaurant in Columbus, Ohio. I was in a restaurant with Fred Saunders in Columbus along with several of his high school coaches and administrators, but at no time did I ever give any amount of cash to Fred Saunders."

Mr. Saunders recalls that while he was standing near the cash register of this restaurant that "Coach Shipley handed me $5.00 and asked me to leave it on the table as a tip to the waiter." He avers that he received no other cash.

In view of these statements, the University must deny this allegation.

The Committee would appreciate receiving the University's explanation and comments concerning the improper inducements allegedly promised or given prospective student-athletes by members of the University's athletic staff or other representatives of its athletic interests. In responding, please indicate whether each allegation is substantially correct and submit evidence to support your response.

Response: The foregoing discussions of the individual allegations contained in this section have shown that there is only one valid allegation in this section, that concerning the transportation of Mr. Greg Procell from Lafayette, Louisiana, to Cameron, Louisiana and back.

It seems odd that with the numerous allegations of monthly payments, cash payments, free apartments, free travel, and so on, never is there an indication of where all this money is coming from in the economy of the late '60s and early '70s.

Question 24: It is alleged that on or about April 24, 1972, basketball coaches Beryl Shipley and Tom Cox contacted then prospective student-athlete Edmond Lawrence at W.O. Boston High School, Lake Charles, Louisiana, without first contacting the high school principal or his authorized representative to explain the purpose of the visit and to request permission to contact Lawrence; further, that during this visit with Lawrence, which occurred during one of the young man's class periods, both Shipley and Cox intimidated and threatened Lawrence in an attempt to influence his decision to attend the University indicating that he would have to go to court and take a lie detector test inasmuch as he had signed two conference and two "national" letters-of-intent. After a few minutes, this visit was terminated by an assistant principal named Palmer, who entered the room where Cox and Shipley were talking to Lawrence and asked the coaches if they had permission to contact the young man on the high school campus. Shipley then acknowledged that they did not have permission and Palmer requested the coaches to leave.

Please indicate whether this information is substantially correct and submit evidence to support your response.

Response: In support of its response to this allegation, the University submits statements from Coach Beryl Shipley, Coach Tom Cox, Mr. William Palmer (currently Principal of W.O. Boston High School), and an unsigned statement from Mr. Edmond Lawrence. Mr. Lawrence was interviewed by one of our student personnel assistants who produced the unsigned statement from his interview notes and brought it back to Mr. Lawrence for his signature. At this point, Mr. Lawrence refused to sign the statement, stating that the last time he had signed something he and his mother had to go to court. Consequently, we present an unsigned statement from Mr. Lawrence which is attested to as a true statement by the person who did the interview. Because of this, we will trust Mr. Lawrence's statement as though it had been signed by him.

Taken together, these four statements tell a vastly different story than that given in this allegation. A brief summary of what actually happened is given below:

Mr. Edmond Lawrence had signed a letter of application for admission to USL, a Southland Conference Scholarship Grant-in-aid to attend USL, and a "national" letter-of-intent to attend USL. A day or two after USL announced that it had signed Mr. Lawrence, McNeese State University (Lake Charles, Louisiana) announced that they had signed Edmond Lawrence. Coach Shipley believed that Mr. Lawrence had signed with us prior to signing with McNeese, and so he and Coach Cox went to W.O. Boston High School to talk to Mr. Lawrence about this problem.

When they arrived at the high school they found Coach Weston (the high school basketball coach) who told them that Lawrence had a physical education class at that time, but was not attending it because of senior privileges. Coach Weston found Lawrence and brought him to Coaches Shipley and Cox. When Coach Shipley requested that Lawrence talk to them about the problem, Lawrence took them to a counselor's room where they talked for some 15–20 minutes. After this time, then Assistant Principal William Palmer came into the room and asked if Coach Shipley and Coach Cox had permission to be on campus talking to Lawrence. After a while it was determined that permission from the head basketball coach was not enough, but one needed to get permission from the principal. So Coaches Shipley and Cox went to the Principal's Office and secured permission to talk to Lawrence. Upon returning from the Principal's Office, they found that Lawrence was in the room with Mr. Palmer. He stayed in the room with Mr. Palmer until classes ended. As Lawrence left, he indicated to Coaches Shipley and Cox that there was nothing further to talk about, and left the school grounds.

Coach Shipley, Principal Palmer, and Edmond Lawrence all state that there was no intimidation or threatening of Mr. Lawrence by either Coach Shipley or Coach Cox.

With due regard for the four statements from which this story emerged, the University very strongly denies this allegation.

Question 25: Information available to the Committee on Infractions indicates that several prospective student-athletes have revealed, demonstrated and displayed their abilities in the sport of basketball while on the campus of the University; further, that student-athletes at the University have engaged in out-of-season workouts in basketball. Specifically, it is alleged that:

a. During his visit to the University's campus in the spring of 1970, then prospective student-athlete Frank Kluz was requested by then graduate assistant coach Allen Van Winkle to participate in a workout in the gymnasium located on campus; further, participating in the workout with Kluz were University student-athletes Payton Townsend, Garland Williams and Marvin Winkler; further, a student manager provided Kluz with workout clothing from the basketball equipment room; finally, coaches Shipley and Cox were present during the entire workout.

Response: In reply to this allegation, the University submits statements from Coaches Beryl Shipley and Tom Cox, Mr. Allen Van Winkle, Mr. Payton Townsend, and Mr. Marvin Winkler.

Mr. Van Winkle states very clearly in his reply that he did not request that Frank Kluz workout during his official campus visit. He also indicates that it is quite possible that Mr. Kluz did participate in a workout since most visiting prospective student-athletes want to be on the court with varsity athletes. Mr. Van Winkle conceded that Mr. Kluz could have been provided equipment for this workout but he couldn't be sure.

Student-athletes Payton Townsend and Marvin Winkler state that they recall playing with many of the recruits during their tenure at USL, but deny that these workouts were arranged by Coach Shipley or Coach Cox or that either of the coaches was present during any of these workouts.

Both Coach Shipley and Coach Cox deny that they requested Mr. Kluz to participate in a workout as well as that they were present during any such workout.

In consideration of the contents of these five statements, the University must deny that Mr. Frank Kluz was requested to participate in a workout as described above as well as the other allegations contained in this section.

> b. Prior to October 15, 1970, members of the University's intercollegiate basketball team were required by coaches Cox and Shipley to take part in a two-mile conditioning run on the track facility at the University; further, the team members were required to complete the run in less than 13 minutes; finally, those who failed to meet the time limit were required to run again the following day.

Response: The University submits statements from Coaches Beryl Shipley and Tom Cox as a portion of its response to this allegation (see Appendix of Statements).

Coach Shipley states, "no members of the University's basketball team were requested to take part in any run prior to October 15, 1970. On October 15 of each year, I required that on that day the members of the basketball team be able

175

to run the mile in six minutes. Those who do not run the mile in the specified time on that day were required to do so subsequently before they were enrolled to practice with the team."

Coach Cox states, "To my knowledge there was no conditioning program prior to October 15, although we requested our boys to begin getting in shape as early as possible on their own."

In consideration of these two statements, the University must deny this allegation.

    c. Prior to October 15 (1970–71 and 1971–72 academic years), members of the University's intercollegiate basketball team engaged in numerous workouts in the University's gymnasium; further, these workouts usually occurred several times each week with coaches Shipley and Cox usually present to observe and give instructions on occasion.

Response: As a portion of its reply to this allegation, the University submits statements from Coach Beryl Shipley and Coach Tom Cox concerning the content of this section.

Coach Shipley states, "I deny this allegation, and further state that at no time prior to October 15 have I observed or gave instructions for any such workouts."

Coach Cox's statement reads, "We did not organize any workouts for the basketball team prior to October 15 (1970–71 and 1971–72 academic years). Again we feel it is probable that the players worked out on their own after entering school before October 15 of each year."

With due cognizance for these statements from Coaches Shipley and Cox, and because the University has not located any other evidence which verifies these charges, we must deny this allegation.

    d. During a campus visit in the spring of 1967, then prospective student-athlete Garland Williams participated in a basketball workout with student-athlete Marvin Winkler in the presence of Tom Cox and Beryl Shipley.

Response: In support of its reply to this allegation, the University presents statements from Mr. Marvin Winkler, Coach Beryl Shipley, and Coach Tom Cox.

Coach Shipley's statement is as follows: "I deny the allegations contained therein and further state that <u>I was not even in the City of Lafayette during the referred to campus visit of Garland Williams and did not even see Williams during his second visit</u>."

Coach Cox adds, "I have no knowledge of a workout in which Garland Williams participated with Marvin Winkler and was definitely not present during any such workout."

Mr. Winkler indicates that while some recruits may have worked out with members of the basketball team, he doesn't ever recall Coach Shipley or Coach Cox coming to any of these.

In view of the three statements referred to above, the University must deny that Mr. Garland Williams participated in a basketball workout in the presence of Coach Shipley and Coach Tom Cox as alleged.

The University would like to point out to the Committee on Infractions that it has not had the opportunity to obtain a statement from Mr. Garland Williams since we have not been able to locate him despite repeated efforts.

> e. During the campus visits of then prospective student-athletes Dwight Lamar and Ed Ratleff, Columbus, Ohio, during the spring 1969, the two young men engaged in a basketball workout with then student-athletes Garland Williams and Payton Townsend in the presence of Beryl Shipley. This workout occurred in the University's gymnasium.

Response: In responding to the charges contained in this allegation, the University will utilize the statements of Mr. Ed Ratleff, Mr. Dwight Lamar, Mr. Payton Townsend, and Coach Beryl Shipley.

Mr. Ratleff states, "It is correct that when I went to Lafayette, Louisiana for the visit, that several of the basketball players at the University, together with Bo Lamar and myself got up a basketball game. As far as I know, this was

177

something we all wanted to do. I did not see Coach Cox or Coach Shipley present at any time during the game."

Mr. Lamar states, "... when I visited USL, I do recall that I worked out with Marvin Winkler, and Ed Ratleff, who was visiting USL along with me. There were several players who got together to play a scrimmage game. I had brought my own equipment for I thought we would probably play some basketball games when I got to the school. The coaches at USL did not request that I do this. I did not see any coaches watching while we were playing."

Mr. Townsend's statement verifies that he took part in some of these "make-up games" where at times some visiting prospective student-athletes also played and Coach Shipley denies this allegation and states that he was not present during any such basketball workout.

In view of these statements, the University must conclude that the playing of these two prospective student-athletes was at their own bidding and that the USL coaches had no part in organizing and did not observe any workout as described herein.

> g. During the campus visits of then prospective student-athletes George McGinnis, Roy Ebron, Wilbert Loftin and Fred Saunders, the young men engaged in basketball workouts with at least one student-athlete, Garland Williams, in the presence of Beryl Shipley. These workouts occurred in the University's gymnasium.

Response: In response to this allegation, the University submits statements from Coach Beryl Shipley, Mr. George McGinnis, and Mr. Fred Saunders.

Coach Shipley states that he was not present for any such workouts and has no knowledge that such workouts were in fact held.

Mr. McGinnis relates that while on his visit to the University, "several players of the University got up a basketball game and I participated. I don't remember who the players were. This game was not arranged or planned by either Coach Shipley or Coach Cox, as far as I know. I certainly did not see them while I was playing." <u>Mr. McGinnis goes on to say that "it would have been ridiculous for the University</u>

to have asked me to play for them" and that he would have resented it had he been asked. He further states that any basketball that he played at USL was because he wanted to play and for no other reason.

Mr. Fred Saunders indicates that he also played basketball with several other fellows on campus when he visited the University. He further states that to the best of his knowledge Coach Shipley had nothing to do with arranging for the game and he did not see any coaches during the workout.

With due regard for these statements, the University must deny the charges contained in this allegation.

> g. During his visit to the campus, July 1970, then prospective student-athlete Frank Kendrick participated in a basketball workout in the University's gymnasium. The workout occurred on a Friday afternoon, and among the student-athletes participating were Marvin Winkler, Dwight Lamar, Garland Williams and Payton Townsend. Kendrick and the student-athletes worked out at the request of Beryl Shipley and Tom Cox. Equipment was issued by the University, and Shipley and Cox watched the entire workout, which lasted approximately one hour and a half.

Response: The University offers statements from Coach Beryl Shipley, Coach Tom Cox, Mr. Frank Kendrick, Mr. Marvin Winkler, Mr. Dwight Lamar, and Mr. Payton Townsend in support of its response to this allegation.

Mr. Frank Kendrick has given the University the following statement concerning this allegation: "I do remember that when I visited the University, in 1970, that a group got together to play. I cannot remember the names of the players. As far as I know, this game was not arranged by either Coach, but was gotten up among the boys who were around the school at the time. I had taken some basketball shoes and other equipment with me and I was not issued any equipment by the University. I did not see either Coach Shipley or Coach Cox during the time we were playing. I do not remember how long the game lasted, but it was probably from one to two hours."

Mr. Winkler, Mr. Lamar, and Mr. Townsend tell basically the same story concerning these alleged workouts. Coaches Shipley and Cox deny any knowledge of these "student games", and specifically state that they were not present during any such workout.

Taking into account these six statements, the University feels it must deny the charges contained in this allegation.

> h. During his visit to the University's campus in the spring 1970, then prospective student-athlete Greg Procell participated in a workout in the University's gymnasium with most members of the basketball team including Dwight Lamar. Beryl Shipley was present during the entire workout.

Response: In support of its position on the charges contained in this allegation, the University submits statements from Mr. Dwight Lamar and Coach Beryl Shipley.

Mr. Lamar observes, "... during the time I attended USL, I frequently played basketball with other players from our team as well as prospective students. I do not ever recall playing with Frank Kendrick or Greg Procell, prospective student-athletes. I do not recall seeing any coaches present during any of the scrimmages or workouts, however, it is possible that they may have walked through the gym from time to time."

Coach Shipley denies this allegation and specifically states that he was not present during any such workout and has no knowledge of such a workout.

The University, in consideration of these statements, must contend that the charges contained in this allegation are totally untrue.

The fishing expedition continues:

The NCAA Committee would appreciate receiving the University's explanation and comments concerning the tryouts and out-of-season workouts which allegedly have occurred at the University. In responding, please indicate whether each allegation is substantially correct.

Response: In its response to the individual allegations of this section, the University has admitted that there were sometimes spontaneous games, workouts, or scrimmages which took place while some prospective student-athletes were on campus. Very often these prospective student-athletes wanted to and were allowed to join these workouts of their own free will. The University has been able to uncover no evidence that these sessions were planned or witnessed by Coaches Shipley and Cox.

Further, the University would like to point out to the Committee on Infractions that a prospective student-athlete's ability as a basketball player is questioned before, not after he is invited to the campus for a recruiting visit. It would seem rather odd to pay a young man's expenses for a visit to your campus on the chance that he is indeed a good basketball player. Perhaps Mr. George McGinnis said it best in the last paragraph of his statement (see Appendix of Statements).

"I would like also to state in this affidavit that when I was invited to visit the University of Southwestern Louisiana, I was not told that I would have to work out. I had been offered scholarships from over four hundred schools and I do not think that the coaches had to watch me work out to determine whether or not I could play for their school. I think it would have been ridiculous for them to have asked me to do this and I would have resented it. Any basketball that I played at the University was because I wanted to play basketball."

Question 26: Information available to the Committee on Infractions indicates that through the arrangements of the basketball coaching staff the University financed more than one visit to its campus for then prospective student-athletes Garland Williams, Roy Ebron, Greg Procell and Frank Kendrick; further, that visits by Williams and then prospective student-athlete Roy Ebron exceeded 48 hours. Specifically, it is alleged that:

    a. Roy Ebron visited the University's campus on May 15, 1970, with J. Milbourne—the transportation and local expenses being provided by the University; further, during August 1970, Ebron, his mother and sister visited the campus with the transportation and local expenses being provided by the University; finally, on this second visit Ebron remained on the University's campus for approximately one week at the expense of the University before being transported to Columbus, Ohio, by Harry Garverick where he traveled via commercial aircraft to his home.

Response: In response to the charges in this allegation, the University submits statements from Mr. Roy Ebron, his mother Mrs. Lulu Burton, Coach Beryl Shipley and Coach Tom Cox.

The University has admitted paying transportation and local expenses for Mr. J. Milbourne for the visit described above (see reply to allegation 7-a).

To answer the second part of this allegation, we look to Mr. Ebron's statement which says, "In August of 1970, when I came down to enroll at the University, my mother and sister came with me so that they could help me to get situated. As far as I know they paid for all of our transportation and expenses while in Lafayette." Mr. Ebron's mother, Mrs. Lulu Burton, states most emphatically that the expenses of the trip described above were borne by herself.

Additionally, Coach Shipley states that he did not arrange nor participate in any arrangements for University financing of more than one visit to the campus for Mr. Ebron. Further, he states that the University did not finance any such extra visits.

Coach Tom Cox's statement reads, "To my knowledge, the only visit that the University paid for, for prospective student-athlete Roy Ebron, was his official visit during May of 1970. I was aware that Roy Ebron did return to the University in August with his mother and sister, but was under the impression that this visit was paid for by his family. He did not stay on the University campus at the University's expense, but to my knowledge stayed with a friend in the city of Lafayette. As far as his being transported to Columbus, Ohio, by Harry Garverick, I had no knowledge at the time but having talked to Roy Ebron since, he advises me that Harry Garverick did offer a ride back home part of the way."

In summary, the University admits to the charge involving Mr. J. Milbourne as described above and to the transportation of Mr. Ebron from Lafayette, Louisiana, to Columbus, Ohio, as described above. The University must, however, deny the other charges related to a second visit to USL by Mr. Roy Ebron since the principals involved with the charge have all denied these allegations.

> b. Then prospective student-athlete Garland Williams visited the University's campus during the summer 1967 at the expense of the University and remained on campus for approximately five days before returning to Washington, D.C.; further, Williams was provided a second institutionally-financed visit to the University's campus during the summer 1967 in order to take an entrance examination.

Response: In support of its response to this allegation, the University presents statements by Coach Beryl Shipley and Coach Tom Cox. The University would like to remind the Committee that it has not had the opportunity to secure a statement from Mr. Garland Williams since it has been unable to locate him despite repeated and persistent attempts to do so.

Coach Shipley denies any knowledge of arrangements to bring Mr. Garland Williams to visit the University on more than one occasion. He further states that the University has not financed any such second trips.

Coach Cox states, "To the best of my recollection, Garland Williams visited the school in the summer of 1967, at the expense of the University. I do not recall his having stayed on the campus as long as five days. If he did so, it was without my knowing it. He was quite an independent individual and we did not have much association with him while he was on campus. To my knowledge, Williams' next trip to campus was to enroll in school. This trip was not financed by the University and the only tests he took were after he enrolled." The ACT or SAT tests were not required at that time, and the only test he needed to take was administered after his registration.

In view of these two denials, the University feels that it too must deny the charges contained in this allegation.

    c. Frank Kenrick visited the University's campus two times at the expense of the institution. The first visit was during July 1970 and the second during August 1970. The second visit was for the purpose of taking an ACT examination to establish eligibility under the NCAA 1.600 rule.

Response: As a portion of its reply to the charges contained in this allegation, the University offers the statements of Mr. Frank Kenrick, Coach Beryl Shipley, and Coach Tom Cox.

Mr. Kenrick's statement concerning his second visit to the USL campus reads, "I do recall visiting again later in the summer to spend a few days with my friend Marvin Winkler, I paid for my own expenses for that visit and while I was there, I took the ACT test. I was never informed of the results of my test, because I decided to attend Purdue a few weeks later."

Coach Shipley again denies any knowledge of a second trip for Mr. Kendrick. Coach Cox's statement verifies that of Mr. Kendrick.

In view of these three statements from the principals in the charges of this allegation, the University must deny this allegation that Mr. Kendrick received two paid visits to USL.

Question 27: Information available to the Committee on Infractions indicates members of the University's athletic staff arranged for payment of the transportation costs incurred by relatives and friends of several prospective student-athletes to visit the campus of the University. Specifically, it is alleged that:

    a. Mrs. Charles Herbert, mother of then prospective student-athlete Wayne Herbert, was provided without charge commercial airline transportation between her home in Cleveland, Ohio, and Lafayette, during May 1970 when she accompanied her son on his official visit to the University. This visit was arranged by the University's basketball coaches.

Response: In its reply to the charges contained in this allegation, the University presents statements from Mrs. Charles Herbert, Coach Beryl Shipley and Coach Tom Cox.

In her statement, Mrs. Herbert makes it quite clear that she paid for her transportation expenses when she accompanied her son on his official visit to the University.

Coach Shipley indicates that he knew Mrs. Herbert accompanied her son on his official visit, but that she paid her own expenses for this trip.

Coach Cox states, "To my knowledge Mrs. Charles Herbert paid for all of her expenses including her commercial airline transportation during her visit to our campus in May, 1970."

In view of these three statements, the University is obliged to deny the charges contained in this allegation.

> b. Mrs. Brenda Turner, wife of then prospective student-athlete Tom Turner, was provided without charge commercial airline transportation between Evansville, Indiana, and Lafayette on or about August 16, 1971, when she accompanied her husband on his official visit to the University. This visit was arranged by Tom Cox.

Response: The University admits that this allegation is substantially correct. Coach Tom Cox indicates in his statement that he arranged for Mrs. Turner to accompany her husband on his official visit to the University. Mr. Tom Turner, husband of Brenda, verifies this in his statement.

> c. Mrs. Lulu Burton, mother of then prospective student-athlete Roy Ebron, and her daughter were provided without charge commercial airline transportation between Norfolk, Virginia, and Lafayette in August 1970 when they accompanied Ebron on his official visit to the University. This transportation

was arranged by the University basketball coaches. Mrs. Burton's daughter received meals and lodging without charge.

Response: In its response to this charge, the University will use statements made by Mrs. Lulu Burton, Coach Beryl Shipley, and Coach Tom Cox.

Mrs. Burton states that she was personally responsible for all expenses in connection with the travel in August of 1970.

Both Coaches Shipley and Cox, in their statements, deny that they arranged for or had any knowledge of the travel as described in this allegation.

Due to the contents of these statements, the University must deny the charges contained in this allegation.

> d. Robert Saulsbury, then basketball coach, Wilbur Cross High School, New Haven, Connecticut, and the coach of then prospective student-athlete Mickey Heard, and his wife were provided commercial airline transportation by the University between New York and Lafayette on or about January 22, 1972, when they accompanied Heard on his official visit to the University. This visit was arranged by the University's basketball coaches. The Saulsburys were also provided without charge room and board while in Lafayette.

Response: The University verifies the charges contained in this allegation. Coach Beryl Shipley, in his statement, confirms that Mr. Saulsbury and his wife did accompany Mr. Mickey Heard on his visit to the University and were provided with commercial airline transportation by the University.

> e. David Court, high school basketball coach of then prospective student-athlete Rick Wasilewski, New Boston, Michigan, was provided without charge commercial airline transportation between Detroit and Lafayette during the summer 1970 when he accompanied Wasilewski on the young man's official visit to the University. This transportation was arranged by Harry Garverick.

Response: The University admits that this allegation is substantially correct.

>   f. Don McGee, junior varsity basketball coach, Thorn-
>   ton Harvey High School, Chicago, Illinois, and for-
>   mer coach of then prospective student-athlete Lloyd
>   Batts, was provided commercial airline transporta-
>   tion without charge between Chicago and Lafay-
>   ette, Louisiana, when he accompanied Batts on his
>   official visit to the University on or about May 22,
>   1970. McGee was provided without charge room and
>   board while in Lafayette. The arrangements for the
>   transportation was made by Harry Garverick.

Response: The University admits that this allegation is substantially correct.

In responding to the charges contained in this allegation, the University has admitted that four of the six sub-
sections of this allegation are substantially correct. It has
submitted evidence which indicates that the remaining two
of these are without foundation.

Question 28: Information available to the Committee
on Infractions indicates that members of the University's
athletic staff or other representatives of its athletic interests
provided cash to prospective student-athletes during their recruitment by the University. Specifically, it is charged that:

>   a. Mickey Heard, then prospective student-athlete from
>   Wilbur Cross High School, New Haven, Connecti-
>   cut, was provided $70 cash at an intercollegiate bas-
>   ketball game which he attended during his January
>   1972 visit to the University. Manny Goldstein, then
>   a graduate assistant serving as a recruiter on the bas-
>   ketball coaching staff, gave Heard $40 cash before
>   the game and an additional $30 cash following the
>   game.

Response: In responding to this allegation, the University will use a portion of the statement by Mr. Manny Goldstein. The University would like to remind the Committee

that Mr. Heard could not be interviewed by the University and it is felt that this did not allow us to fully explore the ramifications of this charge.

Mr. Goldstein denies that he gave Mr. Mickey Heard $70 in cash at an intercollegiate basketball game which Heard attended during his January, 1972, visit to the University.

In view of this denial and the non-availability of Mr. Heard for an interview, the University must find that it knows no reason to believe that this charge is true.

And here's our guy Kluz again.

> b. Frank Kluz, then a prospective student-athlete from Chipola Junior College, Marianna, Florida, was provided $20 cash by Tom Cox in the spring 1970 when Kluz arrived at the Lafayette airport for his official visit to the University.

Response: Coach Tom Cox denies this charge and states, "I did not give Frank Kluz $20 cash during his visit, but to an athlete of the University to entertain him (Kluz) with."

In view of Coach Cox's denial of this allegation, the University must also contend that the cash was not given to Mr. Kluz, but to a student-athlete who used the money to entertain Mr. Kluz.

> b. Tom Turner, then a prospective student-athlete from Vincennes Junior College, Vincennes, Indiana, was provided $20 cash by Tom Cox in August 1971 to pay for any expenses incurred during a trip to the Gulf of Mexico for Turner and his wife during their visit to the University.

How does one go on a trip to the "Gulf of Mexico"?

Response: In reply to the charges contained in this allegation, the University will draw on statements from Mr. Tom Turner and Coach Tom Cox.

Mr. Turner in relating the incident under question states, "At no time did Coach Cox give me $20 to spend during my visit or on this trip." Coach Cox echoes this statement when he says, "I did not give Tom Turner or his wife $20 for a trip to the Gulf of Mexico."

With due consideration for these two statements, the University denies these charges presented in this allegation.

> d. John Mills, then a prospective student-athlete from Laymon High School, Canton, Ohio, was provided $30 cash by Tom Cox in May 1971 when Mills arrived at the Lafayette airport for his official visit to the University. Beryl Shipley and Harry Garverick were present when Cox handed Mills the money.

Response: In order to refute the charges as presented in this allegation, the University will present portions of statements from Coach Beryl Shipley and Coach Tom Cox.

Coach Shipley comments, "I did not witness Tom Cox providing any money to John Mills and deny the allegations of question 28 (d)." Coach Cox states, "I did not give John Mills $30 cash, but did give one of our athletes $20 to entertain him with."

Having been unsuccessful in its attempts to reach Mr. John Mills, the University has not had the opportunity to solicit a statement from him. In the absence of any such statement, and in view of the statements of Coaches Shipley and Cox, the University must deny the charges contained in this allegation.

In responding to the individual charges contained in allegation twenty-eight, the University has presented evidence (statements) which in its mind is sufficient to show that all of these charges are unfounded. Thus, all charges in this allegation are denied.

Well, let's try again. Same question, same "Gulf of Mexico," different phrasing.

Question 29: It is alleged that then prospective student-athlete Tom Turner, Vincennes Junior College, Vincennes, Indiana, was provided without charge the use of a rental car by Harry Garverick during an August 1970 visit to the University's campus by Turner and his wife, Brenda. Turner and his wife were then on their honeymoon and used the automobile for local transportation as well as for a trip to the Gulf of Mexico.

Please indicate whether this information is substantially correct and submit evidence to support your response.

Response: In response to this allegation, the University submits a statement by Mr. Tom Turner.

Mr. Turner's version of this incident follows: "In August, 1970, during my visit to Lafayette, Harry Garverick checked out a rental car that my wife and I used on a honeymoon trip to the Gulf, approximately 75 miles. On returning the car to the rental agency at the airport in Lafayette, I myself paid for the cost of the car rental."

In addition, the records in the University Business Office show no automobile was rented by a University employee during August or September, 1970.

With due consideration for the allegation and for Mr. Turner's version of the affair, the University must deny the truth of this allegation.

Question 30: It is alleged that then prospective student-athlete Lafayette Mitchell, Gary, Indiana, was a guest of the University for three nights in Evansville, Indiana, during the 1971 NCAA College Division Basketball Championship; further, that Mitchell traveled by bus at the University's expense from Gary to Evansville and stayed cost-free with student-athletes Fred Saunders and Steve Greene at the Executive Inn Motel during the tournament before returning to Gary by commercial airline transportation at the expense of the University. All of his expenses on this occasion, including meals and the cost of tickets to the tournament, were paid by the athletic department of the University.

Please indicate whether this information is substantially correct and submit evidence to support your response. If your response is in the affirmative, please provide the following: (a) the number of University financed visits made by Mitchell to the campus; (b) the present status of this young man in relation to the University; (c) the identity of the University representative arranging for Mitchell's trip to Evansville and the source(s) paying for any costs incurred by the young man during this trip including transportation, room and board, and any other expenses.

Response: In reply to this allegation, the University submits statements from Mr. Lafayette Mitchell and Coach Russ Faulkinberry.

Mr. Mitchell's statement emphatically denies that the University treated him as a guest for three nights in Evansville, Indiana, during the 1971 NCAA College Division Basketball Championship. He states that he paid for all his meals and his ticket to the game as well as his transportation to and from Evansville, Indiana.

Coach Faulkinberry's statement corroborates that of Mr. Mitchell.

Since Mr. Mitchell's statement is straight forward in that he denies receiving anything to help pay for the trip referred to in this allegation, the University must accept his version of this incident and contend that this allegation is false.

The University would also like to call the attention of the Committee on Infractions to a copy of a letter which was sent to the NCAA by Mr. Lafayette Mitchell, Sr. As you can see Mr. Mitchell, Sr. also rather forcefully denies this allegation.

Question 31: It is alleged that after a 1972 basketball game played in Alexandria, Louisiana, between W.O. Boston High School, Lake Charles, Louisiana, and Woodlawn High School, Shreveport, Louisiana, prospective student-athlete Edmond Lawrence, a member of the W.O. Boston High School basketball team, was contacted at the site of the competition by Beryl Shipley, who transported Lawrence to a restaurant in Alexandria and provided him with an expense-free meal; further, that following the meal, Shipley and Tom Cox transported Lawrence from Alexandria to his home in Lake Charles.

Please indicate whether this information is substantially correct and submit evidence to support your response.

Response: The University calls the Committee's attention to the statements of Coach Beryl Shipley and Coach Tom Cox in the Appendix of Statements in which they indicate that this information is substantially correct.

Question 32: It is alleged that with the knowledge of or through the improper efforts and arrangements of members of the University's basketball coaching staff, several student-athletes were erroneously certified eligible under the prediction requirements of NCAA Bylaw 4-6-(b)-(1) [1.600 rule], and therefore were permitted to practice, participate and receive athletically-related institutional financial aid while ineligible for such benefits under this legislation. Specifically, it is alleged that:

    a. Tom Cox forged the name of John A. Frehse, principal, Fairborn Baker High School, on the high school transcript of then prospective student-athlete Steve Greene, and altered on the transcript a Biology grade from an "F" to an "A", a World History grade from an "F" to an "A" and a Spanish grade from an "F" to an "A"; further, these alterations by Cox resulted in Greene's grade point average improving from an actual 1.514 to a fraudulent 2.444, the necessary average to enable Greene's prediction and resultant eligibility during the 1970–71 academic year.

Response: Coach Tom Cox denies that he changed the grades on Steve Greene's high school transcript as described above. According to Coach Cox, a former coach (Mr. Harry Garverick) told him that he had permission to sign the principal's name to the transcript in order to speed up the predicting process. In support of the above, Coach Tom Cox has given a signed statement which is included in the Appendix of Statements submitted along with this report.

    b. Student-athletes Glenn Masson and Fred McDonald were not certified eligible as freshmen during the 1971–72 academic year under the prediction requirements of the 1.600 rule by the University's regular eligibility certifying authority; further, Beryl Shipley was familiar with their high school transcripts and permitted them to participate while ineligible; further, institutional financial aid was awarded without a determination of their eligibility for such aid under the 1.600 rule; finally, that when their prediction status was finally checked by Effie Whittington upon inquiry by the NCAA during the fall semester, 1972–73 academic year, neither young man predicted on the basis of his actual high school record.

Response: In reply to the allegation that Glenn Masson and Fred McDonald were not certified eligible as freshmen during the 1971–72 academic year under the requirements of the "1.600 rule," the University must accept the responsibility for a breakdown in the then established procedures for certifying eligibility under the "1.600 rule." Please refer to the reply to allegation number one for an in depth discussion of the University's old and new procedures for establishing the eligibility of student-athletes. We feel certain that these new procedures which are now in effect will prevent this type of breakdown from occurring in the future.

As to the allegation that Mr. Beryl Shipley, Head Basketball Coach, was familiar with the high school records of these two young men and allowed them to participate in the athletic program while ineligible, Coach Shipley has given a signed statement which denies that he had any knowledge that these two young men were not eligible for participation in intercollegiate athletics. Due to the breakdown in University procedure mentioned above, the coaches were not informed that an actual prediction of these two student-athletes had not been performed.

The University must admit that both Glenn Masson and Fred McDonald were awarded institutional financial aid for the 1971–72 academic year without there being an official determination of their predictability. This happened due to the previously mentioned breakdown in the old procedures for determining eligibility of prospective student-athletes.

When the two young men in question were formally predicted using the Southland Conference guidelines, neither was successful. However, since they were recruited prior to USL joining the Southland Conference, the Gulf States Conference prediction tables should have been used in determining their eligibility. Using these tables, Fred McDonald would have predicted and Glenn Masson would not have predicted. The University submits copies of letters from its Supervisor of Testing Services, Miss Effie Whittington, (Exhibits 32-A, 32-B, and 32-C) concerning the official prediction of these two young men.

    c. Student-athlete Terry Martin was certified eligible as a freshman during the 1971–72 academic year on the basis of an erroneous high school grade point average submitted to the University's regular eligibility certifying agent, Effie Whittington, on a form letter signed by Tom Cox. Martin's actual high school grade point average reflected on his high school transcript was a 1.733, and the erroneous average submitted with full knowledge of Tom Cox was 2.26, the necessary average to enable Martin's prediction and resultant eligibility during the 1971–72 academic year.

    d. Student-athlete Robert Burnett was certified eligible as a freshman during the 1970–71 academic year on the basis of an erroneous high school grade point average submitted to the University's regular eligibility certifying agent, Elsie S. Pearson, on a form letter signed by Tom Cox. Burnett's actual high school grade point average reflected on high school transcript was 1.639, and the erroneous average submitted with full knowledge of Tom Cox was 3.18, the necessary average to enable Burnett's prediction and resultant eligibility during the 1970–71 academic year.

Response: Since allegations 32-c and 32-d are very closely related, the University will answer them together.

In reply to the allegations that student-athletes Terry Martin and Robert Burnett were certified eligible as freshmen during the 1971–72 and 1970–71 academic year, respectively, on the basis of erroneous high school grade point averages submitted on form letters signed by Tom Cox, the University would like to point out that neither of these form letters (Exhibits 32-D and 32-E) was actually signed by Coach Tom Cox, and that all coaches had access to these form letters. Additionally, the University wishes to call the Committee's attention to the fact that this type of error cannot occur under the new procedures (see reply to allegation number one) for certifying eligibility of student-athletes now in force at U.S.L.

Coach Cox has replied to these allegations as follows:

"Terry Martin: A standard form letter was sent to the coach at Mr. Martin's high school with instructions to have the principal fill in the grade point average, sign in the appropriate space, and return the form to U.S.L. The form was returned to the Athletic Department with the grade point average 2.26 which was used to predict Mr. Martin. The certification of eligibility procedures in effect at that time did not require that this grade point average be crosschecked against Mr. Martin's high school transcript.

"Robert Burnett: The form letter which specified Mr. Burnett's grade point average as 3.18 was not sent out by myself. A former assistant coach (Harry Garverick) recruited Mr. Burnett and handled the certification of eligibility of this student-athlete. Since Mr. Burnett's actual high school grade point average was 1.639, I can only assume that this former coach arranged for the reporting of the erroneous grade point average."

Coach Cox's signed statement concerning these allegations is included in the Appendix of Statements.

> e. Student-athlete Willie C. Williams was certified eligible as a freshman during the 1971–72 academic year on the basis of a high school grade point average which was not determined on the same basis as the averages of all students at his high school, Fayette County High School, Georgia. Williams' actual high school record was less than a 2.000 and was not sufficient for the young man to predict. He was erroneously certified eligible with full knowledge of Tom Cox on the basis of a 2.19 grade point average which was computed by Jimmy D. White, principal, Fayette County High School, when advised by Cox to include the young man's grades for courses in

physical education, drivers education and teachers aid—grades in these courses not being considered in determining grade point averages for all of the school's students.

Response: The incident to which reference is made in this allegation is reported as follows by Coaches Cox and Shipley:

On the way to see Mr. Willie Williams perform in an All Star game, both coaches stopped by the Fayette County High School for the purpose of obtaining Mr. Williams' grade point average from the principal. In order to have a record of this grade point average they carried with them a blank form (Exhibit 32-F) which is a basketball version of Exhibit 1-I to be filled out and signed by the principal.

The third paragraph of Exhibit 32-F quotes from the 1971–72 Louisiana State Board of Education Athletic Policies (Exhibit 1-B), subsection 13 under Policies and Procedures for Implementation of the 1.600 Rule (page 14), as follows:

"All courses approved by the State Board of Education and applicable toward high school graduation will be used in making this computation."

This was the "rule" to which Coach Cox referred when he told Mr. Jimmy D. White that grades in physical education and drivers education courses could be used in the computation of Mr. Williams' grade point average.

While it is conceded that this procedure may be a violation of NCAA policy in that the grade point average of a prospective student-athlete must be computed in the same manner as that of all other students at that particular school, in Louisiana grades received in physical education, drivers education, etc. are used in the computation of each student's grade point average.

Thus, it would appear that Coach Cox is at most guilty of attempting to apply a rule which is applicable in Louisiana to a student from Georgia. The University, in its investigation of this allegation, has found no evidence of intent to deceive either Mr. White, the NCAA, or the University on Coach Cox's part.

Coach Cox's statement relating to this allegation is included in the Appendix of Statements.

f. Student-athlete Roy Ebron was certified eligible as a freshman during the 1970–71 academic year on the basis of a fraudulent ACT score of 20 which was not actually attained by the young man. The test was administered in Lafayette on October 17, 1970, and arrangements were made by Tom Cox, with full knowledge of Beryl Shipley, for an individual to take the test for Ebron. Ebron received the benefits of institutional financial aid at the beginning of the 1970–71 academic year and practiced intercollegiate basketball before the 20 ACT score was available for a determination of his eligibility.

[NOTE: The Committee wishes for the University to give due consideration to the following information upon which this allegation is based. An evaluation of Ebron's high school transcript and grade point average indicates that attainment of a 20 ACT score is highly questionable if not impossible. Ebron's high school rank was 428/551 and his high school grade point average was 1.52 with grades of "D" in the majority of hard core subjects such as English, Math, History and Physical Science. In light of Ebron's "D" grades in high school, ACT section scores of 19 in Natural Sciences appears to be a unique if not an impossible accomplishment. —Ebron's composite SAT score was 481. Based upon the Chase-Barritt "Table of Concordance", a 20 ACT score is equivalent to a 924 SAT score, a little less than twice the SAT score Ebron actually attained. —At least one individual observed Ebron in his dormitory room on campus during the morning at the time the young man was supposed to be at the test site to take the test. —Roy Ebron's signatures obtained by a representative of the Committee directly from the young man do not match the signature contained on the ACT answer sheet which supposedly was completed by Ebron. —In an interview with a representative of the Committee, Ebron could not provide any information concerning the October 17, 1970 ACT administration including such details as the location of the test site, the room in which it was administered, the time the test began or ended, or the time necessary for its administration.]

Response: In response to this allegation, the University has included statements from Mr. Roy Ebron, Coach Beryl Shipley, and Coach Tom Cox in the Appendix of Statements. In view of these statements, the University must deny knowledge of any fraudulent ACT score for Mr. Roy Ebron. According to his statement, he took the test himself at a local high school in October 1970.

The University has also looked into the relationship between Mr. Ebron's high school record and the 20 composite score on the ACT examination. Our statistics area reports (Exhibit 32-G) that using data from USL students who had taken the ACT examination in 1970 and Mr. Ebron's high school record that the predicted composite for Mr. Ebron was 17.4. Further, under the assumption that the distribution of ACT scores is normal, the probability that Mr. Ebron would achieve a 20 or more is about 23%. In other words, the chances were about one in four that Mr. Ebron would score 20 on his ACT test. The fact that Mr. Ebron has pointed out that he didn't really try to make grades in high school (his statement) should also be taken into account in this case.

To imply that the Chase-Barritt "Table of Concordance" indicates there should be an <u>exact</u> correlation between ACT and SAT scores is somewhat misleading. As you are undoubtedly aware, a student's score on either the ACT or SAT examinations can be very strongly affected by factors other than what he has learned in school—such as mental attitude, degree of fatigue, or state of health at the time the test is taken. As Mr. Ebron indicates in his statement, he "was not too concerned with the SAT score" when he took this examination since he didn't think it would make any difference in his going to college or not.

Mr. Ebron indicates in his statement that he signed his ACT answer sheet. The University has not had the opportunity to examine his signature on Mr. Ebron's ACT answer sheet in order to check whether it is valid or a forgery, but would welcome the opportunity to have this comparison made by a competent authority.

When Mr. Ebron entered the University in the 1970 Fall Semester, he was not immediately placed on an athletic scholarship since he had not taken the ACT examination and hence could not be formally predicted. Instead, he applied for and received a student aid job as a basketball manager. A check of our records indicates that Mr. Ebron was removed from this student aid job and placed on an athletic grant-in-aid scholarship before the ACT score resulting from his taking the October, 1970, test was available for a determination of his eligibility for such aid. Therefore, this portion of this allegation is substantially correct.

> g. Student-athlete Garland Williams was certified eligible as a freshman for the 1967–68 academic year on the basis of a fraudulent test score utilized in the computation of his 1.600 prediction. The test was administered to Williams during the fall of 1967 in a University History Department room located on campus. This test was not administered under the authority of the appropriate national testing service and was not available at that time to the student body in general. Prior to the test, Williams was provided a sheet of paper by Tom Cox which contained answers to the test. The sheet provided by Cox was used by Williams during the test.

Response: The University has been unable to substantiate any portion of this allegation. During the period in question, the University was making use of the "Cooperative Math" and "SCAT" test scores for prediction purposes, so it is assumed that these are the tests in question in this allegation. Coach Tom Cox has denied any knowledge of the circumstances surrounding the event as you report it. His statement to this effect is included in the Appendix of Statements.

Additionally, the University has not been successful in its attempt to locate Mr. Garland Williams.

Question 33: It is alleged that Tom Cox arranged for an individual to take an ACT examination in Lafayette during the summer 1970 for then prospective student-athlete Frank Kendrick in order for the young man to satisfy the prediction requirements of the 1.600 rule to establish eligibility at the University. The resultant ACT score credited to Kendrick enabled him to predict at the University. Kendrick was present on the campus on the date of this test administration, but was not present at the test site.

Please indicate whether this information is substantially correct.

Response: In reply to this allegation, the University submits statements by Mr. Frank Kendrick and by Coach Tom Cox.

Mr. Kendrick states that while he was visiting the University for the second time (at his own expense) he took the ACT examination. He further states that he was never informed of the results of the test since he decided to attend Purdue University a few weeks later.

Coach Cox in his statement emphatically denies that he arranged for someone to ever take an ACT examination for someone else.

The University would also like to call the Committee's attention to the fact that Mr. Kendrick's composite ACT score from the July 18, 1970, testing was 12, hardly the type of score a substitute would make on an exam.

After giving due consideration to the statements and discussion mentioned above, the University must deny this allegation.

Question 34 was a long, involved probing of the academic records of Mike Haney, James Clark, Neal O'Brien, and Payton Townsend. The problems appeared to be technical and procedural in nature and were fully answered by the university.

Question 35 dealt with the university's failure to maintain a required file on three freshmen during the 1972–73 academic year; they were Percy Wells, Andre Brown, and Tyrone Yates. There was some confusion about the question since the NCAA referred to the wrong bylaw number.

The university responded to the question stating the same procedural problems that had been previously discussed.

> **Question 36**: Information available to the Committee on Infractions indicates that several members of the institution's intercollegiate basketball team represented the University in intercollegiate competition while not in good academic standing as determined by the faculty of the University in accordance with the standards applied to all students, and/or while ineligible for participation and athletically-related financial aid under the continuing eligibility requirements of NCAA Bylaw 4-6-(b)-(a) [1.600 rule]; further, these student-athletes participated on the basis of academic records which were the result of improper grade changes. Specifically, it is alleged that:
>
> a. At the completion of the 1970–71 academic year, student-athlete Steve Greene's accumulative grade point average was a 1.483 placing him on academic probation under institutional standards at the completion of his freshman year and ineligible under the continuing requirements of the NCAA 1.600 rule. Subsequent to the completion of the 1971 spring semester, grades attained by Greene in HPEM 151 and MATH 104 were changed improperly to grades of "B". These grade changes along with his 1971 summer school grades resulted in an accumulative grade point average of 1.648 and reinstatement of eligibility under the 1.600 rule and the academic standards of the institution. The grade change in HPEM 151 occurred when Albert C. Simon, head of the department of physical education, changed the grade on a grade change request form by forging the signature of the course instructor, Ed Cavalier, without his permission. The grade change in MATH 104 was made by course instructor D.D. Hebert without the required and necessary permission of Dr. D.R. Andrew, head of the mathematics department. Both grade changes were necessary to result in an accumulative minimum 1.600 average to be eligible for both semesters of the 1971–72 academic year.

b. At the completion of the spring semester, 1970–71 academic year, student-athlete Wilbert Loftin's accumulative grade point average was 1.969 placing him on academic suspension as determined by the standards of the University. On June 11, 1971, a "C" grade attained in MATH 104 was changed to a "B" resulting in an accumulative average of 2.000, removal of academic suspension and restoration of eligibility to participate in athletics. This grade change was made by course instructor D.D. Hebert without the required and necessary permission of D.R. Andrew, head of the mathematics department.

c. At the completion of the 1970–71 academic year, student-athlete Wayne Herbert's accumulative grade point average was 1.379 placing him on academic suspension for one regular semester under the standards of the institution and ineligible under the continuing requirements of the NCAA 1.600 rule. Subsequent to the completion of the 1971 spring semester, an "F" grade attained in HPEM 151 was changed to a "B" resulting in an accumulative average of 1.482 and removal of academic suspension for one regular semester. Herbert attended 1971 summer school. The grade change in HPEM 151 along with his 1971 summer school grades resulted in an accumulative grade point average of 1.680 and reinstatement of eligibility under the 1.600 rule for the 1971–72 academic year. The grade change in HPEM 151 occurred when Albert C. Simon, head of the department of physical education, changed the grade by forging the signature of the course instructor, Ed Cavalier, on a grade change request form without Cavalier's permission.

d. At the completion of the 1970–71 academic year, student-athlete Roy Ebron's accumulative grade point average was 1.399 placing him on academic suspension for one regular semester under institutional standards at the completion of the freshman year and ineligible under the continuing requirements of the NCAA 1.600 rule. Subsequent to the completion of the 1971 spring semester, grades attained by Ebron in HPEM 151 and MATH 104 were changed improperly to grades of "B". These grade changes resulted in an accumulative grade point average of 1.636 and reinstatement of eligibility under the 1.600 rule and alteration of academic suspension to academic probation. The grade change in HPEM 151 occurred when Albert C. Simon, head of the department of physical education, changed the grade and forged the signature of the course instructor, Ed Cavalier, without his permission on the grade change request form. The grade change in MATH 104 was made by course instructor D.D. Hebert without the required and necessary permission of D.R. Andrew, head of the mathematics department. Both grade changes along with grades from the 1971 summer school were necessary to result in the accumulative minimum 1.600 average to be eligible for the fall semester, 1971–72 academic year.

The Committee would appreciate receiving the University's explanation and comments concerning the eligibility of the student-athletes named herein under the NCAA 1.600 rule as well as under the standards of the institution related to good academic standing applicable to all students. In responding, please indicate whether each allegation is substantially correct and submit evidence to support your response.

Response: These four allegations all stem from improper grade changes by two members of the University faculty, Dr. Albert C. Simon and Mr. D.D. Hebert. In order to refute these allegations, we will show that the grade changes referred to in these charges were all accomplished under normal conditions of University procedure at that time. Further, these same procedures and policies were applicable to all students in the University, not just student-athletes. Since this reply does not follow the format of the allegation, the University will deviate from the requested form of response in its reply to this allegation.

In order that you may have a better understanding of the policies and procedures for changing grades which were in effect during the periods in question, we will first state two underlying principles which govern all grade changes at U.S.L.

1) All grade changes, except in very unusual circumstances, must be initiated by and are under control of the instructor of the course concerned. Once a faculty member determines that a change of grade for a student in a course he has taught is warranted, some procedural and policy questions may arise, but his professional decision to change a grade is not questioned.

2) In the event that the instructor of the course in question is no longer a member of the faculty, the department head responsible for the course (after either having made arrangements before the instructor's departure; or confirming his action with the instructor via mail or telephone, if possible; or determining to his satisfaction that the circumstances surrounding the case justify a grade change) has the authority to initiate the grade change and sign the course instructor's name to the "Request for Change of Grade" form.

Let us first discuss the grade changes in HPEM 151 for Steve Greene, Wayne Herbert, and Roy Ebron which are alleged to have been accomplished when Dr. Albert C. Simon, Head of the Department of Physical Education, forged the signature of the course instructor, Dr. Ed Cavalier, without his permission. Since the circumstances surrounding this case are reported somewhat differently by Dr. Simon and by Dr. Cavalier, we will present each version along with our comments:

1) Dr. Albert C. Simon

During the 1971 Spring Semester, the three athletes in question missed quite a few of their HPEM 151 classes, some due to travel with the athletic team and some due to injuries sustained while playing and/or practicing basketball for the University. Dr. Simon recalls that Steve Greene either broke or severely sprained one of his fingers and he believes that Wayne Herbert pulled a muscle in one of his legs. He could not recall the circumstances surrounding Roy Ebron's case. However, he does stipulate that he is sure all three athletes had reason to limit their participation in the weight lifting classes (HPEM 151) for some time during this Spring Semester. Since grades for physical education classes depend to a large extent on class attendance, it was not unusual for Dr. Cavalier to assign a grade of "F" to these three students.

However, Dr. Simon reports that he had talked to Dr. Cavalier concerning these three cases, and that Dr. Cavalier had agreed to change their grades if and when they made up the missed classes. Since Dr. Cavalier left U.S.L. at the completion of the 1971 Spring Semester, it fell to Dr. Simon as Department Head to supervise the make-up work for these three students during the 1971 summer session and to initiate the appropriate grade changes upon the completion of the make-up work.

Obviously, under these circumstances, Dr. Simon signed Dr. Cavalier's name to the "Grade Change Request Form" when he had satisfied himself that these students had made up the missed classes. Then, according to Dr. Simon, no forgery exists in these cases since Dr. Cavalier had agreed to change the grades under the conditions which were met by these students. Dr. Simon is at a loss to explain why Dr. Cavalier denies that such arrangements had been made. Perhaps the fact that during this Spring Semester Dr. Simon was named to the headship of the Department of Physical Education, a post that both Dr. Simon and Dr. Cavalier were being considered to fill, has some bearing on this denial as well as Dr. Cavalier's abrupt departure from the faculty of U.S.L.

It should be pointed out that Dr. Simon has the authority to sign an instructor's name to a "Change of Grade Form" whenever these instructors are no longer on the U.S.L. faculty and Dr. Simon has satisfied himself that a grade change is warranted.

2) <u>Dr. Ed Cavalier</u>

Dr. Cavalier reports that the three students in question missed a large number of his classes in HPEM 151 during the 1971 Spring Semester, and thus he assigned them the grade of "F". He disclaims any knowledge of an "agreement" whereby these students could get their grades changed by making up the missed classes. Dr. Cavalier left U.S.L. for other employment at the completion of the 1971 Spring Semester, and says he heard nothing more about this case until the present time.

Dr. Cavalier denies that he gave permission to Dr. Simon to change the grades of these three students upon completion of the missed classes.

We do not understand the discrepancy between these two accounts of the circumstances surrounding these grade changes. It would appear to be Dr. Cavalier's word against Dr. Simon's word. However, since Dr. Simon had the authority to initiate the grade changes without Dr. Cavalier's permission, the question as to which story is correct is moot. The fact is that these grade changes were accomplished in accordance with accepted University policies and procedures, and do not constitute forgery on the part of Dr. Simon with or without permission from Dr. Cavalier.

We will now discuss the grade changes in Math 104 for Steve Greene, Wilbert Loftin, and Roy Ebron, which are alleged to have been accomplished "without the required and necessary permission" of the head of the Department of Mathematics, Dr. D.R. Andrew.

The "Request for Change of Grade" card in use at U.S.L. at that time has blank spaces for three signatures: the Instructor; the Instructor's Department Head; and the student's Academic Dean. Under normal circumstances, signatures of these three University employees would appear on every change-of-grade card. However, reasonably often the Department Head and/or the student's Academic Dean are away from campus when their signature is needed on a grade change card. In these instances, some person in the departmental office and some person in the dean's office is usually designated to sign such documents for the department head or the dean. Although it is desirable that the proper signatures appear on all documents, this procedure is usually followed in order that routine University documents which require signatures of administrators (purchase requisitions, change of grade cards, travel requests, etc.) can be processed without undue delays.

Although Dr. D.R. Andrew, current Head of the Department of Mathematics, had not specifically designated anyone in his office to sign change-of-grade cards in his absence (the problem of a change-of-grade card needing his signature when he was absent from the campus had not occurred), his secretary Mrs. Annie Leach had his permission to sign purchase requisitions and travel requests in his absence. Furthermore, Mrs. Leach had been allowed to sign change-of-grade cards in the absence of the former department head, Dr. Zeke Loflin. Consequently, since Dr. Andrew was off campus, she had no hesitation about signing Dr. Andrew's name to these cards when they were presented to her. Of course her initials, A.L., appear beneath Dr. Andrew's signatures.

In view of the foregoing discussion, the University must deny that Mr. D.D. Hebert made the grade changes in question "without the required and necessary permission of D.R. Andrew." In fact, these grade changes were made under circumstances which were considered "normal" by the University at that time. (Please note that the academic dean of each student had no qualms about affixing their signatures to these cards after Mrs. Leach had signed Dr. Andrew's name.) Had Dr. Andrew been on campus at the time these change-of-grade cards were presented for his signature, he undoubtedly would have signed them since Mr. Hebert had stipulated that he, as instructor of the course, felt that the grade changes were warranted.

In view of the fact that all grade changes mentioned in this allegation were made according to standard University policies and procedures which were applicable to all students of U.S.L., the University feels it had to utilize the changed grades in determining the eligibility of the four student-athletes under the NCAA 1.600 rule and under University standards for academic good standing. Consequently, the University contends that its certification of these four student-athletes as eligible under the NCAA 1.600 rule and under U.S.L.'s standards for academic good standing for participation in athletics for the 1971 Fall Semester was correct.

Question 38: It is alleged that student-athletes Steve Greene, Roy Ebron, and Wayne Herbert were ineligible under the continuing requirements of NCAA Bylaw 4-6-(b)-(2) [1.600 rule] at the completion of their freshman year (1970–71 academic year), and received institutional financial aid to attend the institution's 1971 summer school. Specifically, even with the benefit of alleged improper grade changes, Greene and Herbert did not have a minimum 1.600 grade average at the completion of their first two semesters. Please indicate whether this information is substantially correct and submit evidence to support your response.

Response: During the spring and summer of 1971, this University was still a member of the Gulf States Conference which did not specifically require that a student maintain a 1.600 average to retain his eligibility. Therefore, under NCAA Bylaw 4-6-(b)-(2), these three continuing student-athletes were "limited only by the official institutional regulations governing normal progress toward a degree for all students, as well as any other applicable institutional eligibility rules, including those of the athletic conference of which the institution is a member."

Since the University maintains that the grade changes on these three student-athletes academic transcripts were valid, their grade point averages at the conclusion of the 1971 Spring Semester were: Roy Ebron—1.653; Steve Greene—1.678: and Wayne Herbert—1.482. According to normal University rules and regulations, all three of these student-athletes were eligible to continue as students at U.S.L. Roy Ebron and Wayne Herbert were on "academic probation"—a warning that their academic performance was not up to par. However, all three were eligible to attend the University and, consequently, eligible for the aid awarded them during the 1971 Summer Session.

Question 39: A review of the University transcripts of student-athletes Steve Greene, Garland Williams, Wilbert Loftin, Wayne Herbert, Mike Haney, Payton Townsend, Roy Ebron and Dwight Lamar indicates that for the most part all of these young men have either been on academic suspension or academic probation during each term of attendance at the University; further, many of these young men were first placed on academic suspension for one semester and thereafter removed to academic probation as a result of timely grade changes which enabled them to be eligible for participation; further, most of these athletes participated in one or more semesters while on academic probation. The Committee is concerned about these numerous grade changes, at the participation of several of these student-athletes while on academic probation for the majority of their undergraduate attendance, and about the possibility of these young men participating while not maintaining normal progress toward a degree. Accordingly, please submit the following information concerning each student-athlete:

a. An explanation of each grade change reflected on their University transcripts, and an indication of whether these grades were changed in accordance with standards applicable to all students rather than just student-athletes.

Response:

1. Steve Greene

a) The two grade changes which appear on Mr. Greene's transcripts (Exhibits 39-A) have been discussed in detail in the reply to allegation 37-a, and will not be discussed further at this point.

2. Garland Williams

a) The grade change "I" to "F" for English 101 (refer to Exhibits 39-B, Mr. Williams' transcript and grade change forms) during Mr. Williams' first semester on campus (Fall, 1967) was an automatic change. At that time the University's policy on incomplete (I) grades was that incomplete work not completed during the next regular semester reverted automatically to an "F". For the current policy concerning incomplete grades, please refer to Section V-A-5, page 374, of the University's 1971–72 Catalog (Exhibit 39-C).

The grade change "I" to "B" for the course HPEM 234 in the 1969 Fall Semester indicates that work not completed during the regular semester was finished and that Mr. Williams' overall grade in the course was "B".

The grade change "C" to "B" in Psychology 311 in the 1969 Fall Semester was made when Mr. Williams completed some course work that he had missed during the regular semester. The course instructor felt that this completed work was of sufficient quality so as to raise Mr. Williams' overall course grade to a "B".

All of the above grade changes were made in accordance with rules and regulations applicable to <u>all</u> students of the University.

3. Wilbert Loftin

a) The one grade change which appears on Mr. Loftin's transcript (Exhibit 39-D) has been discussed in detail in the reply to allegation 37-b, and will not be discussed further here.

4. Wayne Herbert

a) The grade change for HPEM 151 (refer to Exhibits 39-E, Mr. Herbert's transcript and grade change forms) which was completed in the 1971 Fall Semester has been discussed in detail in the reply to allegation 37-C and will not be discussed further at this time.

The grade change from "D" to "B" in Statistics 214 which was completed during the 1971 Summer Semester was made when Mr. Herbert turned in a term project which had been misplaced. This change was made according to the rules and regulations governing all students at this University.

The grade change from "F" to "D" in English 202 which was completed during the 1972 Spring Semester was made when an error in computing Mr. Herbert's grade was brought to the attention of the Head of the Department of English, Dr. Mary E.

Dichmann, by Mr. Herbert. Mr. R. Leyendecker, the instructor in this particular course, had terminated his employment with the University and left the area. Consequently, Dr. Dichmann signed Mr. Leyendecker's name to the "Request for Change of Grade" card—a privilege which is vested in our department heads. This change of grade was made in compliance with rules and regulations of the University which are applicable to all students.

5. Mike Haney

a) Mr. Haney has had two changes on his transcript (Exhibits 39-F). The first was in Psychology 220 which he completed during the 1971 Spring Semester. This grade change was from a "C" to a "B". Mr. Haney had done reasonably well in the course (a low B), but had missed a lot of class because of basketball road trips and other reasons. Dr. Caves felt that this lack of class attendance was sufficient to lower Mr. Haney's grade to a "C". However, he agreed to change the grade to a "B" on condition that Mr. Haney attend all class sessions of this course during the 1971 Summer Session to make-up for the missed class periods. This Mr. Haney did. This grade change was accomplished within the University rules and regulations as applied to all students.

The second grade change on Mr. Haney's transcript occurred for a Physical Education (PHED 100) course, which he completed during the 1971 Fall Semester. The instructor of the course changed Mr. Haney's grade from a "C" to a "B" when Mr. Haney made up some course work, which he had failed to complete during the regular course. This grade change was made in compliance with University rules and regulations, which are applicable to all University students.

6. Payton Townsend

a) Mr. Townsend has no grade changes on his transcript (Exhibits 39-G) in the sense of having one permanent grade changed to another permanent grade. There are two instances where incomplete grades were removed and a permanent grade was entered on the transcript. The first of these occurred after Mr. Townsend's first semester (Fall, 1968) at this University. The instructor of a Speech 100 class changed Mr. Townsend's grade in this course from an "I" (incomplete) to a "B" upon Mr. Townsend's completion of the written work required in the course. The next semester, Mr. Townsend received an incomplete grade in Aerospace Studies 102 from the instructor in the course. The instructor of this course was transferred after this semester. Thus, when Mr. Townsend completed the work required in this course, Colonel David M. Hill, Head of the Department of Aerospace Studies at that time, changed the grade from "I" to "A". In the process, he had to sign the original instructor's name to the "Request for Change of Grade" card, an act which he had the authority as department head to perform. <u>The removal of both of these incomplete grades was accomplished within normal University rules and regulations which apply to all students.</u>

7. Roy Ebron

a) Mr. Ebron has had six grade changes on his transcript (Exhibits 39-H). Two of these have been discussed in depth in reply to allegation 32-d, and will not be further discussed at this point. Consequently, the following discussion will be limited to the remaining four grade changes.

During the 1970 Fall Semester Mr. Ebron received an "IC" grade in a Speech 100 class. This grade meant that Mr. Ebron had not completed the requirements for the course but had a "C" from the work he had completed. (For a complete discussion of the meaning of these incomplete grades, please refer to section V-A-5, page 374, of the University's 1971–72 Catalog—Exhibit 39-C.) Mr. Ebron later completed the work required in the course and the instructor changed his grade from an "IC" to an "A".

This change was accomplished in accordance with standard University rules and regulations applicable to all students.

During the 1971 Spring Semester, Mr. Ebron was enrolled in an elementary typing class (SECS 100) which met five days a week. Since he was traveling with the basketball team, Mr. Ebron missed several days of this class. Ordinarily, these are excused absences, but the instructor in this class was unaware that Mr. Ebron was on the basketball team, and consequently applied the Freshman absence rule (See Exhibits 39-I) to this case. Thus, Mr. Ebron received an "F" in this course unfairly.

When this was pointed out to the instructor of this typing class, she changed the grade from an "F" to an "IC". This change was accomplished in accordance with standard University rules and regulations applicable to all students.

Mr. Ebron was enrolled in a Physical Education course (PHED 208) during the 1971 Fall Semester and received a grade of "F" in this course due to not having completed all the required work. Shortly after the semester ended, Mr. Ebron completed this required work and the instructor changed his grade to a "D". This change was accomplished in accordance with standard University rules and regulations applicable to all students.

During the 1972 Spring Semester Mr. Ebron scheduled Health 312, Personal and Community Health Problems. Very early in the semester Mr. Ebron dropped this course and stopped attending class. However, the records of this action were either lost or not processed for some other reason. After receiving a grade of "F" in the course, Mr. Ebron questioned the whereabouts of his "drop cards", and it was determined that they were missing and had not been processed. When this was discovered the instructor of the course changed the "F" grade to a "W" grade which means that Mr. Ebron had dropped the course without penalty. This change was

accomplished in accordance with standard University procedure applicable to all students.

8. Dwight Lamar

a) There are no grade changes on Mr. Lamar's transcript
(Exhibit 39-J).

b. An explanation of the terms "academic probation"
and "academic suspension", and a statement of the
eligibility of each student athlete to participate in
intercollegiate athletics while on such academic probation or suspension.

The University is required to adhere to the rules
and regulations concerning "academic status" as promulgated by the Louisiana State Board of Education,
its governing body. These rules and regulations are
set forth on pages 378–380 of the 1971–72 University Catalog.

As can be seen, "academic probation" is essentially a warning to the student that he must show
improvement if he is to remain in the University.
As such, "academic probation" would not necessarily prohibit participation in intercollegiate athletics.
"Academic suspension" implies dismissal from the
University. Thus, any student-athlete who is placed
on "academic suspension" would be ineligible to participate in intercollegiate athletics unless he submitted a successful appeal to the Committee on Academic Affairs and Standards (see G in Exhibit 39-K).
In this case, his "academic suspension" would be
rescinded and he would be placed instead on "academic probation" and could possibly retain his eligibility to participate in intercollegiate athletics.

A student-athlete's actual eligibility status is
determined by his academic status in conjunction
with any applicable conference polices governing
continuing eligibility. For example, under the Gulf
States Conference, continuing eligibility for participation in intercollegiate athletics was determined
solely by the student-athlete's academic status since

214

the conference had no specific continuing eligibility requirements. In this case, once a student-athlete had successfully predicted 1.600 or better, his eligibility for participation was determined "only by the official institutional regulations governing normal progress toward a degree for all students" (NCAA Bylaw 4-6-(b)-(2)). On the other hand, the Southland Conference requires a cumulative or past academic year grade point average of at least 1.600 for continuing eligibility.

The continuing eligibility status of the University's student-athletes was determined by the Gulf States Conference rules until the 1971–72 academic year at which time the University became a member of the Southland Conference.

c. A statement of each young man's eligibility to participate indicating whether each young man was maintaining normal progress toward a degree under established institutional standards at the completion of each semester of attendance.

Response: The University has no standards that define "normal progress toward a degree." In fact, it is forbidden by the State Board of Education from enacting and/or enforcing any rule concerning this subject other than those which define "Academic Status" (see 39-b above). As a consequence of this, the University is not able to define "normal progress toward a degree." The fact that a student who earns over a 1.500 but less than a 2.000 grade point average could continue at this University in good standing indefinitely without the possibility of earning a baccalaureate degree (since graduation requirements are a 2.000 grade point average) has been pointed out before. The following statement is taken from the August, 1971, accreditation report of the Engineers' Council for Professional Development, Incorporated, after an inspection visit to the University's College of Engineering:

"The University should revise its policy on suspension for scholastic deficiency and readmission thereafter. Currently, students who earn over 1.5 but less than 2.0 may con-

215

tinue indefinitely without scholastic probation but without the possibility of completing baccalaureate requirements. A graduated scale should be employed so that the quality of educational effort in the junior and senior years will not be diluted with very weak students."

The University is thus forced to equate "normal progress toward a degree" with eligibility to continue attendance at the University. In reality, this means that a student or student-athlete is making "normal progress toward a degree" if he is enrolled in a degree program and eligible to attend the University.

The information concerning continuing eligibility for the eight student-athletes mentioned in this allegation follows:

1. Steve Greene

Mr. Greene was eligible for participation in intercollegiate athletics throughout his academic career at this University. He was placed on academic probation at the conclusion of the 1971 Fall Semester, but made a sufficiently high grade point average during the next regular semester to have this probation removed.

2. Garland Williams

Mr. Williams' record indicates that he was placed on academic probation at the conclusion of the 1967 Fall Semester, the 1969 Spring Semester, the 1970 Spring Semester, and the 1971 Spring Semester. In each case (except the last) his succeeding semester grade point average was sufficient to remove him from academic probation. Mr. Williams was eligible to participate in intercollegiate athletics during his entire tenure as a student at the University since he met all requirements for continuing eligibility of both NCAA and the appropriate conference of which the University was a member.

3. Wilbert Loftin

Mr. Loftin was placed on academic probation after his first semester (Fall, 1970) at this University. However, his grade point average during the next regular semester was sufficient to remove this probation. Thus, Mr. Loftin was eligible to participate in intercollegiate athletics until his academic suspension at the conclusion of the 1972 Spring Semester, meeting all NCAA and conference requirements for continuing eligibility.

4. Wayne Herbert

Mr. Herbert's academic record indicates that he was placed on academic probation at the end of the 1971 Spring Semester. Having failed to make the required grade point average to have this probation lifted during the next regular semester, Mr. Herbert was placed on academic suspension after the 1971 Fall Semester. This suspension was rescinded by the favorable action of the committee on Academic Affairs and Standards on Mr. Herbert's appeal for a waiver of this action. (It is estimated that approximately 75% of all first-time suspendees who appeal to this committee have their suspensions rescinded.) This action left Mr. Herbert on academic probation during the 1972 Spring Semester. Since he failed to make the required grade point average during this 1972 Spring Semester, he was again suspended. A second appeal to the Committee on Academic Affairs and Standards was unsuccessful, and Mr. Herbert became ineligible for participation in intercollegiate athletics as of the 1972 Fall Semester. During those times in which Mr. Herbert participated in intercollegiate athletics at USL, he met all continuing eligibility requirements of the NCAA and the athletic conference to which the University belonged.

5. Mike Haney

Mr. Haney was placed on academic probation at the conclusion of the 1970 fall semester, however his grades during the subsequent 1971 spring semester were sufficiently high so as to remove him from this probation.

Mr. Haney was suspended at the end of the 1971 fall semester for academic reasons. However, the Committee on Academic Affairs and Standards acted favorably on an appeal by Mr. Haney and rescinded this suspension. This action left Mr. Haney on academic probation for the 1972 spring semester and made him eligible to participate in intercollegiate athletics during this semester. It should be noted that this was Mr. Haney's first "suspension," and that the committee usually rescinds about 75% of the suspensions for those suspended for the first-time. Mr. Haney's academic performance during the 1972 spring semester (the next semester) was sufficient to remove him from academic probation and continue his eligibility for participation in intercollegiate athletics under the continuing eligibility requirements of both the NCAA and the athletic conference of which the University was a member.

6. Payton Townsend

Mr. Townsend was placed on academic probation after completing his first semester (Fall, 1968) at this University and again after completing the 1971 Fall Semester. In each instance, his academic performance during the next regular semester was sufficient to remove the probation and allow him to continue his eligibility to participate in intercollegiate athletics.

7. Roy Ebron

Mr. Ebron was placed on academic probation at the end of the 1971 Spring Semester. However, during the next regular semester (1971 Fall Semester) his academic average was high enough to allow this probation to be lifted. He was again placed on academic probation at the end of the 1972 Spring Semester. During the times in question, Mr. Ebron met the requirements for continuing eligibility to participate in intercollegiate athletics of both the NCAA and the conference to which the University belonged.

8) Dwight Lamar

Mr. Lamar was placed on academic probation at the end of the 1970 Fall Semester. However, his academic performance during the next semester (Spring, 1971) was such that this probation was removed. Consequently, Mr. Lamar has been eligible for participation in intercollegiate athletics during his entire attendance at this University.

   d. A statement of the University's standards defining normal progress toward a degree.

Response: As stated in the beginning paragraphs of the answer to allegation 39-c above, the University has no standards which define normal progress toward a degree. Instead the University must consider any student who is enrolled in a degree program and eligible to attend the University to be making satisfactory and normal progress toward a degree.

The NCAA then asked for a detailed description of each of these student athletes and their degree pursuits, semester by semester; the university complied.

Finally the Infractions Committee asked the question concerning where all these alleged funds were coming from. They had alleged monthly payments, free apartments, gasoline, clothing, cash, and so on. Note the phrasing of the question. Since they said these funds existed, they now wanted to know where they were coming from.

Question 40: In light of the considerable amount of money allegedly given to prospective and enrolled student-athletes by members of the institution's basketball coaching staff and representatives of the University's athletic interests as set forth in this inquiry, the Committee on Infractions is concerned about the possibility of an outside fund, or other sources of money not administered by the University, being made available to the department of athletics to assist prospective and enrolled student-athletes.

Accordingly, the Committee requests the University to review carefully these allegations with a view to determining whether such a fund exists; further, that the University's representatives be prepared to discuss the results of this review at the time of their appearance before the Committee; finally, please indicate whether the Century Club, a local University boosters' club, is administered in accordance with NCAA Official Interpretation 107.

Response: Were it not for the fact that the University has emphatically denied the vast majority of the allegations presented in this "Official Inquiry," we too would suspect that our athletic department had access to sources of money not administered by the University. However, the amount of money involved in those allegations which the University has admitted is not very large, and has certainly alleviated any suspicions that we might have had concerning outside sources of funds.

True, the actual funds allegedly distributed was not very large; the amount allegedly promised was.

In order to comply with the request for an indication of whether the Century Club is administered in accordance with NCAA Official Interpretation 107, the University submits a statement from Mr. M.L. Moore, Jr., the Executive Director of the USL Foundation who administers all funds received from booster organizations (Century Club, Champion Club, Redcoat Club, and B.A.M. Club) for use by the USL Athletic Department and also a statement from Mr. Ovey Hargrave, Jr., Business Manager of the University (see Appendix of Statements).

As these two statements indicate, all outside funds (including those of the Century Club) are being administered (properly.)

Question 41: The Committee on Infractions would welcome any additional comments or information.

Response: The University of Southwestern Louisiana feels that it has had ample opportunity to comment and introduce pertinent information while responding to the many allegations contained in this "official inquiry," and will refrain from extending this narrative any further than absolutely necessary.

Thus the inquisition was over. The questions and answers were finally out in the open. The university's responses included multiple examples of evidence. In most instances more than one source (sometimes three) were quoted from sworn statements refuting the anonymous allegations submitted. In many cases the sworn testimony came from sources other than university or athletic department employees and coaches, in direct contradiction of the NCAA's stated belief that all defensive testimony was tainted by selfish motivations.

In the face of such massive defense testimony, most legitimate prosecutors would have been embarrassed to present the charges the NCAA put forward: airline tickets purchased for a woman who had never been in an airplane nor had ever been to the destination where the alleged flight took her; clothing purchases for which no one, including the department store allegedly involved, has any record; illegal scrimmages ordered by and attended by the head coach when records show he was out of town. The list of uncorroborated violations is amazing. It truly was a massive fishing expedition.

The university openly admitted to procedural problems it had experienced in admissions, transcript verification, and minor problems in administration of financial aid. The most serious admissions probably were the three or four incidents of paying travel expenses to family or coaches of recruits or players. Shipley says, "Frankly coaches and family members in the North were skeptical of how their young men would be treated in this Deep South Louisiana school. We felt we had to bring them here to see for themselves." Still, even those violations shrink to insignificance when viewed in the severity of the penalty.

All of the above—all of the testimony, statements, logical explanations— appeals to realism in understanding the actions of governing authorities: multiple denial sources versus single accusations. All were disregarded, totally ignored by the rulers of college athletics, the National Collegiate Athletic Association. They had their case. They could now prove that they could and would properly punish those who would taint the pristine reputation of college athletics. Not only could they punish; they were omnipotent. They could eliminate whole university programs with the "death penalty."

USL's massive response document was probably received near the July 4 holiday. The NCAA never acknowledged receipt of the package. No one from the NCAA ever questioned the university's responses and denials or any of the participants who signed sworn statements refuting almost every allegation.

Less than three weeks after the university mailed the document, the NCAA completed its Case 390 report. The accusations of Garverick, Kluz, and unnamed others were accepted. All of USL's responses were in vain. The university received the case document shortly after July 20. The letter of transmittal read, "The committee on Infractions will submit its report to the Association's Council beginning at 2:30 p.m. at the Hyatt Regency, O'Hare (airport), the American Room, August 4, 1973."

Oddly, or coincidentally, the Resolution that nailed the coffin shut was dated August 4, 1973; the same day the committee supposedly saw Case 390's report for the first time. Obviously the penalty document had been written before the council met.

The most important part of the penalty resolution read:

BE IT FURTHER RESOLVED, that effective August 4, 1973, the following penalties shall be imposed upon the

University of Southwestern Louisiana, it being understood that if the University's membership is not terminated by the 68th annual Convention, these penalties shall remain in full force and effect:

1. The University of Southwestern Louisiana shall be reprimanded and censured, and placed on indefinite probation from this date, it being understood that prior to the expiration of this probationary period, the Committee on Infractions shall review the athletic policies and practices of the institution;

2. For a period of four years from this date, the University of Southwestern Louisiana shall end its sports seasons with the last, regularly scheduled, in-season contest or event, and it shall be ineligible to enter teams or individuals in National Collegiate championship competition and in all other postseason meets and tournaments;

3. For a period of four years from this date, the University of Southwestern Louisiana shall be denied the privilege of being represented on any NCAA committee or the right to vote on any question before the Association, except on the motion before the 68th annual Convention to terminate its membership in the Association;

4. For a period of four years from this date, the University of Southwestern Louisiana's athletic teams shall not be eligible to participate in any national television series or program subject to the administration and control of the Association, and the University shall not make any commitment for any such television appearances before it has been restored to full rights and privileges of membership, and

5. For a period of two years from this date, the University of Southwestern Louisiana shall not permit its intercollegiate basketball teams to participate against outside competition.

BE IT FURTHER RESOLVED, that if the University of Southwestern Louisiana's membership in the Association is terminated by the 68th annual Convention, and thereafter it is re-elected to membership prior to the expiration of the terms of the penalties prescribed herein, the foregoing penalties shall be reinstated; in this event, the terms of these penalties shall be considered to have commenced August 4, 1973;

BE IT FINALLY RESOLVED, that in any event, the Council, in accordance with NCAA Constitution 4-2-(b), directs the Association's membership to refrain from participating in intercollegiate basketball competition against the University of Southwestern Louisiana for a period of two years from this date (August 4, 1973).

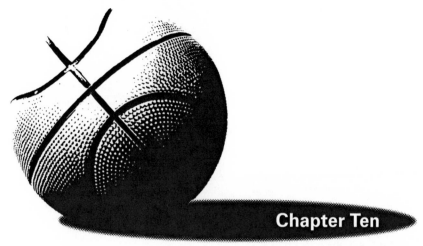

Chapter Ten

Amid the ruins

The university could have appealed the decision. Further litigation could have been pursued, but everyone involved in the defense seemed to be exhausted. Shipley, Cox, and Urban were gone. The infidels who had broken the sacred code of segregation of Louisiana athletics had been punished and banished.

Lafayette and Acadiana were in shock. Basketball fans had accepted the fact that some violations had been discovered but believed the charges were all answerable. They believed the university administration would go to the wall against the NCAA. The announcement of the NCAA decision was met with disbelief. No USL basketball for two years? Four years probation for the entire athletic program? Impossible!

Beryl Shipley had resigned three months earlier, but Tom Cox had been advised by supporters outside of the university to stand his ground and make himself available as Shipley's replacement.

Cox received a phone call from Shipley about two hours after the press conference at which he had announced his resignation. Tom said, "This was in May and all the bad stuff didn't really hit until much later. Everybody was left with the impression that Beryl had left because of the NCAA mess and the heat he was getting about everything. Not true.

"At that time the NCAA did not have the power to tell schools who they could hire and who they could fire; that came later. At that time Beryl could have stayed there. He could have gone back even after he had resigned, if he had chosen. He could have walked back in, if he had decided, and ridden the penalties out as head coach. The people who were in power were [Richard]

Dick D'Aquin [publisher of the daily newspaper the *Advertiser*, and, even more importantly, a member of the state's universities Board of Regents], Senator Sonny Mouton, J.Y. Foreman [businessman and recently named member of the new state board of trustees, governing authority on state universities] and Bob Wright [world-class trial attorney]—and everybody thought the world of Beryl. Beryl had control; he could have done anything at that time that he wanted to do.

"There was no question, Ray Authement and Blanco aspired to run the ship, and they didn't want anybody else there; it was best for them if Beryl was gone. But there were others who could have stood in their way.

"I'll tell you how strong those guys [D'Aquin, Mouton, Foreman] were. When Beryl said he had resigned, I said I was going to resign too—if Rougeau won't support you, he damn sure won't support me. Beryl said, 'No, stay in there and get the job done.'

"I had to make up my mind, and by the time I did, Rougeau had resigned and Authement was the acting president. Anyhow, I went down to Channel 10 and taped my resignation. Then I went to the *Daily Advertiser*, and submitted my written resignation. The next day, Dick D'Aquin called me and asked me what did I think I was doing? I told him that I was resigning—if Ray Authement won't support Beryl, he certainly won't want me. Dick told me, 'Authement is not calling the shots—Ray Authement is not president yet, he is interim, acting president. Until he is officially appointed, he doesn't call the shots. We are calling the shots and I'm telling you to call the TV station and pull that resignation back, and I'm pulling it from the paper.'

"I did as he asked. I retracted the resignation from Channel 10 and then sat there in limbo the whole summer, not knowing what the hell I was going to do."

Former USL executive and former president of Delgado Community College in New Orleans, Jim Caillier, was one of the many members of the black community deeply saddened by the NCAA actions. "The violations that USL were accused of were happening at every university involved in educating black kids. Many schools, including USL at that time, had a committee whose job was to evaluate students on probation and to determine whether they should remain on probation or be removed. This removed the need for grade changes from the teaching professors. This school (USL) didn't use this infrastructure for student athletes that was already in place for other students. Thus, the coaches were forced to deal with the faculty directly and the procedure was more transparent. The NCAA and the state board used that fact against the basketball program, knowing that it was not a unique problem."

In a later conversation, Shipley asked Caillier why, in the face of all the violations, somebody from the administration didn't come to him and ask about them early on. "Nobody came," Shipley said, "not one until the end was near."

Caillier's answer to Shipley was, "The reason no one came was because the administration wanted to make a change. You [Shipley] were getting too much attention. And it worked. Blanco got the president of his choice—Authement. Authement made it by one vote—and that vote was changed the night before the vote was taken. LSU was the designated flagship for the state and the success of the USL basketball program made those in Baton Rouge very angry. LSU and other regional schools were all allied against USL and used whatever influence they had to try to destroy the program. And they all, to some extent, used their influence to demand the NCAA to take some action. The NCAA had a lot of help—a lot of help from Northwestern. That's the school with which the state board's chairman was affiliated. That's why, today, the Sports Writers Hall of Fame is located there. I think the organization promised that Beryl Shipley would never get the recognition he deserves. Galloway is there. He lied. Galloway took the story to the NCAA, but they all did. Stan was the most vocal, but LSU and all of the other schools, as well as those people internally, were very active."

Caillier's reference to Dr. Ray Authement's election by one vote by the State Board of Education as president of USL may come as a surprise to some. The board announced that the vote had been unanimous.

Actually, the day before the vote was taken, another candidate held a one-vote lead. President Clyde Rougeau had suddenly announced his retirement two weeks after Shipley resigned. Authement was named interim president and served in that position for a year.

Board Chairman Jesse Bankston of Baton Rouge was leading the move to elect Winston Riddick as president of USL. Riddick was a native of Crowley, home of then governor Edwin Edwards, Judge Edmond Reggie, Dick D'Aquin, B.I. Moody, Billy Trotter, and other movers and shakers (some called them the Crowley Mafia) in Louisiana. Riddick was a graduate of USL and had been student body president in his senior year. His credentials were spectacular: 1962 Outstanding Graduate, PhD from Columbia University, Juris Doctorate from LSU. He later served as an assistant attorney general for the state and ran for state attorney general in 1991. He is currently a member of the law faculty at Southern University in Baton Rouge.

There were some in Lafayette who were quietly suggesting that the board should not rush into a selection but conduct a legitimate nationwide search for the president to succeed Clyde Rougeau. This group felt that the university had been practicing academic incest by choosing the leadership only from its own ranks. Bankston called one of that group several days before the vote on the new president was to be taken. He urged the Lafayette group to go public in supporting Riddick over the university candidate, Ray Authement. The person Bankston called refused the request, saying he and his associates were not against Authement and not for Riddick; they simply wanted a more legitimate search to be made open to other candidates. Bankston assured him he had the votes to get Riddick elected though the margin was slim, eight to seven.

By the time the vote was taken, one member, Harvey Peltier, Sr. of Lafourche Parish, a major Louisiana political player for many years, had switched his vote from Riddick to Authement, giving him a one-vote margin. This was done in executive session with no media coverage or public participation. The board then ratified its action in a face-saving unanimous vote that was announced to the public.

There are those who say that Raymond Blanco, former assistant football coach, then dean of men, currently vice president for student affairs at ULL and husband of Governor Kathleen Blanco, engineered the Peltier switch with the help of then state senator Edgar Mouton. Mouton, indeed, was a close ally of Peltier and the new sitting governor, Edwin W. Edwards. If this is true, Authement has certainly proved his gratitude to "coach" Blanco through the years. Shipley once referred to Blanco as "a politician masquerading as a football coach."

Caillier's conversation concerning the basketball program went on. "Coach Shipley was fighting the whole state and still running a winning basketball program. Northwestern [now Northwestern Louisiana University at Natchitoches], Monroe [now University of Louisiana at Monroe] and Tech [Louisiana Tech at Ruston], they were all furious. I can remember the talk about bringing in black athletes. They would each bring in one black athlete, then each bring in one more, and gradually bring them into all the schools together. That was merely a story to make maintaining segregation palatable.

"You [Shipley] were just ahead of the times. Even before 1966, you went out of the state to recruit, because you wanted good athletes and that was a part of the problem."

Even before the death penalty was announced, Shipley and Cox had been attempting to assist their young players, who still had eligibility, to transfer to other universities. For the most part, they were successful, and for the most part, the transferees were ultimately successful on their new campuses.

Andre Brown went on to a satisfying career at Mercer University in Georgia. Larry Fogle, the super athlete with the "gangsta" attitude, transferred to Canisius in New York state and led the nation in scoring the following year. Freddie Saunders, one of the most levelheaded and mature of the group, signed on with Syracuse University but ran into the vindictiveness of the NCAA again.

According to Saunders, he was interviewed by an NCAA investigator in June of 1973 at his home in Lafayette. He had called Coach Shipley to tell him about the investigator and was advised by the coach to answer his questions openly and honestly. The NCAA agent was obviously not pleased with Saunders's answers and said if he didn't get "the truth" he was going to "bust him." Saunders stuck to his original statements and the agent left.

When Freddie showed up at Syracuse University, he found that the NCAA had notified the university that Saunders had been named in numerous violations at USL and was not eligible to play or even practice with the team. Syracuse officials investigated the situation and found it to be unfair and capricious and filed a lawsuit against the association. (There's that strong response by a university again.) Saunders sat out the first semester until the court found the NCAA's accusations were not substantiated and the association did not have the true facts. Fred finished his basketball career and graduated two years later. He was drafted and signed by Phoenix of the NBA and later played for New Orleans and the Boston Celtics.

The next two winters were bleak in Lafayette, Louisiana. Thousands of basketball fans had no team to cheer for, no relationships to share with other roundball groupies. The camaraderie between the races that the program had engendered was sadly diminished.

A year in advance of the lifting of the penalty, Jim Hatfield, a member of the University of Kentucky staff, was hired to rebuild. He added Bobby Paschal as his assistant, and they started the difficult task of recruiting to a program that could not play a schedule until the winter of 1975 and could not participate in post-season games for two more years after that.

Hatfield's legacy came in the name of Andrew Toney, a lightning-fast six-three guard from Birmingham, who led the team from 1976 through 1980 before being drafted in the first round of the NBA by Philadelphia and starring for the 76ers for nine seasons. Hatfield spent three years at USL and left with a .573 winning average. He was succeeded by his assistant, Paschal, who had a respectable .643 eight-year run.

Although many of the former stars still lived and/or worked in Lafayette, they were never called on to help in recruiting or coaching. Lamar, Saunders, and Payton Townsend, among others, were all available and eager to help but were not called upon. Lamar was and is still remembered throughout the nation as one of the game's all-time greatest shooters.

Ron Gomez remembers being on a flight from Atlanta to Washington, D.C. in 1999, twenty-six years after the last Shipley season. A seatmate on the plane asked where he was from, and he replied, "Lafayette, Louisiana."

The young man lit up and said, "Isn't that where that basketball player Bo Lamar played? Did you ever see him play? Did you know him?"

It was a very short, enjoyable flight.

One of the succeeding coaches referred to them as outlaws. They didn't deserve that.

With respect to the other coaches and fine players who have worn the vermilion-and-white, it has never been quite the same.

You just had to be there.

Chapter Eleven

Life after the Death Penalty

Having read the writing on the wall, Tom Cox resigned shortly after Dr. Rougeau. Tall, easygoing, and personable, Tom had a lot of friends in Acadiana and probably could have been successful in half a dozen different professions. Fortunately for both, he and State Farm hooked up. His agency is now one of the most successful in the state, and Tom's love for the game of golf is being totally fulfilled. His wife Judy, who suffered along with him during the rough times, was a successful educator in her own right, serving as principal of one of Lafayette Parish's largest high schools, then winning a seat on the parish school board, on which she served two notable terms.

The more fiery and high-strung of the two coaches, Shipley couldn't settle into the good life quite as easily. He was deeply hurt by the accusations, his treatment in the state media, the lack of support by the university administration, and its reluctance to appeal the NCAA decisions to set the record straight. He was profoundly concerned for the reputations and futures of his players and associates. Like Cox, he had a myriad of job offers. He entered the insurance business for a short time, but the love of the game and the itch to redeem himself was powerful.

The relatively new American Basketball Association beckoned to him. Started in 1967, it was giving the NBA much-needed competition. With its red-white-and-blue basketballs and three-point field goals, it brought professional basketball to places like Denver, San Antonio, Indiana, Memphis, and San Diego.

The new league opened franchises anywhere local owners could put up the money. During its nine years, there were such teams as the Anaheim

Amigos, Baltimore Claws, Minnesota Muskies, Spirits of St. Louis, and Pittsburgh Condors.

Hotshot college stars were wooed with big contracts, and many were playing in the new league. Julius "Dr. J." Erving, Connie Hawkins, George McGinnis, Artis Gilmore, Moses Malone, and other future NBA stars started with the ABA.

Dwight "Bo" Lamar was picked in the third round of the NBA draft by the Detroit Pistons, but the San Diego Conquistadors (try to rhyme that in a cheer) made him their number-one draft choice and signed him. Not surprisingly, the nickname was shortened to Q's. It was hoped that Bo's long-range shooting style would fit perfectly with the three-point field goal and wide-open play of the young league.

Lamar didn't disappoint. In spite of his wiry build and his height (he claimed and USL publicists used six-one; five-eleven and a half was probably closer), the rookie had some good days on the ABA courts. Before Shipley arrived on the West Coast, in his first half-season, Bo had a thirty-six-point game in a 122–102 blowout of Utah, a thirty-four-point effort in a loss to the San Antonio Spurs, and thirty-six in a 139–125 win over the Carolina Cougars.

Beryl was hired as the Q's head coach by Alex Groza, who had been serving as both general manager and coach. The previous coach, Wilt Chamberlain, had left before the '73–74 season began. Groza, who died in 1995, was a member of the 1948 Kentucky Wildcat National Championship team. Ironically he was also involved in the point-shaving scandal in 1951 that led to the only other NCAA basketball "death penalty."

Beryl and Lamar teamed up to try to turn around a seemingly lost cause. The loss of Chamberlain as head coach severely diminished the fan-appeal of the club. Now, with a losing season underway and Groza doing double duty as general manager and head coach, fans were staying away in droves. Yet the Shipley-Lamar combo still had its moments: Bo scored twenty-five in a win over Kentucky in late January, then came back to score forty-eight on February 8 in a 120–105 win over San Antonio. He had 30, 39, 33, and 41 points in games through the end of the season, ending with an average of 20.4 points in 84 games for the season.

Shipley recognized early on that the pro basketball life was not for him and that the San Diego franchise was in deep trouble. His pro coaching record of sixteen and thirty was certainly no reflection of the brilliant career he had fashioned at USL. It was time to come home.

Lamar played another season in San Diego, averaging 20.9 points while fighting through injuries in 77 games. He ended his ABA career after a trade to the Indiana Pacers for the '75–76 season, when he averaged sixteen points in forty-three games.

When the NBA and ABA called off their war and merged in 1976, only four of the new teams survived: New York Nets, Denver Nuggets, Indiana Pacers, and the San Antonio Spurs. Lamar was traded to the Los Angeles Lakers and finished his career there in 1977.

Shipley got involved in the booming oil service business in Lafayette and Southwest Louisiana. With his large network of friends and fans and his natural gregariousness, he was hugely successful and eventually retired comfortably. In spite of severe health problems that would have discouraged, if not killed, a lesser person, Shipley, with the staunch support and nursing of his wife, Dolores, is a robust eighty-one-year-old still playing golf as often as the South Louisiana climate and weather will allow.

In 2001 a group of friends in Lafayette, led by former physical education professor Dr. Ed Dugas, put together a Beryl Shipley reunion. It was billed as a "Tribute to a Coaching Legend." His players, assistant coaches, managers, and trainers from 1957 to 1973 were sought out and invited. They came from all over the United States. An incredible number of those invited came; there were doctors, lawyers, teachers, bankers, realtors, coaches, insurance brokers, and contractors. Almost all of Beryl's boys were back. And guess what? They all paid for their own transportation, lodging, registration, and food.

A scholarship program that had been established at Beryl's insistence was announced during the reunion. Called "The Mended Heart Scholarship" (Beryl's heart problems have been diagnosed as virtually untreatable for two decades), the funds are available to students who have survived heart surgery. It is the first of its kind at the University of Louisiana at Lafayette and may be the first in the nation. During the reunion functions, Dr. Ed Dugas presented a check to the scholarship fund for thirty-five thousand dollars received in donations. Proceeds from the reunion were to be added to that.

A Web site was also established at the time: www.coachshipley.com. It is also included on the outstanding UL Athletic Network Website at www. athleticnetwork.net.

In the fall 2004 issue of ULL's magazine, *La Louisiane*, recognition was given, probably for the first time by any official pronouncement or acknowl-edgement of the university administration, to the profoundly positive impact Beryl Shipley and his basketball program had on the institution. In the ar-ticle historian Dr. Michael Wade is quoted as saying, "Coach Beryl Shipley's courageous decision to break the color barrier by recruiting three black high school All-Americans for his 1966 team had far-reaching consequences." For a historian that is an amazing understatement of the facts.

Elsewhere in the article, local journalist and historian Jim Bradshaw, who was a student at the university in the 1960s, wrote:

> Shipley's teams brought the national spotlight to USL and his recruiting in those less-tolerant days of the 1960's brought him the scorn of other coaches. The attention and the scorn caused NCAA investigators to take a hard look at the USL basketball program and that brought big trouble. But, oh, it was fun while it lasted, when Blackham Coliseum rocked to the rafters during a USL game.

Shipley's recognition came slowly and sometimes grudgingly. In 1985, a dozen years after the NCAA penalty, he was named "Mr. Louisiana Basketball" by the Louisiana Association of Basketball Coaches at their tenth annual hall of fame banquet.

Jonas Breaux, a staff writer for the *Advertiser*, covered the event:

> "Beryl was the first coach in our state to really go out of Louisiana to recruit and to do something positive about upgrading his schedule," said LABC Master of Ceremonies Lenny Fant of Northeast, one of Shipley's former coaching foes.
>
> Shipley brought USL into the national limelight in the late 1960's. "I've done some things in my career that some people didn't agree with. But, I'll be honest with you, I really don't give a damn," Shipley said in his acceptance speech.
>
> Fant had nothing but words of praise for his former adversary and recalled one game in particular when he had to play USL in the old Earl K. Long gym.
>
> "Either the roof had blown off Blackham or there was a rodeo going on. Anyhow, we had to play at the old gym on campus. Well they hadn't used the gym for games in years and the scoreboard went out on us in the second half.
>
> "Well, the refs were keeping time and the score, so with the second half winding down I decided to ask about the time and the score. The ref walked over to the scorer's table and shouted back. 'You got four-and-a-half minutes left and we've got you by five, coach,'" Fant quipped.
>
> Shipley made the induction speech for his former player, Flake, a player Shipley said "came to USL measuring 6-7 and

weighing a mere 135 pounds. After four years with us he left measuring 6-8 and weighed 137 pounds."

In 1986 Shipley was inducted into the Louisiana Association of Basketball Coaches Hall of Fame. What the sportswriters would not recognize his peers did.

Reporting on the event, the *Advertiser's* Bruce Brown quoted Beryl's longtime assistant, Tom Cox, who made the presentation:

> "People say it takes 20 years to become an overnight success," said Cox. "Beryl Shipley coached at USL for 16 years and is a legend. He has been like a second brother to me.
>
> "Whatever credit I received as his assistant is too much. I was just a passenger in the vehicle, but I'll never forget the trip. Beryl Shipley was the father of modern day basketball in Louisiana."

The article went on to quote Shipley:

> "The most gratifying thing to me is that I don't know of one of my former players who hasn't done well or isn't well thought of in his community. We can get together later, and if any of you can tell me of one of them who is in need, we can send them a CARE package ... and tell the NCAA to foot the bill."

Chapter Twelve

Parting Shots

As indicated several times in the preceding pages, Beryl Shipley was never one to hide or moderate his true feelings. He would never be accused of speaking in codes or attempting to conceal his opinions.

For a man accustomed to such a forthright and outspoken manner, the last three decades have been torture. He has agonized over the writing of this book for years.

> My side of the 1957–1973 era has lain dormant for all these many years. I have decided to speak up now. I know that the story will be unfavorably received by some, especially those in leadership positions at the university, then and now. I'm sure the NCAA officials might also be in some disagreement with what I've said.
>
> I doubt the present administration has the fear today of the State Board of Education or its replacement, the Board of Trustees, as they had during my tenure. But today, just as it was then, athletics seem to be treated almost as a necessary evil. The administration, in that respect, has performed and is performing as though nothing has changed.
>
> If the administration had spent as much time promoting athletic interests with the student body and community as it has spent on politicizing itself for personal and political gain, we would be in excellent shape, athletically.

I personally feel that during my tenure at USL the student body and community took pride in the athletic program and our success at USL and supported it with a personal interest. During this time the state board used its power, contrary to existing law, to influence the administration on integration and "unwritten law" issues.

Despite the success that we were having and national recognition the university was receiving, the administration, working in collusion with the state board, stopped it all because of the administration's fear of the board and the pressure that it was applying—a prime demonstration of the administration's lack of integrity. The administration was so fearful of the state board that it was willing to sacrifice the reputation of the school to satisfy and placate that political body. Someone in the administration, some individual talented in intrigue, looking for personal and political gain, set the stage for a rocky road, divide-and-conquer mentality unequaled in USL athletic history.

Athletics has always been a vital part of any college campus and always will be; however, if it is to be supported by the community, student body, and alumni, the administration must demonstrate its enthusiasm for the activities with positive actions. The political board is no longer breathing down the administration's neck, yet for over thirty years the student body has been used by the administration as a pawn for personal interests and goals, and athletics has not had so much as a bone thrown in its direction. Every coach, in nearly every sport, has been on his/her own in attempts to raise money and gain support for his/her sport. Any coach will tell you that this hard work is a vital part of any successful athletic program, and the college leadership must come to understand the value to the school that could be derived if the leadership would join in a united effort.

We have a great community, outstanding alumni, and loyal fans. In my opinion, the administration has failed them. During my tenure the advantages to the university, gained from the national attention engendered by the basketball program's success, were clearly demonstrated. In my sixteen years, we moved from a relatively obscure educational institution to become a nationally known, acclaimed university. Despite this evidence, during my over fifty years in this great community, until recently, the administration had never acknowledged the importance of athletics. I fully recognize the university's outstanding computer science and petroleum-engineering programs that are world renowned, but I think the university leaders have failed to recognize that to truly advance nationally, it needs a strong athletic department to help promote the university and its educational program.

I have presented this story as it was, as I experienced it, and what it is today. I know that during my tenure at USL the student body and the community took pride in the athletic program at USL and supported it with a personal interest.

I think you will recognize a pattern with athletics today that I experienced with the administration. For whatever reasons—fear, jealousy, political advancement—the administration has settled for mediocrity in the athletic theater. Today the political fear should be gone, but the university administration is currently carrying on in the same vein—from fear and jealousy of a strong athletic department and a desire for personal enhancement.

Finally, in 2002, Gerald Hebert, former manager for Coca-Cola in Lafayette and a dynamic salesman, was hired by the athletic department to raise money and develop fan interest and loyalty. Gerald's dynamic presence has done more to advance the enthusiasm and overall improvement of the athletic program than anybody in the history of the university. I believe Gerald through his promotional ability, emphasizing student and community support, will successfully promote the beginning of a new era in athletics that has lain dormant for way too many years. It is unfortunate that Gerald's abilities and achievements were not recognized in the recent selection of a new athletic director. I just hope the new president being hired to replace the retiring Dr. Ray Authement will recognize the importance of athletics as well as the academic side.

To all the magnificent USL basketball fans, the players, coaches, and my great friends and family, thanks for the memories.

Beryl Shipley
Fall 2007

The position of athletic director was filled only by an interim appointee for more than two years until the summer of 2007. Gerald Hebert was an enthusiastic applicant for that position. Acting A.D. David Walker was chosen.

In 1973 Ray Authement, who had just become university president, and Dean Sammie Cosper flew to Chicago to meet with NCAA officials to plead the university's case. A brilliant and dedicated academician, Cosper had written the entire 312-page response document presented to the association. He had used most of his summer vacation on the project. The volunteer attorneys accompanied them on the trip.

One of the attorneys says that Dr. Authement urged the group to accept the NCAA's sanctions without objections. The unanimous decision was to defend the program with every means possible.

The arguments presented fell on deaf ears. Senator Mouton, one of the attorneys in attendance, says that midway through the meeting he felt the university's position was pretty solid, that they had successfully defended all of the allegations. He was in the men's room when one of the NCAA officials told him, "You haven't seen anything yet. Wait till the next session."

Mouton says they were hit by allegations in the afternoon session that they had not prepared defenses for. Even today, Mouton wonders if the university administration knew about but chose not to defend the additional allegations. Two days after the meeting, Authement issued this statement:

> On Saturday, Aug. 4, at 2:30 p.m., Dean Sammie Cosper and I appeared before the NCAA Council to discuss the findings of the NCAA Committee on Infractions. Dean Cosper and I were provided the opportunity to discuss both specific findings and internal actions already taken by the University in regard to its athletic program. Penalties imposed by the NCAA Council, of which I was informed by telephone yesterday morning, are in my opinion severe in view of the personnel changes already made in the Athletic Department. After considerable deliberation with members of my staff, I believe that the best interest of the University will be served by pursuing the following course of action:
>
> 1. The University, through its actions in the next few months, will attempt to convince the NCAA membership that the University should remain an active

member of [the] NCAA. We believe this is necessary if we are to aspire to a program of excellence in athletics—a goal to which we are committed.

2. If successful in retaining membership in the organization, the University will make every attempt to remove all athletic programs of the University from probationary status as soon as possible. In these efforts the University will rely on appeal procedures available to all members of NCAA. As the newly elected president of the University, I am reminded of the title of a song which is currently popular—"This Time, Lord, You Gave Me A Mountain." Together, the University and the people of Acadiana can, through diligent work and loyal support, scale this mountain and bring the University's athletic program to a position of excellence.

To the best of Beryl Shipley's knowledge and Tom Shipley's extensive research, no appeal was ever filed, none of the points made by Dr. Authement were ever pursued.

Acknowledgements

Tom Shipley's months of research produced a historical account of events that led to the integration of Louisiana and Deep South universities, in both undergraduate studies and athletics. In doing so, he used the memories of those directly involved, newspaper records of events, Internet sources, and recently acquired University of Louisiana at Lafayette (ULL) archive records. He became involved because he believed the NCAA's serious accusations of misbehavior of his brother had to be false and decided to help him tell the story. Without this belief in his brother Beryl, Beryl's records, his remembrances, and his friends in ULL's library archives, nothing could have been written.

Special thanks to:

- Michael G. Wade, Appalachian State University, ULL historian, *A Half-Century of Desegregated Higher Education: From SLI to the University of Louisiana—Lafayette, 1954–2004*

- The *Lafayette Daily Advertiser*: February 16, 1961; March 6, 9, 10, 1965; March 3, 1968 issues for information and opinions crucial in revisiting events of that period.

- Walter Byers, *Unsportsmanlike Conduct*, 1995, University of Michigan Press. Its contents were revealing and raised interesting questions.

- Internet, Google: *Due Process and the NCAA* for a report on September 2004 House of Representatives hearings on NCAA unfairness. An indication that NCAA procedures remain unfair to this day.

- ULL library for the use of its microfilm collection of Lafayette *Advertiser* newspaper articles.

- Dr. Ray Authement for making available copies of correspondence during the 1970s, including the official university response to NCAA allegations, most of which had never been seen by the coaches and other interested parties.

- Glynn Abel, dean of men, (now ninety-four years old) for his lucid recollections of 1954 student integration procedures, black/white student reactions, and the NAIA tournament debacle.

- Tom Cox's recollections, as assistant coach, of the trials and tribulations of the '60s and '70s.

- Dr. Jim Caillier for his memories as a student and subsequent member of USL's administration.

- Former state senator and attorney Edgar Gonzague "Sonny" Mouton, who represented the state and the university at hearings, filed proceedings, almost missed his daughter's wedding, and provided memories and corrections for these pages all pro bono.

- Attorney John Allen Bernard, who contributed his time and talent in defense of the university and his friend Beryl Shipley and reviewed the legal aspects of this manuscript.

- Dr. Sammy Cosper, retired vice president of ULL who wrote the final 312-page response document for the university and reviewed this manuscript for accuracy.

- Former players and friends of Beryl Shipley who have encouraged the publication of this book.

- Certainly not to be forgotten is the Florence Nightingale of the Shipley household, Beryl's wife Dolores, who has nursed him back from the brink more times than either would like to count. She also knows where all the newspaper clippings, notes, and documents are at all times. Her halo is barely noticeable.

CPSIA information can be obtained at www.ICGtesting.com
Printed in the USA
BVOW042030191211

278753BV00003B/10/P